Re-Forming the State

Interests, Identities, and Institutions in Comparative Politics

Series Editor:
Mark I. Lichbach, University of California, Riverside

Editorial Advisory Board:
Barbara Geddes, University of California, Los Angeles
James C. Scott, Yale University
Sven Steinmo, University of Colorado
Kathleen Thelen, Northwestern University
Alan Zuckerman, Brown University

————

The post–Cold War world faces a series of defining global challenges: virulent forms of conflict, the resurgence of the market as the basis for economic organization, and the construction of democratic institutions.

The books in this series take advantage of the rich development of different approaches to comparative politics in order to offer new perspectives on these problems. The books explore the emerging theoretical and methodological synergisms and controversies about social conflict, political economy, and institutional development.

————

Democracy without Associations: Transformation of the Party System and Social Cleavages in India, by Pradeep K. Chhibber

Gendering Politics: Women in Israel, by Hanna Herzog

Origins of Liberal Dominance: State, Church, and Party in Nineteenth-Century Europe, by Andrew C. Gould

The Deadlock of Democracy in Brazil, by Barry Ames

Political Science as Puzzle Solving, edited by Bernard Grofman

Institutions and Innovation: Voters, Parties, and Interest Groups in the Consolidation of Democracy—France and Germany, 1870–1939, by Marcus Kreuzer

Altering Party Systems: Strategic Behavior and the Emergence of New Political Parties in Western Democracies, by Simon Hug

Managing "Modernity": Work, Community, and Authority in Late-Industrializing Japan and Russia, by Rudra Sil

Re-Forming the State: The Politics of Privatization in Latin America and Europe, by Hector E. Schamis

Re-Forming the State

The Politics of Privatization in Latin America and Europe

Hector E. Schamis

Ann Arbor
THE UNIVERSITY OF MICHIGAN PRESS

FL¡P

2005   2004   2003   2002   4   3   2   1

A CIP catalog record for this book is available from the British Library.

Library of Congress Cataloging-in-Publication Data applied for
ISBN 0-472-11257-0 (cloth)
ISBN 0-472-08850-5 (paper)

To A.A.H.M.

Contents

Tables

Acknowledgments

In writing this book, which has been long in the making, I have incurred many intellectual debts. Over time colleagues read all, parts, or preliminary versions of the manuscript. Others read and commented on related work, which later became integrated into the book. For helpful suggestions and criticisms, as well as their encouragement with the project, I thank Miguel Angel Centeno, Douglas Chalmers, Edward Gibson, Blanca Heredia, Robert Kaufman, Isaac Kramnick, Mark Lichbach, Oscar Muñoz, Guillermo O'Donnell, Etel Solingen, Alfred Stepan, Kathleen Thelen, and Andrés Velasco. I also thank participants in seminars at Brown, Princeton, and Yale Universities whose comments helped me refine the argument, especially Jeremy Adelman, Linda Cook, Geoffrey Garrett, Pauline Jones Luong, Marsha Pripstein Posusney, Victoria Murillo, and Paul Sigmund.

While writing this book, I was simultaneously working on the political economy of exchange rate policy in Latin America. That research was particularly relevant for my work on privatization. I thank Eugenio Díaz-Bonilla, Jeffry Frieden, and Ernesto Stein for their insightful comments during the two-year collective project.

At Cornell, I gratefully acknowledge comments made by participants and colleagues at the Political Economy Research Colloquium and the Latin American Studies Program Seminar. I especially thank Benedict Anderson, Matthew Evangelista, Béla Greskovits, Jonathan Kirshner, and Christopher Way. I also thank Matthew Ferchen, Stephen Jackson, Anirudh Krishna, and Arturo Santa-Cruz for discussing parts of the manuscript with great scrutiny in different seminars.

I also want to thank two anonymous reviewers for the University of Michigan Press for their helpful criticisms, and Jeremy Shine, political science and law editor, for his hard work and support during the process. Finally, my deepest gratitude goes to Anna Eliasson, for her countless readings of the manuscript, criticisms, suggestions, and for everything else.

PART 1

The Approach

Chapter 1

Introduction

The Argument

This book examines the processes leading to, and the political effects of, market reform experiments. Specifically, it focuses on the patterns of collective action and coalition building that drive privatization, and the transformations of institutional domains that stem from these programs in advanced, developing, and postsocialist nations. In doing so, the argument of this study questions established approaches in the discipline of economics and in the fields of comparative and international political economy.

In economics, dominant reasoning treats a liberal economic order as a public good. As such, it is subject to familiar collective action problems: the completion of liberalization benefits all groups in society, but vested interests who enjoy sector-specific protections are tempted to maintain a closed economy. The former are prone to free riding, while the latter have incentives to organize against an open economy. Accordingly, an influential research program within this field, labeled neoclassical political economy, has explained state intervention as the result of the deliberate action of distributional coalitions—rent seekers who benefit from subsidies, tariffs, and regulations.[1] Conversely, since liberalization disperses gains and concentrates costs, marketization efforts are expected to dissipate rents and dissolve distributional coalitions.

A vast literature in political economy, in turn, has followed these propositions and applied them to the study of the politics of economic adjustment.[2]

---

1. The concept "neoclassical political economy" brings together public choice theory, Olson's collective action approach, and the literature on the rent-seeking society. For a review, see David Colander, ed., *Neoclassical Political Economy: The Analysis of Rent Seeking and DUP Activities* (Cambridge: Ballinger, 1984); and T. N. Srinivasan, "Neoclassical Political Economy, the State, and Economic Development," *Asian Development Review* 3, no. 2 (1985).

2. Joan Nelson, ed., *Fragile Coalitions: The Politics of Economic Adjustment* (New Brunswick, N.J.: Transaction Books, 1989); Joan Nelson, ed., *Economic Crisis and Policy Choice: The Politics of Adjustment in the Third World* (Princeton: Princeton University Press, 1990); Stephan Haggard and Robert Kaufman, eds., *The Politics of Economic Adjustment* (Princeton: Princeton

Scholars in this research program have argued that liberalization programs concentrate present costs on the beneficiaries of a closed economy and disperse (initially uncertain) benefits in the future. Hence, losers are prone to engage in collective action, whereas prospective winners, facing uncertainty about payoffs, remain disorganized. The pro-reform coalition is thus seen as fragile vis-à-vis forces that extract rents from protectionism and state intervention. On this basis, eliciting political support for market reform is considered a difficult and improbable task, especially in the early stages of the program. Consequently, while economists have generally highlighted the importance of consistency and credibility for successful reform, political scientists have posited the autonomy and insularity of policymakers as the main explanatory variable. Both approaches see the reforms flowing from above and, thus, overlook a most crucial aspect of the process: how coalitions organize in support of liberalization.

I argue, in contrast, that market reform does not necessarily dismantle rents; in fact, it can generate new ones. Though this is possible in several policy areas, it has especially been the case with privatization reforms. To the extent that divestiture programs result in the uncompetitive appropriation of state-owned assets, the transfer of public monopolies to the private sector intact, and the absence of effective regulatory frameworks, privatization creates a context propitious for the reproduction of rents. Closer analysis of these institutional settings suggests that benefits are concentrated and costs dispersed, generating suboptimal aggregate outcomes and incentives for the formation of distributional coalitions. On the basis of this modified payoff structure, I hypothesize that much of the impetus for marketization comes from the strategic behavior of interest groups in anticipation of market reserves made available by state withdrawal.

These propositions seek to highlight how policy instruments meant to overcome rent-seeking behavior become themselves the source of rents. Accordingly, and in order to capture how these coalitions organize in support of liberalization, I suggest extending the insights of the theories of the rent-seeking society to the study of market-oriented reform. As discussed in greater detail in the following chapters, this book represents an effort to close two prevalent gaps in dominant collective action theories and the literature on reform. The first is the assumption that only interventionist policy contexts generate incentives for groups to engage in rent-seeking behavior and distributional coalition building. The second is the view that, given the previous conditions, reform experiments

University Press, 1992); Robert Bates and Anne Krueger, eds., *Political and Economic Interactions in Economic Policy Reform* (Oxford and Cambridge, Mass.: Blackwell, 1993); John Williamson, ed., *The Political Economy of Policy Reform* (Washington, D.C.: IIE, 1994); and Stephan Haggard and Robert Kaufman, *The Political Economy of Democratic Transitions* (Princeton: Princeton University Press, 1995).

flow from insulated policymakers because it is difficult to organize societal support for liberalization.

As I demonstrate that economic liberalization can generate opportunities for rent-seeking behavior as well, I show different patterns of interaction between policymakers implementing reforms and interest groups benefiting from them. To increase the breadth and explanatory power of these propositions, I select cases across regions and with variation in type of political regime, pre-reform strategy of development, and international position, among others. The evidence presented in this book shows that, for example, in both Chile and Hungary, collusion between policymakers and economic elites who benefited from privatization drove the reforms. In Argentina and Mexico, in turn, explicit or implicit pressure on the part of industrial-financial conglomerates prompted policymakers to embark on divestiture programs, while in Britain political elites initiated privatization with the goal of altering material incentives in order to restructure long-standing coalitions. These examples point to convergence in the behavior of political elites and the goals of interest groups, thus opening the door for distributional coalition building and making state autonomy arguments questionable.

The second set of propositions of this book addresses the political effects of marketization and challenges important contributions to the study of the transformation of state structures associated with these economic changes. For example, a wealth of research on globalization has argued that increasing integration of transnational economic actors and heightened penetration of market forces into the national space diminish, erode, or otherwise weaken the state. Confronted with global production, fully mobile financial capital, and rapid technological change, the argument goes, states lose their autonomy to choose and capacity to implement domestic policy that deviates from the externally induced norm. As a result, the state is in retreat. Moreover, in some versions of this argument, the very idea of the nation-state and the traditional conceptions of sovereignty in contemporary international relations are considered to be severely challenged, if not rendered altogether useless, by openness and large-scale marketization.[3]

---

3. See, for example, Susan Strange, *The Retreat of the State: The Diffusion of Power in the World Economy* (New York: Cambridge University Press, 1996), and *Mad Money: When Markets Outgrow Governments* (Ann Arbor: University of Michigan Press, 1998); Vivien Schmidt, "The New World Order Incorporated: The Rise of Business and the Decline of the Nation-State," *Daedalus* 124, no. 2 (spring 1995); Martin Van Creveld, *The Rise and Decline of the State* (Cambridge: Cambridge University Press, 1999); and Richard Devetak and Richard Higgot, "Justice Unbound? Globalization, States, and the Transformation of the Social Bond," *International Affairs* 75, no. 3 (1999): 483–98. Though less focused on the state than on the homogenization of economic policy due to globalization, see Paulette Kurzer, *Business and Banking: Political Change and Economic Integration in Western Europe* (Ithaca: Cornell University Press, 1993); and Fritz Scharpf, *Crisis and Choice in European Social Democracy* (Ithaca: Cornell University Press, 1991).

This view is consistent with a number of studies on privatization in the advanced industrial, developing, and postcommunist worlds alike. Withdrawing from the market, transferring important allocative functions to the private sector, and downsizing its own administration, the state has allegedly been receding in the face of comprehensive divestiture programs and welfare state retrenchment. Put in a nutshell, if for the literature on globalization, the global market makes the state retreat, for much of the literature on privatization its impact at home makes the state shrink. Starting in the 1980s and well into the late 1990s, "state shrinking" appears to have become a prevalent conceptualization of this phenomenon.[4]

In contrast to this view, I show that concepts like retreat, weakening, and shrinking of the state do not do justice to what really is at stake in current processes of privatization and economic liberalization. These terms are misleading, for they are unable to capture the most critical political dimension associated with marketization: the reassertion of state power. True, through comprehensive reform experiments the state has withdrawn from key markets, leaving a number of allocative functions to the private sector, domestic or foreign. But at the same time these programs involve a stricter specification and enforcement of property rights, the empowerment of new winning coalitions, the reorganization of revenue collection mechanisms, and the centralization of fiscal policy and budgetary procedures, among other institutional consequences. In short, property rights, extraction, and centralization have defined the political boundaries of the marketization drive. On this basis, I suggest that privatization is more about state building than about state shrinking and retreating, and I evaluate this proposition by examining reform experiments in Latin America and Europe.[5]

---

4. For example William Glade, ed., *State Shrinking: A Comparative Inquiry into Privatization* (Austin: Office of Public Sector Studies, Institute of Latin American Studies, University of Texas at Austin, 1986); Dennis Swann, *The Retreat of the State: Deregulation and Privatization in the UK and the US* (Ann Arbor: University of Michigan Press, 1988); Roman Frydman and Andrzej Rapaczynski, *Privatization in Eastern Europe: Is the State Withering Away?* (Budapest and London: Central European University Press, 1994); Harvey Feigenbaum, Jeffrey Henig, and Chris Hamnett, *Shrinking the State: The Political Underpinnings of Privatization* (Cambridge: Cambridge University Press, 1998).

5. Consider that property rights, extraction, and centralization (with its implications over the monopolization of coercion) define state formation in the works of authors with intellectual trajectories as different as Charles Tilly's and Douglass North's, among others. For the former, see *Coercion, Capital, and European States* (Cambridge and Oxford: Blackwell, 1992); "War Making and State Making as Organized Crime," in Peter Evans, Dietrich Rueschemeyer, and Theda Skocpol, eds., *Bringing the State Back In* (Cambridge: Cambridge University Press, 1985), 169–91; and his edited volume *The Formation of National States in Western Europe* (Princeton: Princeton University Press,

In sum, by linking the preferences and strategies of distributional coalitions to market reform experiments, I address a series of questions left unanswered by dominant views in economics and by the literature on the political economy of reform—which overlooked the organization of political support for liberalization. By subsequently looking at the effects of these policies upon the redesign of institutional domains, I seek to show the limitations of prevalent scholarship on globalization and privatization—which missed the state formation character of market reform altogether. And by selecting empirical materials from cases with wide variation across and within regions, I increase the generalizability of these claims.

This study highlights how privatization is a movement from public to private, but also a movement from nonstate to state, as the reduction of state assets leads to institutional changes that increase state capacity for defining and enforcing property rights, extracting revenue, and centralizing administrative and political resources. The experience of privatization shows that public and private are neither contradictory nor mutually exclusive terms, and that power relations between both spheres are not necessarily zero sum. To stress the point, I borrow from the literature on state formation, which has extensively examined the historical processes by which the construction of effective public institutions has generally been accompanied by the empowering of key private groups.[6] The evidence presented in this book shows why and how, by restructuring coalitional and institutional arenas, marketization serves as an instrument through which political order is generated and political power distributed. I thus specify the conditions under which political change is conceived in terms of and channeled through economic policy; in other words, how the state is "re-formed" through privatization.[7]

1975). For the latter, see *Structure and Change in Economic History* (New York: Norton, 1981); *Institutions, Institutional Change, and Economic Performance* (Cambridge: Cambridge University Press, 1990). For a synthesis of Tilly's Weberian approach and North's contractarian view on state formation, see Margaret Levi, *Of Rule and Revenue* (Berkeley: University of California Press, 1988).

6. Particularly revealing is that even the European nineteenth-century liberal state, which one might think was "shrinking" given that its task was to dismantle the absolutist state, was actually an expanding state that achieved high levels of centralization, completed processes of national and legal unification, and created single currencies and fiscal systems, among other important features. See Raymond Grew, "The Nineteenth-Century European State," in Charles Bright and Susan Harding, eds., *Statemaking and Social Movements: Essays in History and Theory* (Ann Arbor: University of Michigan Press, 1984), 83–120; and Gianfranco Poggi, *The Development of the Modern State* (Stanford: Stanford University Press, 1978).

7. To characterize marketization as state formation, and thus to place the study of market reform within the confines of state formation literature, entails going beyond arguments about how economic liberalization has led to the strengthening of the state apparatus or to increases in the

A Political Economy of Market Reform and Privatization

This study adopts a political economy approach based on distributive conflict and on the notion of distributional coalitions, typical in interventionist settings, though it applies this view to market reform experiments. The framework used in this study assumes that, to the extent that asymmetries among interest groups are based on differences in market power, societal coalitions often become distributional ones, as groups seek market reserves, because that is the most effective and least uncertain way to increase their market power. Interest groups thus prefer to redirect existing wealth toward themselves (and, for example, privatize assets) rather than to maximize additional output. On this basis I argue that the supporters of reform experiments generally organize around short-term distributional considerations and, thus, I highlight the political behavior necessary to get their preferences translated into policy.

This view applies to privatization programs, for they lead to transfers of wealth and income across groups in society, but also because divestiture policies are a key component of broader reform efforts directed toward macroeconomic stabilization, microeconomic restructuring, and the redesign of institutions. As I examine these comprehensive reform programs, I specify particular policies under which benefits are concentrated on a small coalition and costs disperse among a larger set of groups, creating conditions favorable for rent appropriation, even in the presence of comprehensive liberalization. In fact, contexts that produce suboptimal outcomes by deviating from aggregate efficiency magnify the primacy of distributional considerations.

A clarification of terms is in order at this point. Following Olson, I define *distributional coalitions* as groups "oriented to struggles over the distribution of income and wealth rather than to the production of additional output."[8]

---

regulatory capacity of the state as in, among others, Andrew Gamble, *The Free Economy and the Strong State: The Politics of Thatcherism* (London: Macmillan, 1988); Thomas Biersteker, "Reducing the Role of the State in the Economy: A Conceptual Exploration of IMF and World Bank Prescriptions," *International Studies Quarterly* 34 (1990): 477–92; Miles Kahler, "Orthodoxy and Its Alternatives: Explaining Approaches to Stabilization and Adjustment," in Joan Nelson, ed., *Economic Crisis and Policy Choice: The Politics of Adjustment in the Third World* (Princeton: Princeton University Press, 1990), 33–61; Albert Fishlow, "The Latin American State," *Journal of Economic Perspectives* 4, no. 3 (1990): 61–74; Steven Vogel, *Freer Markets, More Rules* (Ithaca: Cornell University Press, 1998); and Richard Snyder, "After Neoliberalism: The Politics of Re-regulation in Mexico," *World Politics* 51 (January 1999): 173–204.

8. Mancur Olson, *The Rise and Decline of Nations* (New Haven: Yale University Press, 1982), 44. The end of the paragraph reads: "(or organizations that engage in what, in one valuable line of literature, is called 'rent seeking')."

Following Buchanan, I define *rent* as that part of the payment to an owner of resources above the alternative earning power of those resources, that is, as a receipt in excess of opportunity cost. Rents are profits, but the "in excess" clause indicates that those kinds of profits are realized in activities where freedom of entry is curtailed.[9] In institutional settings where entry is blocked, profit seekers will invest resources in trying to get in, so that they can secure market reserves. As resources are increasingly utilized in politically related activities, and the allocative process is suboptimal, individual efforts to maximize value will generate social waste rather than social surplus. In this context, profit seekers become rent seekers.

Rent-seeking behavior is typical of interventionist-regulatory regimes. This book, however, makes the argument that certain marketization policies can generate incentives for rent-seeking behavior as well. Take, for example, the issue of capital account liberalization. It is a much debated issue whether full financial openness, and the ensuing inflows of capital, is the optimal policy or whether it is instead a self-defeating one.[10] The latter position is generally based on the fact that capital inflows contribute to real exchange rate appreciation and to the accumulation of current account deficits over time. When these inconsistencies become unsustainable, they lead to runs on the currency, while subsequent attempts to defend the parity cause the drainage of central bank reserves, macroeconomic disequilibria, and weak economic performance, especially in small and middle-size economies.[11]

---

9. James Buchanan, "Rent Seeking and Profit Seeking," in James Buchanan, Robert Tollison, and Gordon Tullock, eds., *Toward a Theory of the Rent-Seeking Society* (College Station: Texas A & M University Press, 1980). In the same volume, Gordon Tullock, in "Rent Seeking as a Negative Sum Game," 17, states that "an individual who invests in something that will not actually improve productivity or will actually lower it, but that does raise his income because it gives him some special position or monopoly power, is rent seeking and the rent is the income derived."

10. See, for example, the collective volume "Should the IMF Pursue Capital Account Convertibility?" *Princeton Essays in International Finance* 207 (May 1998).

11. Though also in OECD countries. For example, the British decision to enter the Exchange Rate Mechanism (ERM) of the European Monetary System (EMS) in October 1990 further appreciated the pound. Capital inflows and trade deficit were followed, by mid-1992, by balance-of-payment problems, runs on the pound, and loss of reserves that account for the deepest recession in postwar history and for the decision to abandon the EMS in September 1992. The original theoretical contribution on this type of crisis by Paul Krugman, "A Model of Balance-of-Payments Crises," *Journal of Money, Credit, and Banking* 11 (1979), has been widely applied and extended. For Latin America, see Guillermo Calvo, "Varieties of Capital-Market Crises," in Guillermo Calvo and Mervyn King, eds., *The Debt Burden and Its Consequences for Monetary Policy* (London: Macmillan, 1998) and papers in *Journal of International Economics,* Symposium on Mexico, 41, November 1996. For Western Europe, see Barry Eichengreen and Charles Wyplosz, "The Unstable EMS," *Brookings Papers on Economic Activity* 1 (1993): 51–124. For Eastern Europe, see Zs. Árvai and J. Vincze, "Vulnerability of Currencies—Financial Crises in the 1990s," *Acta Oeconomica* 49, no. 3–4 (1997–98): 243–69.

For the literature on the sequencing of reforms these problems stem from the wrong timing and combination of liberalization policies.[12] As much as this research has examined the impact of different sequences on stability and growth, it has not addressed, however, the factors that explain the choice of one mix of policies over another in the first place. To the extent that this combination of policies and the ensuing crises are not distributionally neutral, the choice of the wrong sequencing of reforms should be attributed to interest-group politics, not just to inconsistencies or credibility problems as is often the case. In fact, I use Olsonian reasoning about the behavior of groups to explain why, within otherwise far-reaching marketization, welfare-enhancing reforms (and their accompanying institutional forms) have been harder to implement than redistributive ones.

For example, the fast and relatively uncontested nature of capital account liberalization in the 1980s and 1990s, especially when compared with earlier attempts to open trade,[13] can be explained by the fact that the former concentrate benefits on mobile asset sectors, while the latter distributes gains rather evenly across society. More specifically, it has been shown that an open capital account increases opportunities for groups to access financial adaptation instruments (currency substitution, dollarization, capital flight), and that in contexts of macroeconomic disequilibria groups with access to these technologies reduce their taxable base and displace the welfare losses toward groups for whom financial adaptation is not available or too costly. Over time the latter groups will relax their conditions, bearing the larger share of the stabilization costs as well.[14]

Thus, even in the case of macroeconomic aggregates, which by definition cut across groups in society, reform scenarios are characterized by distributional conflicts within an intertemporal dynamic. These settings are propitious for the formation of distributional coalitions, in the sense that groups with high asset mobility are more likely to tolerate higher inflation and for longer periods than

12. See, among others, Ronald McKinnon, *The Order of Economic Liberalization: Financial Control in the Transition to a Market Economy* (Baltimore: Johns Hopkins University Press, 1991); Sebastian Edwards, "The Order of Liberalization of the External Sector in Developing Countries," *Princeton Essays in International Finance* 156 (1984); Dani Rodrik, "How Should Structural Adjustment Programs Be Designed?" *World Development* 18, no. 7 (July 1990): 933–47; and Rudiger Dornbusch, "Credibility and Stabilization," *Quarterly Journal of Economics* 106 (August 1991): 837–50.

13. Not just in emerging markets but also in the OECD. See Kurzer, *Business and Banking,* and Geoffrey Garrett, *Partisan Politics in the Global Economy* (Cambridge: Cambridge University Press, 1998).

14. See two papers by Raúl Labán and Federico Sturzenegger, "Distributional Conflict, Financial Adaptation, and Delayed Stabilizations," *Economics and Politics* 6 (November 1994); and idem "Fiscal Conservatism as a Response to the Debt Crisis," *Journal of Development Economics* 45 (December 1994).

groups with fixed assets.[15] If they can "wait and see" during inflation, their exit threats become more credible, increasing the costs to policymakers not willing to defer to such groups when designing reform programs.

These considerations are necessary to a better understanding of privatization, especially because, as argued earlier, this policy lies at the intersection of macroeconomic stabilization, microeconomic restructuring, and the design of institutions. To the extent that they constitute an important source of revenue, affect competition and the price structure of the economy, and bring about the alteration of institutional domains, divestiture programs are instrumental for most of the objectives specified in broader reform programs. The problem, however, is that the pursuit of these multiple and simultaneous goals often translate into policies that neutralize each other or, worse, work across purposes. Thus privatization is key to the overall reform effort but it also exacerbates distributional problems, and, as such, it is very much subject to interest-group politics.

For example, under far-reaching privatization, private sector demand for credit in domestic and international capital markets increases. Privatization thus contributes to open the capital account further, which puts downward pressure on the exchange rate. Currency appreciation will lead to the accumulation of trade deficits, largely financed by the inflow of financial resources, and increase pressure on the real sector of the economy, greatly accelerating industrial restructuring.[16] This setting can be worsened by across-the-board deregulation of the domestic financial sector, for increasing incentives for arbitrage will produce a massive reallocation of resources from the real to the financial sector, generating efficiency losses that partially offset the welfare effects of liberalization.

In addition, if privatization is initiated in the midst of inflation, as in most Latin American and East European nations in the 1990s and, though more moderate, in some West European ones in the 1980s, this context interferes with the microeconomic objectives. Price distortions and macroeconomic instability make it difficult to value assets. Because of this, the price of the firms on the

---

15. This coincides with Jeffry Frieden's proposition that holders of liquid assets are better shielded from unfavorable government policy. This does not mean, as Frieden suggests, that because of this they are "indifferent to policy." See Frieden, *Debt, Development, and Democracy* (Princeton: Princeton University Press, 1991).

16. Sebastian Edwards, *Real Exchange Rates, Devaluation, and Adjustment: Exchange Rate Policy in Developing Countries* (Cambridge: MIT Press, 1989). For the seminal contributions on the real exchange rate during liberalization, see Ian Little, Tibor Scitovsky, and Maurice Scott, *Industry and Trade in Some Developing Countries: A Comparative Study* (London and New York: Oxford University Press, 1970); and Béla Balassa et al., *The Structure of Protection in Developing Countries* (Baltimore: Johns Hopkins University Press, 1971).

block tend to be determined less by their book value and current proceeds than by projected earnings and future market share. The more severe the budget deficit, the more incentives governments have to tender the companies undivided and with monopoly rights. In this context, revenue maximization offsets the expected increases in allocative efficiency associated with decentralized private ownership.

Governments with budget constraints also prioritize the speed of privatization, thus avoiding the breakup of the firms and impairing the design of a regulatory framework prior to the divestiture process.[17] This creates additional incentives for the transfer of public utilities as vertically integrated monopolies. If privatization also takes place in the banking sector, it will lead to concentration of assets and interlocking ownership, often resulting in unhealthy lending practices with significant moral hazard consequences. This context is propitious for collusion between policymakers and business groups involved in divestiture operations. It also allows newly private firms to enjoy skyrocketing rates and windfall profits, without any tangible benefits for consumers. The presence of insiders in the process, in turn, may make things even worse for, as in several East European countries, they can take over the assets through noncash methods, reproducing monopoly tendencies while forgoing the much needed fiscal proceeds.

In sum, the main theoretical implication drawn from this approach is that across-the-board market reform may not be enough to eliminate incentives for rent-seeking behavior; indeed, it can just as well generate new ones. This suggests a criticism of most approaches constructed on the basis of neoclassical collective action assumptions: to expect the problem of distributional coalitions to be invariably resolved by liberalization. Yet it also implies that concepts like rent seeking and distributional coalitions, if extended to market reform experiments, can have even more explanatory power than expected. If this is so, state-autonomy arguments, widely used to explain market-oriented reform, should be reconsidered. In the next section, I examine why, unable to capture the distributional implications of economic reform, dominant explanations developed by economists and political scientists fail to specify the political behavior of interest groups during marketization, thus providing an insufficient account of the process.

---

17. See, for example, V. V. Ramandham, ed., *Privatization and After: Monitoring and Regulation* (London: Routledge, 1994); Brian Levy and Pablo Spiller, eds., *Regulations, Institutions, and Commitment* (Cambridge: Cambridge University Press, 1996); Ravi Ramamurti, ed., *Privatizing Monopolies: Lessons from the Telecommunications and Transport Sector in Latin America,* (Baltimore: Johns Hopkins University Press, 1996).

Economic Policy and the Politics of Economic Reform:
The Intellectual Terrain

In this section I outline the main theoretical foils of this study. The neoclassical political economy approach and the literature on the politics of economic adjustment have analyzed the policy-making process through a payoff structure rooted in neoclassical assumptions. A closed economy concentrates benefits and disperses costs, while openness reverses this distribution; reform is thus treated as a public good. On that basis, both approaches have drawn collective action implications that point to the difficulties of gathering political support for market reform. Thus, economists have generally focused on the consistency and the credibility of reform policies, whereas political scientists have emphasized issues such as the insularity and cohesiveness of reform teams as the main explanatory variables of the process.

These assumptions lead to an incomplete reading of the coalition-building process associated with marketization and, central to a political economy effort, they account for the type of state theory constructed on the basis of that reading. The neoclassical political economy approach invokes the organization of interest groups to explain protectionism and interventionism, leaving largely unexplored any political factors that may explain liberalization. Thus, it provides only a theory of the "interventionist" state. For much of the literature on the political economy of reform, in turn, the alleged weakness of pro-reform groups vis-à-vis forces favoring the status quo highlights the critical importance of the capacity of policymakers to insulate themselves. Thus, this perspective advances merely a theory of the "autonomous" state. Both approaches, therefore, need important modifications to capture the collective action leading to, and the institutional changes driven by, market reforms.

Economics and the Neoclassical Political Economy Approach

For collective action theories inspired by neoclassical economics, it is the strategic behavior of individuals and groups that accounts for political intervention in the economy. Interests have incentives to organize in small groups because organization is costly and large groups facilitate free riding. When these groups ascertain that the benefits they obtain will exceed the costs incurred, they invest resources in seeking protection. Since there is uncertainty as to how additional output will be distributed, distributional coalitions penetrate decision-making arenas only to redirect existing wealth toward themselves, a scenario that increases state intervention in the economy. As Olson put it, "The accumulation of distributional coalitions increases the complexity of regulation [and] the role of government."[18]

Olson's is mainly a capture theory: public officials are targets of well-organized groups, the rent seekers who "demand" protection.[19] But there is also a supply side to this story. To the extent that politicians maximize their utility by exchanging policies for political support, they prefer allocation through political bargaining rather than through market exchanges and, thus, provide rents to their constituencies.[20] Combined and applied to the developing world—Latin America in particular—these perspectives shed light on the persistence of import-substituting industrialization (ISI). In fact, protectionism generally nurtured a system of patronage in favor of domestic-oriented industrialists, organized labor, and public enterprise—the urban and often-populist coalition behind ISI.[21]

Extended to West and East European context, this approach has also explained why different corporatist frameworks are conducive to more or less monopolistic forms of wage bargaining,[22] and how state socialism developed into a system of collusion between company managers and party officials followed by extreme institutional sclerosis,[23] respectively. Across the board, the creation of institutional settings conducive to the proliferation of distributional coalitions is seen as the source of economic decline. The economy wanes because the politicization of economic policies leads to inefficient allocation and because resources are increasingly wasted in efforts to influence policymakers, namely, in directly unproductive profit-seeking (DUP) activities.[24]

---

18. Mancur Olson, *The Rise and Decline of Nations,* 73; and also, idem, *The Logic of Collective Action* (Cambridge: Cambridge University Press, 1965).

19. The theories of the rent-seeking society share the viewpoint. The original contribution is Anne Krueger, "The Political Economy of the Rent-Seeking Society," *American Economic Review* 64 (June 1974). See also Robert Tollison, "Rent Seeking: A Survey," *Kyklos* 35 (1982).

20. For early contributions, see Anthony Downs, *An Economic Theory of Democracy* (New York: Harper & Row, 1957); and William Nordhaus, "The Political Business Cycle," *Review of Economic Studies* 42 (April 1975).

21. Barry Ames, *Political Survival: Politicians and Public Policy in Latin America* (Berkeley: University of California Press, 1987); John Waterbury, *Exposed to Innumerable Delusions: Public Enterprise and State Power in Egypt, India, Mexico, and Turkey* (Cambridge: Cambridge University Press, 1993); and Barbara Geddes, *Politician's Dilemma: Building State Capacity in Latin America* (Berkeley: University of California Press, 1994).

22. Lars Calmfors and John Driffil, "Bargaining Structure, Corporatism, and Macroeconomic Performance," *Economic Policy* 6 (1988): 14–61.

23. Mancur Olson, "The Logic of Collective Action in Soviet-Type Economies," *Journal of Soviet Nationalities* 1, no. 2 (summer 1990): 1–28; Peter Murrel and Mancur Olson, "The Devolution of Centrally Planned Economies," *Journal of Comparative Economics* 15, no. 2 (June 1991): 239–65.

24. Jagdish Bhagwati, "Directly Unproductive, Profit-Seeking (DUP) Activities," *Journal of Political Economy* 90 (October 1982).

It is axiomatic of this approach that government intervention and rent-seeking behavior go hand in hand; that is, virtually any state intervention creates opportunities for rent-seeking behavior. As James Buchanan put it: "Rent-seeking activity is directly related to the scope and range of government activity in the economy, to the relative size of the public sector."[25] Conversely, a government committed to the market will be less penetrable, will discourage the formation of distributional coalitions, and will thus dissipate rents. As a reviewer of this literature conveys: "the best way to limit rent seeking is to limit the government."[26]

Given this framework of incentives, policymakers implementing reform programs must be uncompromising with groups whose market reserves are eliminated by liberalization. However, since losers are supposed to be ready for political organization and winners are prone to free riding, they have to do it pretty much on their own. As a prominent advocate of marketization put it, "in a handful of heroes" lies "the secret of success."[27] This view was echoed by equally prominent advisers and policymakers involved in the postcommunist transformation who argued that "extraordinary" political circumstances are necessary to sustain policy reforms within such an unfavorable collective action context.[28]

Telling as they may be, these metaphors beg important questions about economic policy-making in general and the reform experience in particular. If the foes of an open economy possess such a capacity for collective action, what explains the pace, scope, and length of the liberalization trend? How can reform-minded elites, on their own, launch policies to abolish the privileges of such powerful rent seekers and still survive their pressure, often under conditions of economic crisis and political instability? In other words, what exactly allows these "heroic" policymakers implementing economic liberalization under "extraordinary" political conditions to prevail over well-organized forces seeking protectionism, subsidies, and regulations?

---

25. "Rent Seeking and Profit Seeking," in Buchanan, Tollison, and Tullock, *Toward a Theory of the Rent-Seeking Society,* 9.

26. David Colander, "Introduction," in *Neoclassical Political Economy,* 5.

27. Arnold Harberger, "Secret of Success: A Handful of Heroes," *American Economic Review* 83, no. 2 (May 1993): 343–50. Though more sensitive to their role as coalition builders, a similar emphasis on the talent of the individuals leading the reforms is in Jorge Dominguez, ed., *Technopols: Freeing Politics and Markets in Latin America in the 1990s* (University Park: Pennsylvania State University Press, 1997).

28. See Jan Winiecki, "Why Economic Reforms Fail in the Soviet System—A Property Rights Approach," *Economic Inquiry* 28, no. 2 (April 1990): 195–221; Leszek Balcerowicz, *Socialism, Capitalism, Transformation* (Budapest and London: CEU Press, 1995); Mario Blejer and Fabrizio Coricelli, *The Making of Economic Reform in Eastern Europe: Conversations with Leading Reformers in Poland, Hungary, and the Czech Republic* (Brookfield, Vt.: E. Elgar, 1995).

These questions, however, cannot be answered within this collective action approach, for the strategic behavior of groups is linked to government policy only under conditions of state intervention. The theory of collective action is mostly a capture theory, though a unidirectional one: toward intervention. The reverse situation, however—namely, that interests organize and capture decision-making arenas to induce governments to withdraw from the economy— remains untheorized. It is, in fact, inimical to this approach to consider whether analogous distributional coalitions could organize in anticipation of market reserves made available by marketization, and that collusion between economic elites and policymakers could give a most decisive impetus to liberalization. Based on a profoundly negative view of politics characteristic of neoclassical economics (that is why whenever societal groups engage in political organization, protectionism is invariably expected to follow), this approach brings politics into the picture in order to explain interventionism, but when economic policy adopts a pro-market direction, politics vanishes—policy consistency and credibility, and the heroism of the policymakers, take its place. In sum, as much as the neoclassical political economy approach has attempted to endogenize the state into its models, it succeeded just in a context of market-deviant policies. As such, this approach furnishes only a theory of the "interventionist" state.

Political Science and the State-Autonomy Approach

Implicitly or explicitly, a wealth of research in political economy has started from those unanswered questions and addressed them by the heading "the politics of economic adjustment."[29] Scholars in this research program, mostly political scientists, have provided a rather straightforward answer to the preceding quandaries. Paradoxically, however, and despite their greater sensitivity to political factors, their explanation is based on a payoff matrix rooted in the neoclassical paradigm. Since liberalization concentrates present costs on the beneficiaries of a closed economy and disperses (initially uncertain) benefits in the future, it is generally argued, losers have incentives to engage in collective action but prospective winners, facing uncertainty about payoffs, remain disorganized.

The pro-reform coalition is thus seen as "fragile" vis-à-vis those forces favoring ISI. Consequently, the reform process needs to be politically "managed"— groups favoring the status quo must be thwarted. Lacking effective societal support, reform elites rely on enhancing autonomy, cohesiveness, and institutional

---

29. See footnote 2.

capacities in order to override opposition. Given these assumptions, it has been common in this approach to explain economic policy reform by the inevitability of the adjustment—the consequence of deep economic disequilibria[30]—or by exogenous factors—the pressure of foreign governments and multilateral financial institutions.[31]

Arguably, these factors together have forced governments to adjust, depriving them of domestic political support, especially at the outset of the reform process when economic pain has to be distributed widely in society. Within this payoff structure, these reforms can originate only in the realm of insulated policy-making teams who have to design and implement policy autonomously from society because, as Haggard and Kaufman put it, "compared to those who gain from the status quo, the diffuse beneficiaries of the reforms may have substantial difficulty organizing, particularly when the gains from the policy reform are ambiguous and uncertain."[32]

This view has permeated "the politics of economic adjustment" throughout. John Waterbury, for example, sees the state sector as "the lynchpin of a reputedly powerful coalition of beneficiaries with well-established claims to public resources," whereas "the beneficiaries of reform and privatization remain unorganized," enhancing in this setting the importance of "the coherence of technocratic policy change teams."[33] In this context, argues Joan Nelson, where "the benefits of structural changes are often delayed and accrue to individuals and groups who are not politically organized and may not even recognize their potential gains when the policy is launched . . . it is hard to build a political alliance with them."[34] With these assumptions, it would be logical to limit political

30. See, for example, John Williamson, "What Washington Means by Policy Reform," in Williamson, ed., *Latin American Adjustment: How Much Has Happened?* (Washington, D.C.: Institute for International Economics, 1990); and Anne Krueger, *Economic Policy Reform in Developing Countries* (Oxford and Cambridge: Blackwell, 1992).

31. See, for instance, Barbara Stallings, "International Influence on Economic Policy: Debt, Stabilization, and Structural Reform," in Haggard and Kaufman, *The Politics of Economic Adjustment;* and Miles Kahler, "International Financial Institutions and the Politics of Adjustment," in Nelson, *Fragile Coalitions.*

32. Haggard and Kaufman, *The Politics of Economic Adjustment,* 27. Even if in *The Political Economy of Democratic Transitions,* Haggard and Kaufman consider other variables to explain economic reform—regime type, party systems, corporatist frameworks, and electoral rules, among others—they insist that "the costs of reform tend to be concentrated, while benefits are diffused, producing perverse organizational incentives; losers are well organized, while prospective winners face daunting collective action problems and are not" (157). Because of this, the explanatory power of insulated policy elites remains of a higher hierarchy than the other variables.

33. Waterbury, "The Heart of the Matter? Public Enterprise and the Adjustment Process," in Haggard and Kaufman, *The Politics of Economic Adjustment,* 183.

34. Nelson, *Economic Crisis and Policy Choice,* 359.

analyses to the role of negative interests, that is, to those who oppose economic reforms, and to disregard how interests organize in support of them.

Thus, whereas economists have generally emphasized the importance of consistency and credibility for successful reform, political scientists have stressed the resolve and insulation of policy-making elites, positing these factors as the main causal variable of the process. Both therefore adopt an approach "from above." Whereas under liberalization an explicit conception of power tends to be absent from the work of economists, political scientists underline the importance of negative power, that is, the capacity of the executive to disorganize opposition. For these reasons the "politics of economic adjustment" is often reduced to the "politics of neutralizing the losers." In fact, the lack of a conception of positive power and the neglect of proactive collective action overlooks that coalitions also organize in support of liberalization. The larger politics of economic reform thus remains unexplored, and the collective action driving policy change, undertheorized.

Despite different points of departure, therefore, the approaches reviewed in this section converge in their understanding of the economic policy-making process in general and marketization in particular. While neoclassical perspectives provide only a theory of the interventionist state, the literature on the politics of economic adjustment advances merely a theory of the "autonomous" state. Yet neither the proposition that only interventionist policy contexts generate incentives for groups to engage in rent-seeking behavior and distributional coalition building nor the claim that liberalization flows from insulated policy teams because losers are better organized than winners conform to the empirical materials discussed in this book. In fact, the reform experiments examined in chapters below indicate the existence of increasing opportunities for rent-seeking behavior during marketization, a consideration that would suggest a concentration of benefits and dispersion of costs. On this basis, I suggest modifications to those approaches by bringing interests to the forefront of our theorization in political economy (which state autonomy arguments omit) irrespective of whether the economy is closed or open (which neoclassical perspectives overlook).

Re-Forming the State: Explaining Institutional Change by Policy Change

Economists' claims are based on a negative view of politics characteristic of neoclassical economics. In the literature on the politics of economic adjustment, its propositions about the insularity of policymakers are inspired by what appears to be an increasingly prevalent tendency in the field of political economy:

to view political institutions—particularly the state—as autonomous structures with their own distinctive ideas, interests, and objectives and to treat them as the independent variable that explains various socioeconomic outcomes, government policy among them.[35]

Scholars persuaded by a state-centered approach have sought to reject views of the state as epiphenomenal of societal forces. Government policy does not necessarily reflect the interests of competing societal groups because institutions do more than merely aggregate and transmit the preferences of interest groups; they mediate, combine, and ultimately modify those preferences. The pervasiveness of institutional contexts, that is, their propensity to outlive the factors that have given rise to them, in turn, influences even the way actors perceive their own interest. Since institutions are seen as the carriers of historical legacies, contributors to this research program have generally emphasized patterns of institutional continuity. Thus, the larger contribution of "historical institutionalism" to the field of political economy has consisted of "understanding policy continuities over time within countries, and policy variation across countries."[36] For, if institutions change only occasionally, and if they retain a central role for the explanation of policy outcomes, policy continuity is the only logical consequence to be expected. This approach, therefore, cannot provide an adequate theory of institutional change because institutions are always treated as the independent variable and their autonomy and durability constitute a basic premise of the entire theoretical construct.

Only by placing institutions in the role of the dependent variable can we move beyond an analysis of how institutions shape outcomes and constrain behavior and assess, instead, under what conditions and by what types of processes new constraints are defined. In this book, those conditions are determined by comprehensive market reform experiments, and the specific processes take place within privatization programs. Viewing institutional change as the result of the distributive outcomes of marketization seeks to highlight that the

---

35. The landmark contributions are Peter Katzenstein, ed., *Between Power and Plenty* (Madison: University of Wisconsin Press, 1978) (yet a more heterogeneous set of contributions); Peter Evans, Dietrich Rueschemeyer, and Theda Skocpol, eds., *Bringing the State Back In* (Cambridge: Cambridge University Press, 1985); James M. March and Johan P. Olsen, *Rediscovering Institutions: The Organizational Basis of Politics* (New York: Free Press, 1990); and Sven Steinmo, Kathleen Thelen, and Frank Longstreth, eds., *Structuring Politics: Historical Institutionalism in Comparative Analysis* (Cambridge: Cambridge University Press, 1992). A recent review and statement along these lines is in Paul Pierson, "Increasing Returns, Path Dependence, and the Study of Politics," *American Political Science Review* 94, no. 2 (June 2000): 251–67.

36. Kathleen Thelen and Sven Steinmo, "Historical Institutionalism in Comparative Politics," in Steinmo, Thelen, and Longstreth, *Structuring Politics,* 10.

enforcement institutions of a society—economic, legal, political—are meant not only to secure greater prosperity[37] but also to affect the distribution of wealth. In other words, institutions affect economic performance, but they also provide a framework for struggles over the distribution of the gains. As such, institutions become the battlegrounds for interest-group politics.[38]

Seen in this light, the connection between policy and institutions is apparent. To the extent that actors can anticipate the distributive effects of economic policy, and organize and mobilize accordingly, they can also anticipate that once policy becomes embedded into an institutional setting, future disputes over distributive outcomes are avoided, or at least mitigated. Thus, preferences over policy translate into preferences over institutions. Interest groups seek to invest resources in institutional configurations that stabilize their preferred distributional outcome, for the same reasons that they aim their strategies at redirecting existing wealth toward themselves rather than at maximizing output. Thus, institutions are neither autonomous nor created by actors pursuing optimal choices; rather, they are often the product of actors who seek to gain strategic advantage in ways that secure distributional outcomes. This comprehensive process of institutional redesign highlights the state-building character of marketization.

If interest groups anticipate the distributional consequences of institutional designs, political elites often anticipate their political effects. Reform governments are said to become excessively reformist less because of straightforward economic results they expect and more because they attempt to resolve reputation problems. They seek to signal agents in a specific direction[39] and to enhance credibility by committing to an emerging normative order. The consolidation of new institutional arrangements, however, has a more immediate political incentive: it facilitates a reconcentration at the center, largely achieved by increasing power in the executive. In this context, cementing winning coalitions and dislocating opposition groups become more feasible.

---

37. Douglass North, *Structure and Change in Economic History* (New York: Norton, 1981); and *Institutions, Institutional Change and Economic Performance* (Cambridge: Cambridge University Press, 1990).

38. For a distributive approach to institutions, see Robert Bates, *Beyond the Miracle of the Market* (Cambridge: Cambridge University Press, 1989); George Tsebelis, *Nested Games: Rational Choice in Comparative Politics* (Berkeley: University of California Press, 1990); Jack Knight, *Institutions and Social Conflict* (Cambridge: Cambridge University Press, 1992); and Jack Knight and Itai Sened, eds., *Explaining Social Institutions* (Ann Arbor: University of Michigan Press, 1995).

39. Dani Rodrik, "Promises, Promises: Credible Policy Reform via Signaling," *National Bureau of Economic Research Working Paper* 2600 (May 1988). This and other influential papers on signaling were brought together by Federico Sturzenegger and Mariano Tomassi, eds., *The Political Economy of Reform* (Cambridge, Mass.: MIT Press, 1998).

In Latin America, for example, the rent-seeking behavior of industrial-financial conglomerates and the consolidation of distributional coalitions shaped the pace and content of much of privatization. One common feature in military (Chile), civil authoritarian (Mexico), and democratic (Argentina) contexts as well, has been that, along with economic reforms, governments embarked on unprecedented institutional changes—new constitutions, autonomous central banks, and private social security systems, to name just a few—that translated into increasing executive authority.

In Britain, in turn, the electoral calendar and the goal of making inroads among the working-class electorate shaped and accelerated Margaret Thatcher's privatization efforts, particularly in regard to the share distribution and council housing programs. An alteration of coalitional incentives gave the Conservative government an opportunity to engage in massive institution-building tasks: welfare state reform and civil service reorganization, among others, in the context of an increasing centralization of decision-making power in the office of the prime minister.

In several countries of East-Central Europe, well-positioned ex-communists have become wealthy entrepreneurs by taking over state assets. "Nomenklatura privatization"—the distribution of assets among former company directors and party officialdom—appears to have been effective in eliminating the nomenklatura as a political mechanism, particularly in Hungary and Poland. The transition from "soft to hard property rights" became pivotal for the transition from "soft to hard budget constraints." It contributed to the reconstruction of the fiscal base of the state and the very institutions of capitalism and democracy, but it also cemented a coalition of winners that allowed for a relatively rapid and benign recomposition of the control and oversight functions of the state.

It is in this context, and on the basis of the theoretical considerations discussed previously, that this book explains institutional change by policy change. A detailed examination of marketization across regions highlights what and how particular factors that are likely to affect institutions come into play. More specifically, the emergence of a new edifice of property relations has triggered vast processes of institutional change, ones whose scope and nature point to the classic themes of state formation. As argued earlier, this would be of no surprise for historians of state formation, for they have shown that the construction of effective public institutions has generally been accompanied by the empowering of private groups. The key to this process is the specification and enforcement of property rights—in this study, the politics of privatization—because rulers must offer positive benefits to a minimum winning coalition in order to sustain revenue production systems over time, ensure stable rule, monopolize coercive means so as to provide protection, eliminate rivals, and centralize administrative and political resources.[40] The state is thus "re-formed."

Logic of Comparison and Case Selection

The type of analysis adopted in this book relies on a method of controlled comparisons among a small number of cases. On this basis, I examine the hypothesized causal relationship between distributional coalitions and privatization programs across cases. As I argue that liberalization is not enough to eliminate incentives for rent-seeking behavior, I examine variation in the type of interaction between interest groups and policymakers, and differences in the mix and sequence of marketization policies pursued. Thus, the cases are selected on the basis of the relevance of the event to be explained. A limited number of cases allows for a detailed analysis of the causal flow of events and for a systematic examination of similarities and differences. Yet the number of cases (or observations) is high enough, and diverse enough, to keep the number of explanatory variables advanced by the theoretical argument to a minimum.[41]

In this sense, the first set of empirical observations comes from the examination of the Chilean policy reform experience after 1973 and until the 1990s, and I inductively fine-tune the argument on the basis of the Chilean experience. The reason is that, long before the wave of economic liberalization policies in the 1980s and 1990s, Chile constituted the first country to embark on comprehensive market reform programs and to turn them into the part and parcel of state strategy and purpose. It is common social science practice to stylize explanations of different phenomena on the basis of a crucial, often early, case and draw insights from that case for comparative analysis. Consider, to name just a few examples, the importance of England for the larger study of capitalist industrialization, the primacy of the case of Russia for the broader analysis

---

40. See footnotes 5 and 6, and Michael Hechter and William Brustein, "Regional Modes of Production and Patterns of State Formation in Western Europe," *American Journal of Sociology* 85, no. 5 (1980); Frederic Lane, *Profits from Power: Readings in Protection Rent and Violence-Controlling Enterprises* (Albany: SUNY Press, 1979); Allan Silver, "The Demands for Order in Civil Society: A Review of Some Themes in the History of Urban Crime, Police, and Riot," in David Bordua, ed., *The Police: Six Sociological Essays* (New York: John Wiley & Sons, 1967); 1–24; Youssef Cohen, Brian Brown, and A. F. K. Organski, "The Paradoxical Nature of State Making: The Violent Creation of Order," *American Political Science Review* 75 (1981).

41. See Adam Przeworski and Henry Teune, *The Logic of Comparative Social Science* (New York: Wiley, 1970); Arend Lijphart, "Comparative Politics and the Comparative Method," *American Political Science Review* 65 (1971): 682–93.

of social revolution and state socialism, and more recently, the centrality of the Spanish case for the scholarship on democratic transitions.

In the same vein, I treat the Chilean case as the modal political economy of privatization, not because other cases may have emulated the Chilean reforms—though that factor should not be underestimated among several "late reformers"—but because the causal connections among distributional coalition building, marketization, and institutional redesign appear consistently throughout the country's broad reform experiment. On that basis, as I introduce more cases in my narrative I assess whether the argument retains more or less power in explaining later reform experiments. Thus, I subsequently examine the reform processes in Britain, Mexico, Argentina, and Hungary in that order. In so doing, I reproduce the "most different systems" design; that is, a strategy based on expected similar outcomes across a range of different contexts.

To the extent that the cases examined in this book stand out as significant reform experiences, the logic of case selection can be charged with sampling on the same value of the dependent variable and, thus, can be subjected to the much debated problem of selection bias.[42] Allowing for variance in the dependent variable, while selecting observations on the basis of the independent variable, is considered to enhance the reliability of the propositions advanced, for it makes them falsifiable on the basis of the frequency of presence of the hypothesized causal factor in the absence of the outcome expected. By allowing for a probabilistic assessment of the causal relationship under investigation, this selection method enhances the generalizability of the empirical findings, thus increasing the robustness of the theory.

However, three observations are pertinent in anticipation of criticisms along the lines of selection bias arguments. First, as a number of recent contributions have pointed out, selecting on the dependent variable has value in order to specify necessary, as opposed to sufficient, conditions of the outcome to be explained, as well as in order to eliminate a range of plausible causes, which is standard procedure under the scientific method.[43] The rival approaches of this study have argued that collusion leads to state intervention and, on the basis of

---

42. For two examples of this discussion, see Barbara Geddes, "How the Cases You Choose Affect the Answers You Get: Selection Bias in Comparative Politics," *Political Analysis* 2 (1990): 131–52; and Gary King, Robert Keohane, and Sidney Verba, *Designing Social Inquiry* (Princeton: Princeton University Press, 1994).

43. See Douglas Dion, "Evidence and Inference in the Comparative Case Study," *Comparative Politics* 30 (January 1998): 127–46; David Collier, "Letter from the President: Comparative Methodology in the 1990s"; and Charles Ragin, "Comparative Methodology, Fuzzy Sets, and the Study of Sufficient Causes," both in *American Political Science Association, Comparative Politics Newsletter* 9 (winter 1998): 1–5 and 18–22, respectively.

the payoff assumptions made, liberalization dissipates rent-seeking behavior. To prove those propositions wrong—one of my main theoretical goals—selecting on the dependent variable is probably the most effective strategy. In fact, the more cases where market reform is present and distributional coalitions persist, the weaker those explanations become.[44]

Second, along with the main cross-regional analysis, I address another subset of more or less explicit comparisons. Whereas Chile, Mexico, and Argentina are seen in the context of the terminal crisis of ISI in Latin America, the British case is generally treated as a manifestation of the general problem of Keynesian decline in Western Europe, and the Hungarian case is examined under the light of the broad postcommunist transition in East-Central Europe. With this type of comparative analysis, I complement the previous selection method based on the dependent variable. By assessing possible variance in outcome among roughly similar cases, I sample on the independent variable. I thus add to the analysis a "most similar systems" perspective.[45]

Third, as I proceed from the examination of the factors that explain market reform and privatization to the analysis of the institutional consequences of those policy changes, I develop a sequential narrative in support of the theoretical argument. With this procedure, I hold economic reform constant across the cases, to address variance in the mode and timing of institution-building strategies and state formation processes emerging from similar marketization programs in different countries. By developing a more complete picture of the politics of economic reform over time, I thus attempt to reduce the risks of selection bias.

Plan of the Book

Consistent with the methodology outlined, the second part of the book stylizes the argument on the basis of the Chilean experience. Thus, chapter 2 discusses the specifics of the Chilean economic policy reform process after 1973 and into the 1990s. Chapter 3 isolates the main explanatory variable of the process: the reproduction of opportunities for rent-seeking behavior and the

---

44. In other words, theoretically, there is no need for selecting cases with different values of the dependent variable in this study, for the causal primacy of distributional coalitions upon state interventionism has already been established in the literature. Yet, by developing a historical narrative, I do introduce variation in the dependent variable by examining the behavior of interest groups and rent seekers under different political economies—ISI in Latin America, Keynesian in Western Europe, and state and reform socialism in Eastern Europe.

45. For a recent example of this combination of methods of analysis, see Valerie Bunce, *Subversive Institutions* (Cambridge: Cambridge University Press, 1999).

impact of interest groups organized in distributional coalitions on the reform program in general and privatization in particular. And chapter 4 examines how, cast and designed as institution-building instruments, these policies subsequently triggered vast state formation strategies.

The third part of the book introduces a broad comparative perspective in order to evaluate the argument. The subsequent chapters introduce wide variance across regions and within region as well. An assessment of the main propositions in cases with different positions in the international system, types of political regime, levels of development, and pre-reform strategies of development enhances the explanatory power of the approach while simultaneously introducing nuances to the argument. Chapter 5 examines the British experience from 1979 on, chapter 6 examines Mexico in the 1980s and 1990s together with the Argentine liberalization experience in the late 1970s and again in the 1990s, and chapter 7 approaches the postcommunist transition by focusing on Hungary since the late communist period. The narrative used for the Chilean story is reproduced in the structure of each of the three comparative chapters: first, a historical political economy analysis that sets up the long-term trends behind reform policies; second, the examination of the main, and more or less distributional, coalitional-building practices leading to privatization; and third, the effects of these policies on comprehensive institutional changes.

The last chapter summarizes the theoretical and empirical analysis and outlines a general framework about the politics of economic reform and privatization. Having established the state formation character of marketization, this chapter also introduces some speculations, and future avenues of research, regarding the tensions between tendencies toward the reassertion of state power, centralization, and concentration of power in the executive—all distinctive of state-building activities—and parallel democratic processes. These reflections take us back, once again, to state formation literature, and to possible ways of reconciling this literature with the scholarship on democratic transition and consolidation.

PART 2

Stylizing the Approach

Chile's Reform Experiment

Chapter 2

From State to Market

The Chilean Policy Reform Experiment

As discussed in the introductory chapter, the argument of this book is stylized on the basis of the Chilean reform experiment. The main reason for this approach is not that Chile has pioneered the implementation of comprehensive market reforms in the developing world, nor that its liberalization experience has received close attention by "late reformers" in the developing and the postcommunist worlds—though these two factors should not be underestimated. I have inductively developed the argument based on the fact that the hypothesized causal relationships—those between the behavior of distributional coalitions and the sequence and content of the policy process, and between privatization and the emerging institutional redesign—appear consistently throughout the country's long economic reform.

This is the first of three chapters that examine the Chilean case. Here, I describe the overall process of reform, its different policies, the sequence of implementation, and its economic and political consequences. Thus, I place the analysis of privatization within a larger policy framework. This is another reason for a detailed analysis of the Chilean experiment. The implementation of privatization through several phases and different methods was consistent with broader policy objectives and had, in turn, different institutional implications. Thus, the evidence presented in this chapter highlights how, to the extent that they provide revenue and affect the price structure of the economy, divestiture programs are at the core of policy efforts directed toward macroeconomic stabilization and microeconomic restructuring.

This chapter also shows that the simultaneous pursuit of macro- and microeconomic goals through privatization often translates into policies that neutralize each other, or even work across purposes, thus leading to suboptimal aggregate outcomes. As such, privatization magnifies the primacy of distributional considerations: it is very much subject to interest-group politics—this I discuss in chapter 3. In addition, to the extent that privatization programs bring about the alteration of crucial institutional configurations, they also constitute a state-building strategy—an issue I examine in chapter 4.

This chapter provides the necessary empirical background of the policy process. The findings are presented in two sections. The first describes the main economic policy reforms implemented throughout the period 1974–90. The second examines the different privatization programs implemented and the various methods employed in the country's comprehensive divestiture effort.

The Market Reform Experiment

I review in this section the central characteristics and phases of the comprehensive policy reform experiment in Chile. The periodization is based on the main policy instruments used. Regardless of their effects on economic performance, differences in policy instruments are seen here as a reflection of the politics of the process and are considered to have distinctive implications for emerging institutional configurations.

Normalization, 1973–74

Upon seizing power, the military government's economic goals were to reverse the policies of the Allende administration and restore macroeconomic stability. Given the previous levels of inflation and public deficit,[1] as well as widespread food shortages, emphasis was placed on restoring market mechanisms. Prices were freed up and the exchange rate was devalued in October by 230 percent. In addition, taxes were increased and public expenditures reduced in an effort to correct the large public sector deficit. A new value added tax (VAT) was introduced, while direct taxes on capital gains were eliminated and taxes on corporate profits reduced. As it struggled to control inflation, the government tended to repress demand by both contracting the money supply and reducing wages.

The military government's initial approach was characterized by policy pragmatism, the result of a broad and heterogeneous support coalition with rather contradictory economic interests. Nevertheless, the authorities disclosed their long-term goals of structural transformation. Early on, the possibility of reproducing the pre-1970 traditional impost-substituting industrialization (ISI) was ruled out, even if the across-the-board liberalization Chile pioneered in

---

1. By September 1973, the fiscal deficit exceeded 20 percent of GDP and inflation mounted to an annual rate of 1,000 percent.

Latin America and in much of the developing world was not fully implemented until 1979.[2] At this time, government officials also established the future lines of social security policy and outlined the fundamentals of a far-reaching reform, implemented in 1980.[3] In this phase, property under state control (though not legally nationalized) was returned to legal owners, and the government announced a calendar for the reprivatization of commercial banks and firms nationalized by the socialist government (Popular Unity, UP). Finally, the government banned the activities of unions and suppressed collective bargaining, allegedly to bring inflation down, but also to curb the power of organized labor.

These measures backfired. Reflecting previously repressed inflation, abrupt deregulation of prices led to a peak 128 percent inflation in the last quarter of 1973, stabilizing at around 45 percent quarterly in 1974, in any case far above the expectations of policymakers. Recessionary measures in turn had an impact on production, wage, and employment levels. With inflation and recession aggravated by the fall of copper prices, which resulted in $375 million loss of reserves in the last quarter of 1974 and, subsequently, a severe balance-of-payments crisis, the government was ready for the adoption of new policy instruments.

Shock Treatment, April 1975–June 1976

The failure of the gradualist strategy to bring down inflation, reduce trade and fiscal deficits, and increase output and reserves brought a group of monetarist policymakers to office. In October 1974, Jorge Cauas, then vice president of the central bank, was appointed finance minister, replacing navy officer Leonardo Gotuzzo. Pablo Baraona took Cauas's post at the central bank. And in April

---

2. In the words of the first minister of finance: "The Government estimates that the reform of the tariff structure should be completely effective in less than three years. . . . High tariffs favor the subsistence of inefficient monopolies, which are incompatible with the free competition that should characterize a market economy. Instead, low tariffs will oblige domestic monopolies to confront international competition, with evident benefits for the Chilean consumer." Vice Admiral Leonardo Gotuzzo, January 7, 1974, reproduced in *Somos Realmente Independientes Gracias al Esfuerzo de Todos los Chilenos: Documento de Política Económica* (Santiago: Budget Directorate, 1978), 61.

3. Note the statement by the minister of the economy: "Competitive systems under labor control will be created. Workers will not be forced to contribute to a pre-determined social security fund but rather to the one that will offer greater efficiency. This system will imply a reduction of maintenance costs. At the same time, it will imply a large accumulation of resources which can produce a true revolution of capital markets." Fernando Léniz, *La Tercera,* July 14, 1974. In its final form, the reformed system was put under control of the state, and it was mandatory for workers to choose only among private firms.

1975, Sergio de Castro substituted Fernando Léniz in the ministry of the economy. This reshuffle of the economic team signaled a move toward more theoretical consistency, which in turn led to the deepening of the stabilization program. In this phase, policymakers sought a drastic reduction of public expenditures, an increase in income tax revenues, and an even tighter monetary policy.

Cabinet reorganization, however, meant more than a mere rehash of functions. Driven by the goal of securing the economic reform in the long term, the appointment of Cauas in the ministry of finance was accompanied by a decree that granted "extraordinary powers to the minister of finance to materialize in a unified form economic and financial policy" above the authority of other policy agencies such as the ministries of the economy, agriculture, mining, and public works.[4] This decision revealed the consistency between the policy reforms and the necessary legislative and institutional outcomes. In a deregulated, open market economy, in which prices are determined by competition and allocation is conducted solely by market exchanges, the need for sectoral policies is said to decrease. The role of government is limited to the maintenance of macroeconomic equilibrium, and the institutional capacity of agencies responsible for macroeconomic policy—the ministry of finance and the central bank—logically grows at the expense of other, formally equal, agencies with a more sectoral orientation. In chapter 4, I discuss how this redistribution of power within the Chilean bureaucracy contributed even further to the centralization of authority—a process with long-term effects on the redesign of institutions and the exercise of state power. In chapters 5 to 7, I examine how very similar trends developed in other reform experiments. For now, the focus is on its consequences for the policy process.

Under the newly expanded institutional capacity of the ministry of finance, the recessionary package displayed an even more drastic character. Total public expenditures fell 27 percent during 1975 with a drop of 50 percent in public investment. As a result, industrial production at the end of 1975 was 35 percent below the 1974 level and, despite the implementation of a "Minimum Employment Program," unemployment mounted to almost 20 percent. Tax revenues increased when the government imposed a surcharge on income tax, removed exemptions in the VAT, and increased public utilities rates. A real 45 percent drop in the price of copper and a three-time increase in the price of oil imposed a dramatic decline in the terms of trade. Despite the severity of the recession, inflation, whose reduction was the main goal of the package, remained

---

4. *El Mercurio*, April 13, 1975, commenting on Decree No. 966, April 10, 1975.

inflation

at 29.4 percent for the last quarter of 1975, increasing to 38.8 percent for the second quarter of 1976.

In this phase, the pace of longer-term structural reforms accelerated. As discussed later in more detail, privatization proceeded through the sale of banks, the financial system was deregulated, and tariff reductions were hastened, surpassing the levels initially planned. Despite the more than modest success in controlling inflation, other indicators showed an improvement. The ongoing recession led to a decrease in imports, which ameliorated the reserves crisis. Nontraditional exports compensated, at least partially, for the loss of copper export revenues.

Curbing Costs and Taming Inflationary Expectations,
June 1976–June 1979

At the beginning of 1976, the economy was experiencing high inflation (198 percent annually), rampant unemployment (15 percent), and exiguous international reserves ($107 million). The economic team shifted the policy focus and announced a "Program of Economic Recovery" in June of that year. The program pursued the resolution of two specific problems: the persistence of inflation and the deep disequilibria in the balance of payments. The anti-inflationary strategy shifted from contracting demand to reducing production costs and expectations. To this end, the currency was revalued 10 percent.

Additionally, to tame inflationary expectations a thirty-day preannouncement of exchange rates was determined in February 1978. The adoption of an active crawling peg was meant to reduce inflation by shaping expectations about future inflation and by directly influencing the prices of tradables through slowing the rate of nominal devaluation. This practice of revaluation and preannouncement of exchange rates continued throughout this phase, leading to a stabilization of inflation at a quarterly rate between 7 and 9 percent in 1979. During 1976 and 1977 tariff reduction continued and the average 10 percent goal—to be reached in 1979—was announced.

The balance of payments, in turn, the other issue explicitly addressed by the recovery plan, exhibited ups and downs as a result of subsequent revaluations (June 1976 and March 1977) and devaluations (September 1977 and December 1977) in a context in which the fall of copper price further contributed to the deterioration of reserves. By the first semester of 1979, however, inflows of foreign capital led to a surplus of $550 million. Under these circumstances, the next policy phase would signal the apogee of the policy reform experiment.

Open Economy Monetarism and Institutional Reform,
June 1979–mid-1981

With a balance-of-payments surplus and a more moderate rate of inflation, the economic program entered a phase of deeper reforms, now under Sergio de Castro as minister of finance. A novel approach to stabilization and a sweeping liberalization effort took place along with unprecedented changes in the country's main economic institutions. In the political front, the new constitution was approved, and Pinochet achieved exceptional levels of concentration of authority in his office, even by the standards of authoritarian rule.

June 1979 was the momentous juncture. The opening up of the capital account was concluded. Reaching a homogeneous 10 percent tariff completed trade liberalization. And following a devaluation of 5.7 percent, the exchange rate was fixed at 39 pesos to the dollar, a rate that would hold for the next three years. Complete liberalization of international trade thus combined with a stable exchange rate. The strategy of full openness to international trade and the adoption of a nominal anchor became the pivotal anti-inflationary instrument. The expectation was that domestic prices would converge to world levels, on the basis of the monetary approach to the balance of payments, which stipulates that as domestic inflation decreases, the exchange rate can be held constant and price levels are set automatically.[5]

The application of the monetary approach to the balance of payments signaled a significant departure from conventional monetarism and constituted an innovative technique for Latin American stabilization, used in the southern cone as a whole. While previous methods regarded control of the money supply as the critical variable, it became irrelevant once the fixed exchange rate replaced the crawling peg as the optimal exchange rate policy. Foreign reserve accumulation, in turn, also ceased to be a problem, since the adjustment of domestic inflation to international price levels was expected to resolve balance-of-payments deficits.[6]

---

5. For an exhaustive analysis, see Nicolas Arditto Barletta, Mario Blejer, and Luis Landau, *Economic Liberalization and Stabilization Policies in Argentina, Chile, and Uruguay: Applications of the Monetary Approach to the Balance of Payments* (Washington, D.C.: A World Bank Symposium, 1983). For a criticism, see Alejandro Foxley, *Latin American Experiments in Neoconservative Economics* (Berkeley: University of California Press, 1983), 114–19. This policy framework resulted in real appreciation vis-à-vis the country's main trading partners, due to inflation rates still above industrialized nations and a continuous appreciation of the dollar in the early 1980s. Sebastian Edwards and Alejandra Cox-Edwards, *Monetarism and Liberalization: The Chilean Experiment* (Chicago: University of Chicago Press, 1987), chapter 2, calculated a real appreciation of 31 percent during the fixed exchange rate period, from June 1979 to September 1982.

6. See a comparative examination of these programs in Vittorio Corbo, Jaime de Melo, and James Tybout, eds., special issue of *World Development* 13, no. 8 (August 1985); and Sebastian

These were the years of the so-called Chilean "miracle." Between 1977 and 1981, the economy grew at an average of 7.9 percent per year, and inflation came down to 9 percent in 1981. With a stronger economic performance, stabilization goals under way, and microeconomic reforms completed, the government concentrated on its comprehensive program of institutional reforms, meant to reorganize society, change lawmaking procedures, and secure the economic model. The "Seven Modernizations" was the title given to this ambitious effort. It included a new labor code, the privatization of the social security and the health systems, the introduction of market incentives in education (which implied a de facto privatization), a reversal of past land reform policies, regional decentralization, and the design of new legislative acts. All these pieces of legislation would come together in the 1980 constitution.

2nd phase [handwritten margin note]

The labor plan and the privatization of the social security system were the two most significant modernizations. The former reestablished collective bargaining but limited it to the firm level. The latter allowed for a system of individual capitalization under the administration of newly created private retirement firms, most of which were linked by ownership to the main banks. Under a recently established domestic capital market, neither competitive nor transparent, this measure led to the centralization of large amounts of capital in the hands of a few financial conglomerates.

Crisis, 1982–84

By mid-1981 the economy was accumulating a wide array of disequilibria. The adoption of a nominal anchor to the exchange rate conflicted with the macroeconomic fundamentals. Fixing the exchange rate while nominal wages and contracts were indexed to past inflation resulted in real appreciation. In addition, domestic financial deregulation and capital account liberalization increased opportunities for and drastically reduced the cost of foreign borrowing. A large increase in credit fueled a rapid growth in domestic expenditure, 10.5 percent in 1979, 9.3 percent in 1980, and 11.6 percent in 1981.

As described by the literature on "exchange-rate-based stabilization," this policy context led to the boom years, but it was followed by a bust phase. It came when, under less propitious international conditions, increases in interest rates led to a sharp decline in the availability of foreign loans. The fixed exchange rate had continuously increased the disparity between international and domestic prices. By 1981 the current account deficit reached 90 percent of the

---

Edwards and Simon Teitel, eds., special issue of *Economic Development and Cultural Change* 34, no. 3 (April 1986).

value of exports. Doubts about the sustainability of the exchange rate regime were additionally reinforced by consistently unfavorable terms of trade. A period of negative capital flows thus began in 1981.[7]

With interest rates around 25 to 30 percent, the deterioration of economic activity led to an increase of nonperforming loans, which by the end of 1981 equaled one quarter of the banks' capital and reserves. Full liberalization and ineffective supervision of the banking system exacerbated moral hazard problems, as financial institutions engaged in lending practices that, under deposit insurance conditions, qualified as plain rent-seeking activities. In fact, banks were used to lending to companies related by ownership, to the extent that by the time their loan portfolios began to exhibit difficulties, the largest debtors were often the bank owners themselves.

The default of a private sugar monopoly in May 1981 constituted the first serious warning on the unsustainability of the policy regime. In November the government placed eight banks in receivership. The takeover avoided the collapse of the entire system, but it could not reverse a massive flight to the dollar, facilitated by unrestricted capital account transactions. A rapid depletion of central bank reserves forced the government to undertake a series of nominal devaluations as of May 1982. The devaluation indicated a departure from the existing rules and was taken as a clear signal of the loss of economic governance on the part of the authorities and increased the real value of the financial liabilities. Output thus fell 14 percent in 1982 and unemployment reached 26 percent.[8]

A widespread crisis developed thereafter. By 1983 private domestic indebtedness amounted to an equivalent of more than twice the capital and reserves

---

7. The literature on exchange-rate-based stabilization has shown that the initial consumption boom fed by real appreciation is often followed by current account deficits that, unfinanceable in the medium term, lead to inconsistent fiscal policies that affect the credibility of the peg. At that point, attacks on the currency may become widespread, usually with important losses in foreign exchange reserves and subsequent devaluation, inflation, and recession. See, for example, Guillermo Calvo and Carlos Végh, "Exchange-Rate-Based Stabilization under Imperfect Credibility," *International Monetary Fund Working Paper* 91/77, no. 21 (August 1991); Miguel Kiguel and Nissan Liviatan, "The Business Cycle Associated with Exchange Rate-Based Stabilizations," *World Bank Economic Review* 6, no. 2 (May 1992): 279–305; and Alexander Hoffmaister and Carlos Végh, "Disinflation and the Recession-Now-Versus-Recession-Later Hypothesis: Evidence from Uruguay," *International Monetary Fund Working Paper* 95/99, no. 20 (October 1995). Beyond the Chilean and southern cone experience in the 1980s, it is important to stress that similar cycles are present in the more recent Mexican (1994), Asian (1997), Russian (1998), and Brazilian (1999) currency crises. See, among others, Guillermo Calvo, "Varieties of Capital Market Crises," in Guillermo Calvo and Mervyn King, eds., *The Debt Burden and Its Consequences for Monetary Policy* (London: Macmillan, 1996); and "Capital Markets and the Exchange Rate," unpublished ms.

8. Joseph Ramos, *Neoconservative Economics in the Southern Cone of Latin America, 1973–83* (Baltimore: Johns Hopkins University Press, 1986), 22–23.

of the whole financial system. To avoid massive default, in January the government closed down three institutions and placed another four in receivership, including the two leading private banks that were at the core of the two largest economic conglomerates. In spite of the long-term proclaimed neutrality of the state in the economy, the presumed superiority of automatic adjustment, and the advocacy of a complete depoliticization of economic transactions, the then superminister of finance and the economy justified the intervention on the grounds that "the situation was such that it demanded political decisiveness on the part of the authority."[9] This government takeover caused some critics of the economic reform program to refer, ironically, to the monetarist experiment as "the Chicago way to socialism."[10] Through these bailouts, in fact, the government took control of 67 percent of the deposits, 57 percent of the accumulated pension funds, and 70 percent of the firms privatized between 1974 and 1981.

Recovery, 1985–90

The preceding crisis had, to a great degree, been the result of a gradual declining competitiveness of Chilean industry. Sharp tariff reductions, the overvaluation of the currency, the rise of interest rates, and a major decline of demand drove business to resort to heavy indebtedness in order to avoid bankruptcy. By 1981 the suspension of foreign loans and the increase of international rates augmented the real value of those debts. Thus, just between the end of 1980 and the end of 1982, in terms of proportion of GDP, private sector indebtedness had grown from 42 to 70 percent.[11]

The policies initially implemented in response to the crisis were uncertain. As the crisis progressed, pressures for reversing the liberalization trend intensified, especially on the part of the traditional sectoral associations. In April 1984 Pinochet appointed a rather protectionist team, led by Arturo Escobar and Modesto Collados, to navigate the crisis. Finance minister Escobar, an old-time ally of the ISI lobby, increased tariffs by a factor of three and launched an aggressive fiscal stimulus to invigorate the economy. These policies eventually backfired. Economic performance was sluggish, and inflationary trends followed

---

9. Rolf Lüders, "La razón de ser de la intervencion del 13 de Enero," *Economía y Sociedad* 35 (March 1985): 27.

10. Based on the fact that several policymakers were graduates from the University of Chicago, this criticism cynically rephrases the Allende government motto, "the Chilean way to socialism," which summed up the attempt to introduce socialist reforms within the boundaries of a democratic political regime.

11. José P. Arellano, "De la Liberalización a la Intervención: El Mercado de Capitales en Chile, 1974–83," *Colección Estudios CIEPLAN* 11 (December 1983): 5–49.

fiscal expansion. Only with the appointment of Hernan Büchi as minister of finance in February 1985 was a consistent policy package put together.

Büchi's strategy for economic recovery entailed three groups of policy instruments.[12] The first one consisted of stabilization through the realignment of relative prices. Under the so-called automatic adjustment mechanism, the combination of extremely high interest rates with a homogeneous 10 percent tariff and with a long-term deterioration of the real exchange rate had produced a significant distortion of relative prices. This distortion began to be corrected after 1982 by means of several devaluations complemented by government targeting of interest rates (done through active monetary policies) and increases in public investment (instead of public expenditures). Real exchange rate management in combination with tariff reductions was meant to create an environment propitious for export-oriented activities. These changes in incentives, supported by improvements in international prices, opened a period of export-led growth that lasted for the rest of the 1980s and well into the democratic phase in the 1990s.[13] Ironically, this successful performance was also the result of policies largely repudiated by the military government: successive phases of land reform since the 1960s—which increased the efficiency and productivity of the agricultural sector in the long term—and the nationalization of copper in the 1970s—which provided the treasury (as opposed to private companies) with hard currency revenue necessary to confront the difficulties of the postdebt crisis.[14]

The second set of policies aimed at resolving the financial crisis. These included the recapitalization and normalization of the financial system, and the renegotiation and restructuring of the foreign debt. To this end, the central bank bought the banks' bad portfolios through the issuing of domestic debt. Complementing this effort, the government implemented a comprehensive debt reduction policy, based on buy-back instruments and debt-equity swaps.[15]

The third mechanism consisted of the prompt return to the private sector of the banks under control of the state since the 1983 crisis, and an ambi-

---

12. Oscar Muñoz, "Crisis y Reorganización Industrial en Chile," *Notas Técnicas CIEPLAN* 123 (November 1988).

13. GDP growth for the second half of the 1980s was 6.2 percent average and continued strong in the 1990s.

14. For agricultural exports, see José Miguel Cruz, "La Fruticultura de Exportación: Una Experiencia de Desarrollo Empresarial," *Colección Estudios CIEPLAN* 25 (December 1988): 79–114. For copper-generated revenue in this phase, see Patricio Meller, "El Cobre y la Generación de Recursos Externos Durante el Régimen Militar," *Colección Estudios CIEPLAN* 24 (June 1988): 85–111.

15. See Raúl Labán and Felipe Larraín, "The Chilean Experience with Capital Mobility," in Barry Bosworth, Rudiger Dornbusch, and Raúl Labán, eds., *The Chilean Economy: Policy Lessons and Challenges* (Washington, D.C.: Brookings, 1994).

tious privatization program that this time included all the natural monopolies and significant firms in the tradables sector traditionally owned by the state. Divestiture operations had been an intrinsic part of the government's economic program from the outset. However, they received a most significant impetus after the recession. The next section discusses the different phases, the issues at stake in each of them, and the sequence of the overall privatization process in detail in order to highlight its centrality within the larger reform experiment and its concurrent institutional changes.

Privatization

The stated goal of the military government in terms of privatization was to return companies arbitrarily confiscated by the Allende government to their original owners. Soon after that, however, important policymakers of the Pinochet government openly accepted that the goal was to go far beyond a return to 1970. The main objectives were not only to redefine the lines along which allocation takes place but also to recast the framework within which social interaction is regulated. These goals demanded institutional changes whose completion was necessarily associated with the design and implementation of far-reaching privatization programs. Table 1 shows the evolution of the public sector in Chile and the magnitude of the divestiture effort between 1974 and 1990.

The government sought not only to roll back the structure of state intervention in the economy but also to eliminate its redistributionist role. The state thereby moved from serving as the locus of class compromise—or class struggle, as some would render the process—to an instrument leading a structural, market-oriented transformation. This move was a true developmental U-turn for Chilean society, one that terminated a long and significant history of state intervention.

TABLE 1.   **Share of Public Sector in GDP and Number of State-Owned Enterprises (SOEs) in Chile**

	Share of SOEs in GDP (%)	Number of SOEs
1965 (copper private)	14.2	44
1970 (copper private)	14.0	75
1974 (copper public)	39.0	202
1990 (copper public)	15.9	35

Source: Pontificia Universidad Católica de Chile, Instituto de Economia, "Aspectos de la Privatización de Empresas Públicas," December 1989; Cristián Larroulet, "Reflexiones en Torno al Estado Empresario," *Estudios Públicos* 14, (fall 1984): 129–51; and World Bank, Public Sector Management Division, "Public Enterprise Reform in Chile," 1990.

Note: The share of the public sector in GDP for 1974 and 1989 includes the copper public holding CODELCO, which was not privatized by the military government and accounts for about 60 percent of the total of the public sector share in GDP.

The Chilean Entrepreneurial State (*Estado Empresario*) had grown steadily and uninterruptedly since the mid- to late 1930s until 1973. In the aftermath of the Great Depression, whose impact in Chile was worse than that in the rest of Latin America, governments created state institutions in order to intervene in the economy with greater effectiveness. The prime example of this trend of institutional innovation is the case of the development agency *Corporación de Fomento de la Producción* (CORFO), created in 1939.[16]

The creation of CORFO was meant to create a closer interaction between the government and business.[17] For example, in the 1940s CORFO's main goal was to create industries—public, private, and mixed ones. In the 1950s, it focused on the administration of public credit as a way of stimulating industrialization. In the 1960s, during the heyday of planning techniques, it emphasized the formulation of development programs. In the 1970–73 period of the UP government, CORFO was the main instrument for the formation and administration of the "social property area" created with the nationalized firms. Yet for most of the 1970s and 1980s CORFO was precisely the agency placed in charge of carrying out the divestiture program. The different phases of the privatization program should thus be seen as the concluding chapter in the history of the Chilean entrepreneurial state.

Phase I: Restitution, Reprivatization, and the "Social Sector,"
1974–81

The first step in the extended privatization program consisted of returning to original owners 259 companies confiscated or taken over by the socialist government between 1970 and 1973. These restitutions were not true privatizations because in legal terms these companies were never part of the public sector;

---

16. For CORFO and the entrepreneurial state, see Marcelo Cavarozzi, "The Government and the Industrial Bourgeoisie in Chile: 1938–1964" (Ph.D. diss., University of California, Berkeley, 1975); Oscar Muñoz and Ana María Arriagada, "Orígenes Políticos y Económicos del Estado Empresarial en Chile," *Estudios CIEPLAN* 16 (1977); and Luis Ortega Martínez et al. *Corporación de Fomento de la Producción: 50 Años de Realizaciones, 1939–89* (Santiago: Universidad de Santiago de Chile, 1989). It is important to stress the innovative character of CORFO, which paralleled similar experiments in other parts of the world. For instance, the Italian Institute for Industrial Reconstruction (IRI) was created in 1933, although its role became really significant in the postwar period. IRI, in turn, inspired other efforts at state-led industrialization such as the National Enterprise Board (NEB) in the United Kingdom. See, for this, Stuart Holland, ed., *The State as Entrepreneur: New Dimensions for Public Enterprise, The IRI State Shareholding Formula* (London: Weidenfeld & Nicolson, 1972).

17. For CORFO as a corporatist forum for business-government intermediation, see Constantine C. Menges, "Public Policy and Organized Business in Chile: A Preliminary Analysis," *Journal of International Affairs* 20, no. 2 (1966): 343–65.

they had been under control of or had been confiscated by the government but had never been nationalized. The companies were returned to their former owners under the condition that they would not pursue legal actions against the state.

In September 1973, under Decree Law No. 88, government representatives were appointed in each of the previously confiscated companies in order to bring them back to normal operation. In February 1974 Decree Law No. 333 authorized those companies to normalize their debts with a subsidized interest rate. Simultaneously, CORFO created a new division, the Department of Business Administration (*Gerencia de Empresas*), which was conceived of to steer the privatization process. In 1976 the Department of Business Administration was renamed the Department of Normalization (*Gerencia de Normalización*), focusing entirely on the divestiture process.

The devolution process was completed at the end of 1978 in all but two of the 259 companies. Of these 259 firms, 63 were in the primary sector, 157 in industry, and 29 in services. These firms were received by their legal owners with very little working capital, excessive labor force, and lack of adequate maintenance. Large investments for restructuring them were needed, and the government sought to facilitate the acquisition of these funds by granting credits to these companies. Assets returned to owners amounted to $1 billion.[18]

A simultaneous effort involved a real divestiture of assets. In this second step the government sold state participation in 207 companies (majoritarian in 91), 19 of which were banks. The enterprises that were divested included only CORFO's subsidiaries but none of the enterprises created by law. In addition to the funds needed to restructure the enterprises returned to previous owners, the newly reconstituted private sector further increased the demand for credit in order to execute the new purchases. Consequently, the real interest rate reached 65 percent in 1976, and even when it began to decline thereafter, it did so at a very slow pace until 1979. This led to a disproportionately large indebtedness of the private sector.

The method of privatization called for public auction or tender of the enterprises and assets. When an offer was considered acceptable, a direct negotiation between the government and the prospective buyer was established. In theory, the proponents in auctions and tenders had to present evidence of their financial solvency. In practice, however, qualifications for auctions were easy to obtain, and financial solvency did not apply in most cases. The purchases were ultimately done with a down payment from a direct loan from CORFO,

---

18. Data from CORFO, *Privatización de Empresas y Activos, 1973–78,* Gerencia de Normalización de Empresas, 1978. Figures refer to current U.S. dollars unless otherwise noted.

with subsidized interest rates, and a maturity of up to fifteen years. Furthermore, these loans were guaranteed by the stock of the privatized companies themselves. Assets sold in this phase equaled $1.2 billion.

This divestiture method and the simultaneous privatization of industrial-commercial firms with the banks, in a context of severe economic recession, created the conditions for a marked concentration of ownership in a few financial-industrial conglomerates. The simultaneous strategy of domestic liberalization led to a reallocation of resources to exportables and nontradables. Many of the newly privatized companies could not face this competitive structure and bankruptcies increased steadily, especially in the manufacturing and tradable sectors. With credits provided against the very assets of the privatized companies, these nonperforming loans meant severe losses for the state.[19]

In this phase, the government also executed the so-called modernizations, that is, a set of administrative-institutional reforms among which the privatization of the social security and the health systems stand out as two of the most relevant ones. Decree Laws 3500 and 3501 of November 4, 1980, created the new social security system. The public pay-as-you-go framework was replaced by an individual savings account pension system administered by private pension fund management companies, known in Chile by the acronym AFPs. And the nationally administered health system was decentralized by the creation of, and the transfer of resources to, private health insurance companies known as ISAPREs (*Instituciones de Salud Previsional*).[20]

Phase II: Reversal of Privatization, 1982–83

By the end of 1981 macroeconomic conditions began to deteriorate and the economy went into a recession the next year. This was accompanied by a widespread financial crisis, defaults throughout the economy, and problems in servicing the foreign debt. As discussed earlier, in December 1981, two important banks, one of which was tied to a conglomerate, and six other financial institutions were placed in receivership. As the economic situation worsened through 1982, the financial crisis culminated with the government takeover of five banks, the closing of three, and the direct supervision of another two.

---

19. Foxley, *Latin American Experiments*, 66; and Fernando Dahse, *El Mapa de la Extrema Riqueza* (Santiago: Aconcagua, 1979).

20. For an overview, see Peter Diamond and Salvador Valdés-Prieto, "Social Security Reforms," in Bosworth et al., *The Chilean Economy*, 257–328. For an account by the architect of these reforms, ex-minister José Piñera, see his *El Cascabel al Gato: La Batalla por la Reforma Previsional en Chile* (Santiago: Zig-Zag, 1991).

These ten institutions represented 45 percent of the capital and reserves of the financial system. Among the banks in receivership were the two largest private banks that together held 32 percent of the outstanding loans of the financial system in December 1982, each of them belonging to the two largest conglomerates.[21]

By January 1983 the government controlled 67 percent of the deposits of the entire system. With the intervention in the banks, a large number of commercial firms were also taken over or returned to the public sector, either because the banks were their most important creditors or because they were related through ownership. Among those taken over were four pension fund companies, including the largest two, which in turn belonged to the two largest conglomerates. Together, these two pension funds had, by December 1982, 50.7 percent of the workers and employees affiliated with the new system and 57.5 percent of the accumulated funds of the entire system.[22]

The privatization program conducted in 1974–78 was at the root of this crisis. The explanation comes from the very methodology of the divestiture process. The big flaws were, among others, an undercapitalized private sector, which could not absorb the amount of capital privatized on a sound debt-equity relationship; the coincidence of commercial and financial sector privatizations, which worsened the indebtedness of buyers and led to excessive integration and concentration; and the simultaneous opening of trade and the capital account, which had a greater impact on the competitiveness of the newly privatized companies than the rest. Last, but not least, the decision to privatize during the recession years of the stabilization program in turn affected the sale values of the enterprises, which had an additional negative impact on fiscal proceeds.

Phase III: Reprivatization and Traditional SOEs, 1985–90

Upon coming to office in early 1985, finance minister Büchi announced the reprivatization of the banks, pension funds, and firms taken over during the financial crisis—the so-called odd zone (*area rara*). A new method was introduced in the divestiture of the two largest banks and pension fund companies: people's capitalism. This system consisted of the direct sale to individuals of small packages of shares to diffuse ownership. An explicit goal of this phase of privatization was to avoid the mistakes of the past, namely, to avoid the

---

21. Arellano, "De la Liberalización a la Intervención," table 7.
22. Mario Valenzuela Silva, "Reprivatización y Capitalismo Popular en Chile," *Estudios Públicos* 33 (Summer 1989): 175–217.

concentration that had occurred in the 1970s, and to spread ownership among a large number of shareholders. In the case of the banks, given their financial fragility, the reprivatization also demanded a recapitalization of the institutions.

While sensible from an economic perspective, popular capitalism was also an effective symbolic instrument. In a context marked by the highest unemployment and the sharpest fall in real wages since the Depression, the military regime was pledging to distribute equity among the public. To implement people's capitalism, the government created a series of attractive incentives. CORFO gave loans to individual investors with maturities of fifteen years at zero real interest rates and with 5 percent down payments. Timely payments of the debt obtained an additional 30 percent discount, and buyers could obtain a fiscal credit equivalent to 20 percent of the total investment. The two largest private banks, under government control, and 50 percent of the pension funds equity were privatized under this scheme. The remaining 50 percent were sold to foreign investors.

A second method of privatization entailed direct sale to private investors. Trying to avoid the defects of the 1970s, the selection of participants in the bidding process was more carefully supervised by the government. At the same time, when the enterprise was purchased by a conglomerate, there was no reliance on debt. Cash payment was required for all sales through open bids.[23] A third method entailed sales to foreign investors. The mechanism was not direct investment but foreign debt-for-equity swaps through the debt-reconversion program steered by the central bank since 1985. Participation in this program entailed a capital gain for the investor because it was done with a smaller discount than the discount on Chilean debt available in the secondary market.[24]

The reprivatization of the odd area and people's capitalism reinvigorated the, by then, discredited privatization program. The government thus gained momentum and in 1986 launched the privatization of the large public utilities companies. Initially it projected privatizing 30 percent of twenty-three natural monopolies. Yet the revitalization of privatization as such, the association between privatization and the recovery of the economy, and the use of privatization as a vehicle for keeping political initiative in the hands of the government in a

23. Dominique Hachette and Rolf Lüders, *La Privatización en Chile* (San Francisco: CINDE, 1992), 89–92.

24. Ricardo Ffrench-Davis, "Debt-Equity Swaps in Chile," *Notas Técnicas CIEPLAN* 129 (May 1989).

critical political juncture contributed to the expansion of the program's goals. By the end of 1989, virtually all of the most important state-owned enterprises (SOEs) were privatized completely, with the exception of the copper holding CODELCO.

Prior to divesting them, the government implemented changes in the management of several SOEs. Many of them went through a rationalization process and foreign liabilities and debts were transferred to CORFO to make the companies more attractive to potential buyers. For example, in early 1986 foreign loans of the electricity company ENDESA, amounting to $500 million, were transferred to CORFO.[25] The divestiture program thus entailed the natural monopolies in telecommunications (CTC and ENTEL), electricity generation, transmission, and distribution (the three subsidiaries of the holding Chilectra and ENDESA), and toward the end water and sewage services. It also included some of the largest corporations producing tradables in nitrates (Soquimich), sugar (IANSA), and steel (CAP). The government collected about $2 billion for these SOEs.

In this phase, the divestiture process was carried out through a combination of different methods. The first one entailed the sale of shares to pension funds (AFPs). As new monies became available from workers' savings, new privatizations could be undertaken. The previous privatization of social security accelerated the privatization of SOEs over time, for as more funds were available in the private pension system, more firms were subject to be privatized.

In addition, using the workers' savings to privatize enterprises introduced a significant change in the pattern of socialization of the working class that was consistent with the political goals of the military regime. Previously unionized and militant workers thus became shareholders in now private companies, directly if they bought shares or indirectly through stock owned by the private pension funds. As a practitioner of privatization in Chile put it: "for these formerly socialist workers, now the most important news to read in the paper every morning is the evolution of the stock exchange . . . they are becoming capitalists by need."[26]

Share distribution also took place under "labor capitalism," that is, the sale of equity among current employees of the privatized companies. While this method was also intensely promoted by the government as a great achievement,

---

25. Since the holding CORFO assumed the debts of most public utilities enterprises, the institution incurred severe losses during the program. Some studies suggest that the losses amounted to $1.9 billion. See *Análisis,* January 14, 1991, "Así Arruinaron la CORFO," 11–14.

26. Interview with high official of CORFO, not for attribution.

its relative importance has been quite limited. Workers became full owners of enterprises in only two cases, while their overall share in the first sale of SOEs' equity amounted to 20 percent. Furthermore, actual practice has shown that employees acted more as rentiers than shareholders, as their voting rights were not exercised, due to the transfer to managers who formed investment trusts.[27] In the end, the method most frequently used was the sale of shares in the stock exchange. Actually, 50 percent of the shares were sold through this method in the last phase of privatization. Reportedly, none of these methods prevented concentration of enterprise control in a few hands.[28]

Conclusion

This chapter has focused on the economic reform and privatization policies in Chile between 1973 and 1990. The main goal has been to examine the different combinations and sequences of the policy instruments employed during the long reform program. Privatization has been seen as a key component of this overall process. Given that they pursue increases in revenue collection and changes in the price structure of the economy, divestiture operations lie at the intersection of macroeconomic stabilization and microeconomic restructuring. Thus, this chapter has examined privatization within this broader policy framework.

As the evidence discussed highlights, however, one important problem is that the pursuit of these simultaneous goals may translate into a mix and/or sequence of policies that work across purposes. Revenue maximization through privatization frequently offsets the expected gains in microeconomic efficiency associated with decentralized private ownership. This affects the timing and the methods employed in privatization, creating policy contexts that facilitate increases in the productive efficiency of the firms divested, often at the expense of aggregate allocative efficiency.

In this sense, two conclusions are in order. First, as shown on the basis of the Chilean experience, these suboptimal outcomes magnify the primacy of distributional considerations. Rent-seeking opportunities thus persist, and the organization of distributional coalitions retains great explanatory power for the overall pace and content of the reform process—a subject I examine in the next

27. World Bank, Public Sector Management Division, "Public Enterprise Reform in Chile," 1990. In following chapters, I compare the Chilean program with similar ones in Britain (wider share ownership program), Argentina (participatory property program), and Hungary (employee-share ownership programs).

28. Patricio Rozas and Gustavo Marín, *1988: El Mapa de la Extrema Riqueza Diez Años Después* (Santiago: CESOC, 1989).

chapter. Second, to the extent that those policy contexts give rise to specific institutional settings—in terms of property rights, extractive methods, and administrative blueprint—I argue that privatization leads to state-building processes. I develop this proposition in chapter 4. Once the approach on the connection among distributional coalitions, privatization, and the ensuing institutional effects is stylized on the basis of the Chilean experiment, I evaluate the argument in three consecutive chapters, where I compare the British, Mexican, Argentine, and Hungarian experience with market reform and privatization.

Chapter 3

Distributional Coalitions and the Politics of Market Reform and Privatization in Chile

The evidence presented in this chapter highlights the need to introduce modifications to two important theoretical foils of this study. Consistent with dominant reasoning in economics, the field of neoclassical political economy treats a liberal economic order as a public good. While the completion of liberalization benefits all groups in society, vested interests who enjoy tariffs and regulations benefit from a closed economy. The former are prone to free riding, but the latter, organized coalitions of rent seekers, induce the state to intervene in the economy. Thus, liberalization will dissipate rents and dissolve those distributional coalitions. The literature on the politics of economic adjustment, in turn, has departed from a similar payoff matrix and argued that liberalization programs concentrate present costs on the beneficiaries of a closed economy and disperse benefits in the future. Hence, losers are prone to engage in collective action, whereas prospective winners, facing uncertainty about the gains, remain disorganized. On this basis, much of this research has argued that economic reform flows only from autonomous and insulated policy-making teams, especially in the early phases of the program.

One of the main arguments of this book is that this payoff structure is inexact. Economic reform and privatization programs can lead, and have often led, to institutional settings where benefits are concentrated and costs dispersed, generating suboptimal aggregate outcomes and incentives for the formation of distributional coalitions, despite far-reaching marketization. If this is so, much of the impetus for these programs comes from the strategic behavior of these interest groups who, in anticipation of the distributive consequences of these policies, collude with policymakers to get their preferences translated into policy.

This is precisely the case of the privatization experiment in Chile between 1974 and 1990. In this chapter, I show how one of the most comprehensive, forceful, and enduring processes of market-oriented reform has created, through the privatization of public enterprise, an environment at least as prone to rent seeking as in an interventionist state. Privatization in Chile was precisely about the uncompetitive appropriation of existing state-owned, monopoly wealth by small lobbies. The process reproduced the same type of Olsonian collective action that is necessary to obtain favorable tariffs, subsidies, or any other form of protection. Privatization is also about rents in exchange for political support. Distributional coalitions thus proliferate to profit from the market reserves made available by state withdrawal. This chapter provides evidence in support of these propositions.

The Politics of Structural Change: Chile, 1950–73

To tackle these theoretical questions, I first examine the changing structural context that led to the economic reform and privatization programs and the accompanying social coalition-building process. Social structures are important because they shape the boundaries and the possibilities of political action. They frame the context in which some policy options may be advanced and others dismissed. On this basis, I spell out the main traits of the Chilean political economy prior to 1973. Those were the mutually destabilizing relationships among increasing social mobilization, economic slowdown, and political and ideological polarization. Over time, the combination of these three factors exposed the inherent fragility of the so-called State of Compromise (*Estado de Compromiso*)—the post-1930s multiclass political arrangement that had been the carrier of import-substituting industrialization (ISI).

Social Mobilization

In the postwar period Chilean society began to exhibit many indicators of high social mobilization, characteristic of processes of rapid modernization. The rate of population growth increased from an annual average of 1.47 percent before 1950, to a 2.56 percent between 1950 and 1960. This growth was accompanied by significant internal migrations that translated into a rapid urbanization. In the 1950s the rate of growth of the urban population was 5.9 percent, that is, more than two times the growth of the overall population.[1]

Unionization increased sharply as well. In the urban areas it did so at an annual average of 17.3 percent in the 1965–70 period against an annual average of 0.5 percent for the 1950–65 period. In the countryside, and to a large extent due

---

1. Javier Martínez and Eugenio Tironi, *Las Clases Sociales en Chile* (Santiago: Ediciones Sur, 1985), chap. 1.

to the land reform programs of Presidents Frei and Allende, the number of rural unions increased from 11 in 1953, to 33 in 1965, to 580 in 1970.[2]

In this context, suffrage expanded, though not as rapidly as one would have expected. The stability and durability of Chilean democracy had, in fact, been based on low participation rates. Consider, for example, that it was not until the 1970 election that the right to vote was extended to nonliterate and eighteen-year-old citizens. It has been argued, therefore, that precisely because of this limited suffrage, democracy was able to survive several decades of social mobilization and increasing expectations, avoiding the political crises seen in, say, Argentina and Brazil, at least until the 1970s.[3]

Economic Slowdown

In the 1930s and 1940s—especially after 1938 when the center-left Popular Front defined a more activist role for government in orienting the overall economic process—ISI was a consensual strategy of development. The key factor in this model was the central role played by the state, based on increasing revenues from its participation in the mining sector and on the administration of credits, subsidies, and tariffs. A continuous expansion of public expenditures, services, and employment incorporated wide sectors of the lower-middle groups while its active sectoral policies favored a clientelistic relationship with business.[4] As a result, the share of industry in GDP rose from 13.6 percent in 1940 to 24.9 percent in 1954. Employment in the manufacturing sector grew 70 percent during this phase, and industrial output grew at an average annual rate of 7.9 percent while the GDP evolved at an average annual rate of 3.3 percent.[5]

In the second half of the 1950s, however, this so-called easy phase of import substitution, based on low-technology production of consumer goods, became exhausted. The competitiveness of Chilean trade deteriorated because

2. See Alan Angell, *Politics and the Labour Movement in Chile* (New York: Oxford University Press, 1972); Robert Kaufman, *The Politics of Land Reform in Chile* (Cambridge: Harvard University Press, 1979); and Ruth Berins Collier and David Collier, *Shaping the Political Arena* (Princeton: Princeton University Press, 1991), 555–70.

3. Atilio Borón, "La Evolución Electoral y sus Efectos en la Representación de los Intereses Populares: El Caso de Chile," *FLACSO Documento de Trabajo* (1971); Van R. Whiting "Political Mobilization and the Breakdown of Democracy in Chile," *Latin American Issues* 1, no. 1 (1984).

4. Luis Ortega Martínez et al., *CORFO: 50 Años de Realizaciones,* 1939–1989 (Santiago: Universidad de Santiago de Chile, 1989); and Marcelo Cavarozzi, "The Government and the Industrial Bourgeoisie in Chile, 1938–1964" (Ph.D. diss., University of California, Berkeley, 1975).

5. Markos J. Mamalakis, comp., *Historical Statistics of Chile: National Accounts* (Westport, Conn.: Greenwood Press, 1978); Patricio Meller, ed., "Resultados Económicos de Cuatro Gobiernos Chilenos, 1958–1989," *Apuntes CIEPLAN* 89 (October 1990).

the price of copper fell and led to balance-of-payments constraints. Fewer revenues led to economic slowdown, the rise of price levels, and, subsequently, the utilization of stop-go strategies whose cyclical phases fueled economic tensions even further. As a result, the pace of industrial growth dwindled, evolving at rates below those of the previous decade. More or less permanent balance-of-payment constraints implied increasing pressures on foreign exchange reserves. Ongoing social and political mobilization explains growing distributional conflict across classes and sectors. Recurrent and rapidly accelerating inflation constituted the visible manifestation of the precarious accommodation of diverse groups with different policy priorities.[6]

An inverse relationship between private and public investment developed throughout the 1960s and until 1973. Whereas in 1961 the former accounted for 86.4 percent of the fixed capital investment in industry, by 1973 it represented just 10 percent of that total in a gradually declining trend.[7] The decline of dynamism in the manufacturing sector put intense pressure on the employment structure. Between 1952 and 1960 the manufacturing sector absorbed one-third of the new economically active population, commerce and services absorbed 36 percent of such an increase, and the self-employed absorbed about another third. Between 1960 and 1970, however, industry absorbed 1.1 percent of the new jobs, services and commerce 68 percent, and the self-employed sector around 30 percent. Unemployment was thus concealed by a dramatic expansion of public employment to which governments of varied political orientations resorted to keep the structure of the State of Compromise intact. Between 1940 and 1970, in fact, public employment increased by twice the national average.[8]

Ideological Polarization and Political Crisis

The structure of representation based on the multiparty system and the State of Compromise had been consolidated during the period of rapid industrialization and increasing employment. By the 1960s, however, it became unsuccessful in channeling the augmenting demands of groups that continued to be incorporated, mobilized, and politicized, though in a context of increasingly fewer economic opportunities. The Christian Democrats (DC) came to office in 1964 with a re-

---

6. Albert Hirschman, "Inflation in Chile," in *Journeys Toward Progress* (New York: Norton, 1973).

7. Ricardo Ffrench-Davis, *Políticas Económicas en Chile, 1952–70* (Santiago: Nueva Universidad, 1973); and Barbara Stallings, *Class Conflict and Economic Development in Chile, 1958–1973* (Stanford: Stanford University Press, 1978).

8. Oscar Muñoz, Jaime Gatica, and Pilar Romaguera, "Crecimiento y Estructura del Empleo Estatal en Chile, 1940–70," *Notas Técnicas CIEPLAN* 22 (January 1980).

vitalized agenda of social and economic reform, one meant to resolve these apparent failures. President Eduardo Frei's reformism included the acceleration of industrialization, aimed at reaching the production of durable and capital goods, redistributive income policies, to conclude the process of incorporation, and land reform, to modernize the countryside. Land reform contributed to widening the DC's social basis of support by organizing the peasantry and new farmers, and by incorporating them as effective members of the ruling coalition.[9]

The implementation of land reform led to a growing sentiment of insecurity on the part of propertied groups. Landed elites became politicized and thus created the National Party, soon the dominant expression of Chilean conservatism.[10] Industrialists, in turn, fearful of further expropriations, provided less than mild support to the DC, despite the comprehensive protectionist policies they enjoyed during this period.[11] These conflicts were exacerbated by another episode of inflation followed by a balance-of-payments crisis and, after 1967, a stabilization program. The ensuing recession affected employment and wages, prompting the parties of the left to criticize Frei's reformism and embrace an open revolutionary rhetoric. Economic slowdown, class divisions, and ideological polarization account for the end of the consensual politics associated with the State of Compromise. The election of a socialist coalition (Popular Unity, UP) in 1970 signaled, in fact, the impossibility of reproducing the politics of social compromise.[12]

The UP government prioritized what was seen as the need to correct three interrelated structural deficiencies of the economy: external dependence, monopolistic organization of industrial production and land tenure, and a distorted and limited internal demand. To this end, the program of the Allende government was based on three sets of policies: a complete nationalization of copper resources, extensive expropriations of land and industries, and expansive fiscal and monetary policies meant to achieve redistributive goals.[13] What worked out

---

9. Arturo Valenzuela, *The Breakdown of Democratic Regimes: Chile* (Baltimore: Johns Hopkins University Press, 1978), 3–21; and Timothy Scully, *Rethinking the Center: Party Politics in Nineteenth and Twentieth Century Chile* (Stanford: Stanford University Press, 1992), chap. 4.

10. Sofía Correa, "La Derecha en Chile Contemporáneo: La Pérdida del Control Estatal," *Revista de Ciencia Política* 11, no. 1 (1989): 5–19.

11. A constitutional amendment on property rights was necessary to carry out the land reform program. In combination with the overall notion of "social function of property" advocated by the Christian Democrats, this new legal framework was interpreted as an imminent threat by most propertied groups. See Kaufman, *Politics of Land Reform,* chap. 5.

12. Tomás Moulian, "Desarrollo Político y Estado de Compromiso: Desajustes y Crisis Estatales en Chile," *Colección Estudios CIEPLAN* 8 (July 1982): 105–58.

13. Felipe Larraín and Patricio Meller, "The Socialist-Populist Chilean Experience: 1970–1973," in Rudiger Dornbusch and Sebastian Edwards, eds., *The Macroeconomics of Populism in Latin America* (Chicago: University of Chicago Press, 1991), 175–221.

for a brief period soon led to an even higher inflation, dramatically plummeting production and investment levels, and food shortages and undersupply of most consumer goods.

In the end, therefore, the UP government worsened the tendencies it was supposed to mitigate. The result was a faster economic decline, a greater number of unsatisfied social demands, and an uncontrolled political militancy that ran against the UP government itself. The rest of the story has been amply documented and goes beyond the scope of this work. The military coup of September 1973 caused great international surprise. In Chile, however, except for the violence with which it was carried out, it was hardly an unexpected event.

The Social Basis of Market-Oriented Reform

The policymakers of the Pinochet government aimed at resolving the political and social conflicts previously described by reversing entrenched patterns of protectionism and dismantling the entrepreneurial state—in a nutshell, a U-turn from the previous thirty years of economic history. The economists who produced *El Ladrillo,* the document that served as basis for the military government economic policies, were as opposed to import substitution as in favor of deregulation of prices and fiscal conservatism, which, given high and persistent inflation, was impossible to avoid. They also proposed the privatization of social security and the creation of competitive capital markets, along with the reversal of past nationalization of industrial firms and expropriation of land; namely, a more assertive specification of private property rights.[14]

One of the legacies of Allende's policies was that they had dismantled the ISI regime and destroyed its multiclass political base. As a result of ambitious nationalization and expropriation programs, most propertied groups—landowners, industrialists, middle classes—came together against the UP government. As it became clear that the policies of the military government would favor the interests of propertied groups, the relationship between the state and capital turned into a less mediated, less institutionalized, and thus more transparent one. One illustrative example was the decision of the right-wing National Party to dissolve itself voluntarily shortly after the coup of September 1973. Once the armed forces had eliminated the threat of communism, their perception was that there was "no need for politics." Giving up the political representation of capitalists on these grounds, a paradigmatic and extreme case of Brumairean abdication,

---

14. This can be seen in *"El Ladrillo": Bases de la Política Económica del Gobierno Militar* (Santiago: CEP, 1992), with a foreword by former finance minister Sergio de Castro.

implied an overt recognition of the military as the ultimate representative of the interests of the dominant sectors.[15]

Once participation in the military government as leaders of Chilean conservatism was eliminated, the upper social strata could do so only as representatives of capital. Initially, they found opportunities through the influence of sectoral associations. In fact, the gradual approach to stabilization and the moderate position vis-à-vis liberalization adopted in the early days of the military government reflected the need to accommodate a rather heterogeneous coalition of groups with different policy priorities. At that stage, and aside from the armed forces, the main institutionalized source of support for the authoritarian regime came from the traditional associations of industry, agriculture, mining, and commerce.[16]

The core constituency of the military government, however, rested on a coalition of a handful of diversified economic conglomerates whose main firms were in export activities (mining, fishing, agriculture), manufacturing in internationally competitive industries (food processing, paper), and liquid-asset sectors (finance, insurance, real estate).[17] Tight links between the upper echelons of these conglomerates and the armed forces had been forged prior to the coup, when big business mobilized against the Allende government and their leaders participated in the design of economic policy for the projected postcoup phase.[18] When the military took power, important executives and directors of these firms joined the gov-

---

15. Tomás Moulian and Isabel Torres examine this in "La Problemática de la Derecha Política en Chile, 1964–1983," in Marcelo Cavarozzi and Manuel A. Garreton, eds., *Muerte y Resurrección: Los Partidos Políticos en el Autoritarismo y las Transiciones del Cono Sur* (Santiago: FLACSO, 1989), 335–93. For a characterization of this "Brumairean moment" in Chilean political development, see Alfred Stepan, "State Power and the Strength of Civil Society in the Southern Cone of Latin America," in Peter Evans, Dietrich Rueschemeyer, and Theda Skocpol, eds., *Bringing the State Back In* (Cambridge: Cambridge University Press, 1985), 317–43.

16. Two studies provide a detailed account of this process: Guillermo Campero, *Los Gremios Empresariales en el Período 1970–1983* (Santiago: ILET, 1984); and Eduardo Silva, *The State and Capital in Chile: Business Elites, Technocrats, and Market Economics* (Boulder: Westview Press, 1996).

17. An economic conglomerate (or group) is defined as an organization that centralizes property, management, and control of a set of diversified and integrated companies. The goal is the maximization of utility for the group as a whole, irrespective of the performance of the particular companies of the group. Given their size and diversification, the conglomerates try to exercise influence over policymaking outside of the institutionalized channels provided by sectoral associations. Their diversified character makes them inadequate for sectoral representation—they speak for several sectors and none at the same time—for they seek political influence on behalf of the conglomerate. See Nathaniel Leff, "Industrial Organization and Entrepreneurship in Developing Countries: The Economic Groups," *Economic Development and Cultural Change* 26, no. 4 (July 1978): 661–75. For the notion of "core constituency" in conservative coalitions, see Edward Gibson, *Class and Conservative Parties: Argentina in Comparative Perspective* (Baltimore: Johns Hopkins University Press, 1997).

18. Several of the contributors to *El Ladrillo* were linked to three economic groups: Edwards, Matte, and BHC (later split in two, Cruzat-Larraín and Vial). For detailed accounts of these links by insiders, which document the company affiliations of the main actors involved, see

ernment, for the most part in second-tier positions. Their rise to top cabinet and central bank posts toward the end of 1974 signaled the end of gradualism: trade and financial liberalization accelerated and the stabilization program deepened.

As of that moment, the level of aggregation for the exercise of interest representation was reduced to the level of the firm or economic conglomerate. The *grupos* benefited from being noncorporatist capital; in fact, they soon bypassed business associations and became the key interlocutors of the policymakers. Exposed to the vicissitudes of the market and with no political protection by sectoral organizations, they would represent, in the days of the economic boom toward the end of the 1970s, the success story of the Pinochet policy experiment.

The focus on the role of this handful of enterprises does not imply that they constituted the only basis of support of the military government, nor does it suggest that the government was reduced to a mere instrument of that sector. This focus only recognizes the existence of hierarchy among members of a coalition. This hierarchy was determined by the differential access to policy-making arenas. Furthermore, the capture of key policy-making posts by the large conglomerates led to the implementation of an economic reform program by which these firms took over market reserves, even in the presence of comprehensive marketization. And by reproducing patterns of rent-seeking behavior, this group became a distributional coalition.

Distributional Coalitions and the Politics of Economic Reform

As argued in the previous section, most of the contributors to *El Ladrillo* were linked to the Edwards (*El Mercurio* daily), Matte (paper producer monopoly), and BHC (Banco Hipotecario de Chile) conglomerates, and several of them were, plainly, their representatives. Initially, these economists/executives held second-level positions in the government, mostly in charge of the design of programs. It did not take long for them to occupy more important policy-making posts. By the end of 1974 they began to take first-level positions, and they were soon fully in charge of the design *and* implementation of the economic reforms. Several of them held positions at the conglomerates prior to their coming to office. Jorge Cauas, Pablo Baraona, and José Piñera, for instance, had executive posts at the Cruzat-Larraín conglomerate before taking top ministerial and central bank posts. Rolf Lüders was the second largest shareholder of the BHC (or Vial) group when he became minister of finance in 1982. Fernando Léniz was a top businessman at the Edwards group and had ties to the Matte group when

Arturo Fontaine Aldunate, *Los Economistas y el Presidente Pinochet* (Santiago: Zig-Zag, 1988); and Arturo Fontaine Talavera, "Sobre el Pecado Original de la Transformación Capitalista Chilena," in Barry Levine, ed., *El Desafío Neoliberal* (Bogotá: Editorial Norma, 1992).

he was appointed minister of the economy. Planning minister and retired navy officer Roberto Kelly was a long-term Edwards man. And Sergio de Castro became a top executive of the Edwards group in 1982 after serving as minister of the economy and finance for almost eight years. In a nutshell, during much of the military regime, a revolving-door relationship was established between the largest segments of capital and the government.

The explanation for the rapidly increasing structural power of these conglomerates has to be traced to some unintended consequences of the economic policies of the UP government. During the heyday of the socialist policies in the 1970–73 period, the majority of small- and middle-sized businesses and the bulk of traditional import-substituting industrialists had no capacity to resist government pressures and gave in to nationalization. With production mostly directed to domestic markets and with no substantive diversification of their holdings, these companies lacked major financial reserves and could not access foreign credit, which, given the government control of the entire banking system, implied no credit at all. In this context, they were forced to sell.

The opposite was the case for the larger and diversified conglomerates. When the Allende government pushed them to sell their assets, many refused.[19] The diversification of their holdings and their export activities granted them access to foreign currency and allowed them to resist expropriation, even under strong governmental pressure and in an extremely unfavorable policy context. Eventually, they used their international contacts to obtain financial resources overseas. Unable to purchase their companies, the UP government resorted to takeovers, requisitions, and interventions in order to gain operational control of these companies that, in legal terms, remained as property of their original owners.

After the coup, the military government's first priority was to return a large number of firms to the private sector. The companies that were under government control, a total of 259, were returned to their owners quickly, mostly during 1974. The companies that had been *legally* nationalized under Allende, in turn, went through a longer and more complex process of privatization, and they were not necessarily repurchased by the original owners. More often than not the larger

---

19. The most relevant and politically sensitive example was the attempt to nationalize Matte's paper monopoly producer Compañía Manufacturera de Papeles y Cartones (CMPC). The president and CEO of the company was the ex-president of the country Jorge Alessandri (1958–64). The event ended up becoming an exercise of conservative mobilization and coalition building in support of Alessandri and "La Papelera." Since one of the major consumers of paper was the Edwards group, owner of the conservative daily *El Mercurio*, the projected nationalization was portrayed as an antidemocratic attempt to curtail press freedom. It served to reinforce the strategic alliance between the Matte and Edwards groups, which was maintained throughout the military regime and into the democratic period in the 1990s.

economic conglomerates that had resisted nationalization purchased those reprivatized companies. The reason was that when the privatization program was initiated following the return of the firms under state control, the groups that had been able to resist nationalization were in an advantageous position vis-à-vis small- and medium-sized companies and traditional import-substituting industrialists. They had recovered control of many of their assets, had received state subsidies granted to them in order to bring the companies back to normal operation, and, under the ongoing financial liberalization, had turned a good part of their fixed assets into liquid assets, thus securing access to foreign exchange. In a context of stringent undersupply of capital, this sequence gave them the upper hand when the sale of state-owned stock in 188 firms and 19 banks was announced. In addition, they had their own people in key decision-making arenas.

Although technically this privatization phase lasted until 1982, by the end of 1978 the government had completed the sale of its participation in a total of 193 units—firms, banks, and rural property. The agency in charge of privatization reported to have collected $543 million between 1974 and June 30, 1978.[20] A look at the largest conglomerates' share of this process reveals that a substantial part of the concentration of wealth in this period occurred through the privatization of state-owned stock. From the $543 million sold, $352 million was distributed among eight economic groups. Thus, 65 percent of the assets privatized between 1974 and 1978 was distributed among eight economic groups. Table 2 describes this tendency.

TABLE 2. Privatization of State-Owned Stock among the Largest Conglomerates in Chile, 1974–78

Conglomerate	Amount (millions of 1978 dollars)
Cruzat-Larraín	164.93
Vial	90.81
Angelini	36.39
Luksic	21.89
Edwards	17.30
Galmez	14.56
Matte	3.43
Briones	2.95
Total	352.26

Source: Corfo, "Privatización de Empresas y Activos, Gerencia de Normalización, 1978; and Fernando Dahse, *El Mapa de la Extrema Riqueza.*
Note: Total privatization in the 1974–78 period amounted to $542.84 million.

20. CORFO, *Privatización de Empresas y Activos, 1973–78,* Gerencia de Normalización de Empresas, 1978, appendix 31. Due to the recessionary impact of the simultaneous stabilization program, in general, there was a 40 percent loss from the book value of these companies. That is why the government estimated a revenue of $1 billion from this program.

Financial sector regulations further contributed to reinforce this pattern of concentration. Most banks were not allowed to take the exchange rate risk and had to document their loans in foreign currency, with the final borrower assuming all of the exchange rate risk. Some financial institutions, however, could access credit denominated in foreign exchange but were able to lend in domestic currency. This policy generated a highly segmented credit market where in the end only some of the agents (largely associated with the groups) had access to credit denominated in foreign exchange. By this mechanism, large rents were captured by the financial intermediaries associated with the conglomerates who had access to foreign funds and lent in domestic currency.[21]

In the process the relative size of the conglomerates increased. From the 250 largest companies of the country in 1978 after that phase of privatization with liberalization, 83 were in the hands of four economic conglomerates. The assets of these 83 companies, belonging to the Cruzat-Larraín, Vial, Matte, and Edwards groups, in turn, represented 48 percent of the holdings of these 250 firms and their assets amounted to $1.84 billion.[22] Table 3 shows the economic power of these groups at the end of 1978.

TABLE 3.   Degree of Concentration of the 250 Largest Private Companies in Chile, 1978

	Companies		Assets Dec. 1978	
Conglomerate	Number	Percent	U.S. $ million	Percent
Cruzat-Larraín	37	14.8	936.88	24.72
Vial	25	10.0	477.30	12.61
Matte	12	4.8	325.31	8.59
Angelini	8	3.2	141.80	3.74
Luksic	8	3.2	139.06	3.67
Galmez	2	0.8	98.23	2.59
Edwards	9	3.6	95.95	2.53
Yarur Banna	4	1.6	92.02	2.43
Lepe R.	3	1.2	67.58	1.78
Hochschild	4	1.6	70.73	1.87
Briones	3	1.2	54.89	1.45
Another 30 groups	63	25.2	432.87	11.43
Foreign groups	35	14.0	493.09	13.01
Individual Firms	37	14.8	363.16	9.58
Total	250	100.00	3,788.87	100.00

Source: Fernando Dahse, *El Mapa de la Extrema Riqueza* (Santiago: Aconcagua, 1978), 147.

21. See Roberto Zahler, "The Monetary and Real Effects of the Financial Opening Up of National Economies to the Exterior: The Case of Chile, 1975–78," *CEPAL Review* 10 (April 1980); and Julio Gálvez and James Tybout, "Microeconomic Adjustment in Chile during 1977–81: The Importance of Being a 'Grupo'," *World Development* 13 (August 1985).

22. To have a more accurate idea of the significance of these conglomerates one should recall that in 1978 the country's GDP was $9.6 billion and the external debt equaled $11.25 billion.

Economic Recession and Crisis
of the Dominant Distributional Coalition

The sequence and mix of the reforms implemented in the 1970s led to a wide array of inconsistencies, accumulated over the course of several years. The combination of an overvalued exchange rate, the liberalization of trade, and high interest rates had a negative impact on production and employment levels and drove many firms into debt. Trade and current account deficits increased interest rates, further widening the differential between domestic and international rates. Inflows of capital were necessary to finance the growing deficits, but interlocking ownership, concentration, and deregulation induced the newly private banks to engage in excessive risk-taking practices, most typically lending to related companies within the groups (*auto-préstamo*) or to undercapitalized firms. This context had "Dutch-disease" effects, as a massive reallocation of resources took place, from the real to the financial sector. Financial assets rose from 19.7 percent of GDP in 1975 to 48.1 percent in 1982, and private indebtedness grew from 42 to 70 percent of GDP between 1980 and 1982 alone. By that time the two largest banks (Banco de Santiago and Banco de Chile), owned by Cruzat-Larraín and Vial groups, respectively, controlled 42 percent of credit.

The collapse of a private sugar monopoly in May 1981 represented the first serious warning on the unsustainability of the microeconomic regime, especially when compounded by increases in international interest rates toward the end of that year. Once the balance-of-payments deficit could not be financed, the nominal anchor was no longer credible. In June 1982 the government had to devalue the currency. Given the volume of dollar-denominated debt, these events resulted in a large number of nonperforming loans, representing about one quarter of the banks' capital and reserves. The economy thus shrunk by 14 percent and unemployment reached 26.4 percent for the year.

In the midst of the economic crisis, Pinochet sought to distance himself from the financial conglomerates. In August 1982 he appointed Rolf Lüders as both minister of the economy and minister of finance. Lüders had been number two in the line of command until March of that year (but was still the second largest shareholder) at the Vial group. Given the virtual collapse of the sector, the government deemed it necessary to have somebody with detailed knowledge of the operations of the main financial concerns. On January 13, 1983, in a decision that remains controversial to this day, Lüders decreed the dissolution of three banks and placed another four in receivership.[23] Through

---

23. For Lüders's assessment, see "La Razón de ser de la Intervención del 13 de Enero," *Economía y Sociedad* 35 (March 1985). At the time Pablo Baraona, Jorge Cauas, and José Luis Zabala—contributors to "El Ladrillo" and key policymakers of the government in the 1970s—

these bailouts the government took over 67 percent of the deposits, 57 percent of the accumulated pension funds, and 70 percent of the firms privatized between 1974 and 1981, which were related to the banks either by ownership or because they were their debtors. The rent-seeking opportunities created by the privatization-cum-liberalization program led to a familiar moral hazard scenario, though one of a monumental magnitude.[24] To be more precise: when the Banco de Chile was placed in receivership, its main debtor was the president of the bank himself.

Pressures for reversing the liberalization process intensified thereafter. Political scandals added to the economic crisis, contributing to the alteration of the balance of power inside the business community. Reflecting these pressures, Pinochet appointed a rather protectionist team led by Arturo Escobar and Modesto Collados. The demands of the traditional sectoral associations were heeded: interest rates were lowered and tariffs increased to a 35 percent average.[25] In addition, the authorities began to prioritize a more adequate level of the real-exchange rate, established foreign exchange controls, and achieved an effective renegotiation of the external debt.[26]

By 1983–84, several observers thought that the project of market-oriented reform had collapsed, along with the social coalition that had articulated and supported it.[27] With the political opposition literally in the streets, it seemed at the time that the comprehensive project of economic liberalization was finished, if not that the government was about to fall. The government, however, did not have plans to modify, much less to discard, the essential components of its economic model. In February 1985 the appointment of Hernán Büchi, a young economist with impeccable orthodox credentials, as finance minister signaled that there was no return to ISI. The previously mentioned protectionist measures had been implemented to recover political oxygen rather than to reverse the strategy of development in its fundamen-

were presidents of the Unido de Fomento, Santiago, and Concepción Banks, respectively; these group-related institutions were liquidated or placed in receivership.

24. Fiscal resources used for the bailouts equaled 5 percent of GDP for five consecutive years. See Andrés Velasco, "Liberalization, Crisis, Intervention: The Chilean Financial System, 1975–1985 *International Monetary Fund Working Paper* 88/66 (July 1988); and José P. Arellano, "De la Liberalización a la Intervención: El Mercado de Capitales en Chile, 1974–83" *Colección Estudios CIEPLAN* 11 (December 1983).

25. For a detailed analysis of this phase, see Campero, *Los Gremios Empresariales,* chap. 5.

26. Oscar Muñoz, "Crisis and Industrial Reorganization in Chile," *Journal of Interamerican Studies and World Affairs* 31 (spring-summer 1989).

27. Chilean sociologist Pilar Vergara entitled an otherwise insightful book on the period the "Rise and Fall of Neoliberalism in Chile," *Auge y Caída del Neoliberalismo en Chile* (Santiago: FLACSO, 1985).

tals. As soon as the crisis was controlled the dominant coalition reconstituted itself, as in the 1970s, along the lines of a deregulated, open market economy. Once again, privatization was the instrument used to make this reconstitution politically feasible.

Reshaping Distributional Coalitions:
Distributing Rents While Distributing Shares

The reorganization of the financial-industrial conglomerates after the government takeovers—reprivatization and recapitalization of the so-called odd area—and the privatization of the large public utility companies were the specific conduits through which the dominant coalition was recomposed. The methodology employed in this phase of privatization was based on two mechanisms that each, in turn, had important coalitional implications. The first mechanism consisted of the implementation of different programs of diffusion of ownership of the privatized firms through which the government attempted to widen its social base by creating a constituency of "popular capitalists." The second mechanism consisted of the transfer of state-owned enterprises (SOEs) to newly formed partnerships between reconstituted businesses and policymakers—mostly in the natural monopolies—which indicated the continuation of rent-seeking behavior and the recreation of similar distributional coalitions. *again . . .*

People's Capitalism

The government launched three different alternatives within the large category of people's capitalism. The first program, called *Capitalismo Popular,* consisted of highly subsidized loans for the purchase of stock primarily in the two largest banks and the two largest private pension funds (AFPs), which were under government control. Any person or entity that was current with its tax payments and was purchasing less than $280, could contract a fifteen-year interest-free loan with a one-year grace period and 5 percent cash down payment. Large investors could not buy more than 2 percent of the stock and with a shorter maturity. Twenty percent of the stock purchased was tax deductible and dividends were tax free. The second program, named *Capitalismo Laboral* (labor capitalism), aimed to distribute public company shares among employees of the firms divested, often through the formation of investment trusts. The third program, called *Capitalismo Popular Indirecto* (indirect popular capitalism), relaxed previous restrictions on private pension fund portfolios and allowed the AFPs to purchase stock in state-owned companies in the process of privatization.

The rationale behind the different versions of people's capitalism was political as much as economic. The ministers of finance and the economy had, in this sense, different interpretations on the role and ultimate goal of the program. While for the former, Hernan Büchi, the main goal was "to stimulate greater issuance of stock by productive firms, thus permitting their capitalization," for the latter, Modesto Collados, the program was designed, instead, to "create a national consensus around the idea of the unrestricted respect owed to the right to property."[28] Both objectives ultimately coalesced and reinforced one another.

A few considerations are in order with respect to the actual impact of each of the versions of people's capitalism. The recapitalization of the banks and the AFPs was achieved due to the large subsidy of the interest-free loans that, in some cases, represented 70 percent of the whole operation. The spread of shareholders, in turn, was more than modest. In spite of the 40,000 workers who benefited from popular capitalism, as a proportion of the total adult population, the number of individual shareholders only increased from 0.3 to 2.1 percent between 1985 and 1988. Only in the Santiago and Chile banks did individual shareholders have a significant participation in the total stockholding: the top five shareholders owned under 10 percent. The remaining reprivatized banks were sold to other banks or firms.

The success of labor capitalism is dubious, too. In spite of the substantial capital gains of the shares sold and the sevenfold rise of workers owning shares in their corporations, measured at the peak of the program, the number of workers holding shares ascended to no more than 1 percent of the salaried labor force of the country. The extent to which the program had any significant redistributive effect is also questionable, especially since, as has been reported, in no company did workers hold more than 10 percent of the stock.[29] In most privatized firms, in fact, managers formed trusts under their administration, and in several cases they repurchased stock from the workers relatively fast—after employees made a quick profit—becoming major shareholders.[30]

28. Modesto Collados, "Fundamentos Sociales y Económicos del Capitalismo Popular;" and Hernán Büchi, "El Capitalismo Popular y el Sistema Financiero," in *Capitalismo Popular: Análisis y Debate,* versión completa de las Jornadas Bursátiles realizadas en Abril de 1985, Bolsa de Comercio, Santiago, Chile.

29. Enrique Errázuriz and Jacqueline Weinstein, "Capitalismo Popular y Privatización de Empresas Públicas," *Programa de Economía del Trabajo,* Documento de Trabajo 53 (September 1986); and Mario Marcel, "La Privatización de Empresas en Chile, 1985–88," *Notas Técnicas CIEPLAN* 125 (January 1989).

30. That was the case for the general manager of the electricity distribution company CHILECTRA Metropolitana (later named ENERSIS S.A.), Jose Yuraszeck, who became one of the major shareholders and a member of the board once the two trusts under his administration

The program that completed most of the goals proposed was indirect popular capitalism. By 1988 the AFP system had committed almost 7 percent of its portfolio to corporate stocks and gained control of 25 percent of the stock of the firms privatized after 1985. In this sense, since the funds of each AFP are formed with the savings of the contributing workers, they indirectly own 25 percent of the newly privatized companies. Since workers' funds are mobile, that is, they can take their savings from one pension fund to another as many times as they want during their active worklife, the AFPs have to operate in a highly competitive environment that forces them to maximize the returns of their investors.

The Rent-Seeking Pattern of Privatization: The Sale of SOEs

The reorganization of the economic conglomerates was, in coalitional terms, "the people's capitalism of the top." The first step toward the recomposition of the dominant distributional coalition was the reorganization of the financial sector, under state control since the crash of 1982–83. The two largest banks to be reprivatized, Bank of Santiago and Bank of Chile, had been owned by the two largest economic conglomerates, Cruzat-Larraín and Vial, respectively, who purchased them in the privatization phase of 1974–78. To avoid the concentration that characterized that previous episode of privatization, the government resorted to the distribution of shares through people's capitalism and thus more than 40,000 individuals purchased stock in these two institutions.

This was not an obstacle, however, to reaching an agreement with the large shareholders, which reproduced the revolving door kind of link that characterized the relationship between the economic policy-making agencies of the military government and large business. In the Banco de Santiago an ex-solicitor general of the central bank, an ex-official of the ministry of health, and a former executive of the Cruzat-Larraín group took positions on the board of directors right after its privatization. In the Banco de Chile, an ex-minister of finance, two ex-ministers of labor, and one ex-budget director assumed places on the board.[31]

(Inversiones Los Almendros and Luz y Fuerza) concentrated 21 percent of the stock after privatization. He also became director of the electricity generation company ENDESA, since ENERSIS became a major stockholder of the former. Report by María Olivia Monckeberg, "De Cómo la Luz se Hizo Privada," *La Epoca,* August 28, 1988, 10–11.

31. Patricio Rozas and Gustavo Marín, *1988: El Mapa de la Extrema Riqueza Diez Años Después* (Santiago: CESOC, 1989), 56–57.

This pattern was further reproduced during the privatization of the large SOEs, both CORFO's subsidiaries and the natural monopolies. In those cases, a rapprochement between the government and the main economic groups was a way of recomposing the ruling coalition through the distribution of, in most cases, monopoly rents. For example, in 1988, José Piñera, ex-minister of labor and architect of people's capitalism, and, at the time, president of ENERSIS S.A., became vice president of the electricity generation company ENDESA when ENERSIS became a major stockholder. Piñera also became president of the electricity distribution company Chilectra Metropolitana, once ENERSIS became the largest shareholder of Chilectra. Hernán Errazuriz, foreign affairs minister of the military government, also appeared on the board of ENERSIS.[32] In the case of the long-distance telephone company ENTEL, the board was filled with the names of contributors to *El Ladrillo,* such as Adelio Pipino and Eduardo Undurraga, and ex-minister and Cruzat-Larraín executive Jorge Cauas among others.[33] Cauas also became a member of the board in the privatized CAP, Companía de Acero del Pacifico (Pacific Steel Company).

The distribution of rents became even more evident in the case of the nitrate company SOQUIMICH. In that firm, the presidency after privatization was filled by General Pinochet's son-in-law, Julio Ponce Lerou, and posts in the board were filled by, among others, ex-minister Sergio de Castro, ex-budget director Juan Carlos Méndez, and ex-minister of mining Enrique Valenzuela, who also was a member of the board in the privatized telephone company CTC, initially bought by the New Zealand investor Alan Bond and later purchased by Telefónica de España.[34] This association between policymakers and investing groups sheds light on why, particularly in extraordinarily sensitive sectors such as energy and telecommunications, the industries were privatized as vertically integrated monopolies, including basic concessions on property rights of water for the former and the exclusive access to the satellite for the latter. This perpetuated the monopoly position of the now-private companies, which secured market reserves for the purchasing groups.

The lack of an appropriate regulatory framework further reinforced this rent-seeking pattern. Purchasing groups sought the appropriation of these companies as monopolies and the integration of different segments, such as in the energy sector the concentration of ownership in generation, transmission, and dis-

---

32. Chilectra Metropolitana and ENDESA, *Annual Reports,* 1986–1990. ENERSIS S.A., *Annual Report,* 1988.

33. ENTEL, *Annual Reports,* 1986–1989.

34. SOQUIMICH, *Annual Reports,* 1985–1988, and María Olivia Monckeberg, "Las Amarras del Poder," *La Epoca,* September 25, 1988, 4–5.

tribution of electricity. They appropriated existing wealth, lobbied intensely against further liberalization, and, later on, sought to capture regulatory agencies by political pressure against regulation and often by attracting regulators into their industries, that is, by privatizing human resources largely taking advantage of large wage differentials.[35]

In sum, the privatization-cum-liberalization experiment in Chile shows a distinctive collective action pattern: key policymakers of the Pinochet government served on the boards and in the executive offices of large economic conglomerates before and after holding cabinet and central bank positions, leading to collusion between economic power and political power.[36] Beneficial policy contexts allowed these firms to extract rents and consolidate positions of leadership, often monopoly ones, in their respective sectors. Moreover, these policy contexts led to a series of crises in which negative aggregate outcomes were borne by the fiscal sector, thus representing a redistributive transfer from taxpayers to firms and banks. On this basis, I have claimed that organized political support for the economic reform process came from a coalition of beneficiaries of the reform process, a coalition that qualifies as a distributional one, even in the presence of across-the-board liberalization.

Conclusion

As discussed in the first chapter, for the field of neoclassical political economy, distributional coalitions are groups concerned with the distribution of existing wealth among themselves rather than with increasing output. In this approach, rent-seeking behavior and the organization of distributional coalitions go hand in hand with government intervention in the economy. To the extent that a closed economy concentrates benefits among those who enjoy sector-specific protections and disperses costs among consumers, liberalization will dissipate rents and discourage the creation of distributional coalitions. On the basis of this payoff

---

35. For the original treatment of regulatory capture, see George Stigler, "The Theory of Economic Regulation," in *The Citizen and the State* (Chicago: University of Chicago Press, 1975), 114–44. For a discussion of the problem in Chile, see the following articles in Oscar Muñoz, ed., *Después de las Privatizaciones: Hacia el Estado Regulador* (Santiago: CIEPLAN, 1992): Ricardo Paredes, "Privatización y Regulación: Lecciones de la Experiencia Chilena," 215–48; Eduardo Bitrán and Eduardo Saavedra, "Algunas Reflexiones en Torno al Rol Regulador y Empresarial del Estado," 251–80; and Vivianne Blanlot, "La Regulación del Sector Eléctrico: La Experiencia Chilena," 283–321.

36. With Chile's return to democracy in 1990 and a center-left coalition in office ever since, the participation of policymakers of the military government on the boards of the largest firms expanded, which suggests that the alliances forged during the long economic reform experiment were built to last. This is the general tone of a revealing article in the conservative weekly *Qué Pasa,* May 4, 1992.

structure, a vast literature on the politics of economic adjustment has pointed to the difficulties of gathering political support for market reforms. Thus, the insularity and cohesiveness of reform teams become the main explanatory variables of successful economic reform experiments.

What these two approaches have overlooked, however, is that rent-seeking behavior is not restricted to contexts of state intervention, and that it may also occur under comprehensive marketization. This chapter has provided empirical evidence in support of this claim and has thus emphasized the need to introduce modifications to collective action propositions rooted in those neoclassical assumptions. The Chilean experiment shows that collusion between political power and economic power, revolving-door relationships between corporate executive posts and government executive posts, and policymakers simply taking over state assets and reproducing parasitic behavior are key characteristics of state divestiture. In this process benefits are concentrated and costs dispersed. Thus, the organization of societal support for economic reform is the kind of coalitional context that explains the impetus given to privatization. An implication of this is that, in so doing, these coalitions became distributional ones. That is, they appropriated for themselves existing, and in this case state-owned, wealth; obtained market reserves in the process; and reproduced rent-seeking behavior in order to secure them.

In the next chapter I provide evidence in support of the second set of propositions advanced by this book. To the extent that actors can anticipate the distributive effects of economic policy, and organize and mobilize accordingly, they can also anticipate that once policy becomes embedded in an institutional setting, future disputes over distributive outcomes are avoided, or at least mitigated. Thus, preferences over policy translate into preferences over institutions; interest groups seek to invest resources in institutional configurations that stabilize their preferred distributional outcome. Accordingly, this comprehensive process of institutional redesign highlights the state formation character of marketization.

Once the theoretical argument about the connection among distributional outcomes, policy, and institutional design is stylized on the basis of the Chilean experience, in subsequent chapters I evaluate the argument by examining the privatization experiments in Britain, Mexico, Argentina, and Hungary in that order. As argued in chapter 1, the comparison cuts across region, type of political regime, international position, and the dominant strategy of development prior to the reform. The generalizability of the main propositions of this study is thus enhanced.

Chapter 4

Re-Forming the State

Privatization, Centralization of Power, and Institutional Change in Chile

This chapter provides evidence in support of the theoretical claims of this book regarding the long-term institutional consequences of privatization. As a market-oriented reform process deepens, and as the policies advance from the domain of stabilization to that of structural transformation, they are cast and assessed less in terms of a cluster of economic indicators and more in terms of institutional design. Thus, by reshaping the very structure of the state, economic reform in general, and privatization in particular, affect the way political order is generated and political power is distributed. Accordingly, I argue that privatization is not merely an exercise of economic management; it becomes a true effort at institution building.

On this basis, chapter 1 discussed why the term state "reform" is not enough to capture what is at stake in marketization—much less formulations like state "shrinking," state "retreat," and the like. Policy reform elites aim at changing the economic rules of the game; that is, they establish independent central banks and balanced budgets, and they harden private property rights, among others. Governments seek to change their reputation in economic policy-making, and to do so they create new institutional arrangements: rules, norms, and agencies. A great part of the success of those reform packages, therefore, depends on their capacity to generate credibility among economic agents about the effectiveness and immutability of those rules and norms. Market reform and privatization are thus exercises in institutional destruction and institutional innovation; that is, they are episodes of state formation.

Hence, this chapter examines the mechanisms by which individual and collective preferences and strategies lead to institutional change, and it treats policy as the strategy by which those preferences are mobilized to define new rules and constraints. On this basis, I analyze whether and how policymakers anticipate the institutional consequences of their policies. An examination of the process of policy design and implementation reveals the institutional preferences of interest groups and policymakers. This way I bring the argument of the previous chapter—about the impact of rent-seeking behavior on market reform—in support of this one. The thrust of this chapter is that, to the extent that anticipation of the kinds of outcomes institutions produce transforms preferences over policy into preferences over institutions, distributive considerations are part and parcel of institutional redesign processes.

With these considerations in mind, I focus on the institution-building practices (and their legacies) resulting from the privatization and market reform process in Chile under Pinochet. The policy reforms of those years triggered an unprecedented process of institutional transformation. At first glance, the evidence examined in this chapter—centralization of executive authority, constitutional reform, and the imposition of a private social security system—may suggest that only a military regime like Pinochet's could have executed them. A comparative view of these processes in subsequent chapters, however, will show that other equally repressive market-oriented regimes (Argentina and Uruguay in the 1970s) failed to leave any significant institutional legacy behind, while some established and transitional democratic regimes (Britain in the 1980s, Argentina and Hungary in the 1990s, respectively) have embarked on institutional reforms that qualify as state formation projects. The key to this process, I thus argue, resides in the form and content of market reform; that is, in the extent to which policy changes are locked in new rules, norms, and organizations, regardless of the nature of the political regime.

The Centralization of Authority

During the weeks and months immediately after the coup, military leaders stressed two main issues. They highlighted, first, that the regime would be temporary, aimed at restoring the institutional traditions broken by the socialist government and, second, that the government would be based on a collegial rule under the joint responsibility of the commanders of the four branches of the armed forces. The *Junta de Gobierno* was thus created.

The language of a transitory interruption of democracy, however, soon changed to a discourse that, just like the ongoing economic reform experiment, specified goals instead of deadlines and emphasized the necessity of a new political order to "extinguish political demagoguery once and for all." The idea of creating a political framework that would have long-lasting legacies in Chilean society became particularly evident in the case of General Pinochet, appointed first president of the junta—not yet of the nation—even if, at the time, he did not have a precise blueprint of that institutional configuration, or a clear road map of how to get there. This is revealed by the decision to create a "constitutional commission" in October 1973 (though one without a clearly specified mandate) and in the publication of the "Declaration of Principles of the Chilean Government," a document commissioned by Pinochet and published in March 1974, which constituted the first attempt to outline a refoundational project for the military government.[1]

Once the government specified a long-term project of institutional change, the temporary character of military rule could no longer be claimed. As those institution-building activities entailed important degrees of centralization of authority in the state apparatus, collegiality inside the junta began to strain. As of that moment, Pinochet began to position himself as *primus inter pares,* often pre-empting the other junta members. Given Chile's strong presidential tradition, he greatly benefited from having been designated first in the alternating post of president of the junta. On this basis, in June 1974, Pinochet sponsored Decree Law No. 527, which determined that the junta had constitutional and legislative powers but that executive power was exercised by the president of the junta, who then became "Supreme Chief of the Nation." In practical terms, the junta could hardly exercise legislative control on the executive functions of the Supreme Chief because, while increasing executive power, Pinochet retained veto powers over the junta, simply because it was stipulated that decisions had to be reached by unanimous agreement among the four members and he was one of them. Moreover, by Decree Law No. 806 of 17 December 1974, the title of Supreme Chief of the Nation was changed to that of President of the Republic.

Issues related to the distribution of power, responsibilities, and the ideological definition of the government became frequent sources of internal conflict. Resorting to his title of president, Pinochet distanced himself from his peers in the junta, building ties with the civilians in the economic policy-making teams and exercising leadership over the security apparatus. The leeway given to the intelligence agencies served to imbue the regime with a language of national security and anticommunist war. The influence granted to the free-market policy elites provided the government with the social and economic policies needed to give

---

1. "The Government of Chile has taken upon itself the task of giving Chile new governmental institutions . . . to provide our democracy with solid stability, cleansing our democratic system of the vices which made its destruction easy." Declaration of Principles, reprinted in Juan C. Méndez, *Chilean Economic Policy* (Santiago: Budget Directorate, 1979), 36. For early accounts on the refoundational character of the government, see Tomás Moulian and Pilar Vergara, "Estado, Ideologías y Políticas Económicas en Chile, 1973–78," *Colección Estudios CIEPLAN* 3 (1980), and Manuel A. Garretón, *Proceso Político Chileno* (Santiago: FLACSO, 1984).

shape to the still vague institutional configuration, as well as with a key societal coalition of support.

As of April 1975, Pinochet began to show full endorsement of the economic liberalization policies. At that time, the government adopted a "shock therapy" approach to stabilization under finance minister Jorge Cauas who, by Decree Law 966, was granted extraordinary powers over other ministers. The stabilization program led to a deep recession that year, but the economy began to show signs of recovery by 1976. At the end of 1976, a cabinet reshuffle—when Sergio de Castro became minister of finance—increased the ideological homogeneity of the reform team and deepened the character of structural reform policies. Pinochet solidified his political links with the policymakers and with the business elites associated with them. At this point the authoritarian regime had become a civil-military one.

By 1977 the economy showed high growth rates and the reform program signs of consolidation, especially due to the completion of most of the privatizations in the banking and manufacturing sectors. The repeatedly announced *nueva institucionalidad* began to take more defined contours. In July, Pinochet announced the creation of a new institutional framework leading to a "new democracy," one that would be "authoritarian, protected . . . [and] rooted in the principle of subsidiarity . . . which is the basis of economic freedom."[2] He also announced that the process would be slow-paced and lead to the drafting of a new political constitution. A United Nations' denunciation of Chile for violations of human rights gave Pinochet an unexpected opportunity for political gain. Despite the opposition of other junta members, Pinochet used his executive prerogatives and called for a referendum (*consulta*) on January 4, 1978, "in defense of the dignity of the country." Intimidation, propaganda, and fraud notwithstanding, due to the way the ballots were phrased, a large majority of Chileans ended up endorsing "President Pinochet's institutionalization of the country."

Pinochet capitalized on the referendum. Subsequently, the junta's internal conflicts exacerbated to a point of no return. General Gustavo Leigh, the air force commander, was the staunchest critic of Pinochet's growing centralization of power and his main, if not only, rival in the junta. Throughout his tenure in the junta, Leigh strived to reinforce the predominance of collegial rule, which he saw as the source of all legitimacy of the military government. He advocated a decidedly provisional character for the regime and favored only minor modifications to the 1925 constitution. In an attempt to reverse the existing direction

---

2. Pinochet speech in Chacarillas, July 9, 1997, in Augusto Pinochet, *Pinochet: Patria y Democracia* (Santiago: Editorial Andres Bello, 1984), 86–87.

in the government, in May 1978 Leigh expressed his own views on the future institutional framework in an internal memorandum, urging a return to democratic rule in no more than five years and within the context of the existing constitution. Furthermore, Leigh expressed these viewpoints openly in an interview given to the Italian daily *Corriere della Sera* and published on July 18.

The interview gave Pinochet grounds to outmaneuver Leigh once again, though this time for good. On July 24, with the support of his generals and the defense and interior ministers, and in a display of force that qualified as a coup d'état, Pinochet ousted General Leigh from the junta and forced him to resign as commander of the air force. Pinochet condemned Leigh for divulging disagreements on such sensitive matters to foreign media and charged him with lacking patriotism and threatening the unity of the junta. In light of these accusations and the decree of Leigh's expulsion presented as a fait accompli, the other two members of the junta sided with Pinochet. Eighteen air force generals expressed solidarity with Leigh, but they were also forced into retirement—some by Pinochet, some by political isolation. Pinochet had the support of the army, had divided the air force, and counted with strong support in the civilian camp, the policymakers and their allies in the large financial-industrial conglomerates. Amid political isolation, Leigh had to depart.[3]

The removal of General Leigh from the government was a major victory for Pinochet on several grounds. First, Leigh represented an important obstacle for economic reform inside the military junta. He advocated a middle-of-the-road strategy, retaining an active role for the state in directing the development process, and avoiding shock therapy and excessive privatizations.[4] Second, Leigh was a consistent defender of what he used to call, in reference to the coup of September 11, 1973, "the spirit of the eleventh," namely, a defense of shared authority among the four members of the junta and opposition to the "personalization of power." Third, Leigh advocated a fast-track restoration of democracy within the context of only minor reforms to the 1925 constitution. He opposed a long political process contingent upon the design of a new institutional framework—including a new constitution—as Pinochet had advocated.

Without Leigh, all three processes—economic reform, centralization of power, and institutional reform—received a most significant impetus in that

---

3. A revealing account by General Leigh and a reprint of important documents on that crisis are found in a series of interviews conducted and published by Florencia Varas, *Gustavo Leigh: El General Disidente* (Santiago: Editorial Aconcagua, 1979). For a thorough analysis of military politics during the Pinochet government, see Genaro Arriagada, *Pinochet: The Politics of Power* (Boston: Unwin, 1988).

4. For Leigh's views on these matters, see Varas, *Gustavo Leigh,* 63–71.

order. As Sergio de Castro became firmly in place as the country's economic czar, the structural reform accelerated and widened. Trade liberalization entered its definitive phase and institutional transformations were about to take place in the social sector. Thus, on December 26, 1978, José Piñera was appointed minister of labor and social security. Known for his revolutionary ideas of institutional modernization, Piñera would design a new labor code and implement the privatization of social security. By October of that year the constitutional commission was completing its work and, subsequently, turned the draft to a previously created consultative body—the Council of State—for comments.

Collegial rule vanished and Pinochet thus consolidated his leadership. In the initial phases of the regime, the main rhetorical devices were coated in terms of "war against communism." As the economic reform process advanced, it served to redefine property rights and revamp extractive methods, while simultaneously creating the winning coalition that would provide sustained societal support to the regime. At that point, the language of a new institutional configuration emerged. Pinochet's capacity to outmaneuver his peers in the junta, in turn, allowed him to achieve the centralization of power that was deemed necessary to accomplish the projected institutional changes. These factors together account for the emergence of true state-crafting tasks. Toward the end of the 1970s, therefore, the new architecture of the state was taking a well-defined shape.

Economic Reform and the 1980 Constitution

The new constitution was seen as a prerequisite for the stability of the Pinochet government and the construction of a long-term political order, one projected to be "immune to demagoguery." It was also the result of the policy reform process and deemed critical to secure the economic transformation under way; that is, protect private property, roll back state intervention in the economy, and reestablish market-based allocation processes. Jaime Guzmán, a prominent member of the constitutional commission, brought both dimensions together in straightforward terms: "the fact that it was possible to adopt an outright collectivist and marxist economy without any need to reform the constitution [under the Allende government 1970–73], highlights in eloquent fashion the vulnerability of our old democracy."[5]

---

5. "La Definición Constitucional," *Realidad* 2, no. 3 (August 1980); reprinted in a collection of his writings edited by Arturo Fontaine Talavera, "El Miedo y Otros Escritos: El Pensamiento de Jaime Guzmán Errázuriz," *Estudios Públicos* 42, especial issue (fall 1991): 398. Guzmán, a constitutional lawyer and key ideologue of the Pinochet government, was of traditionalist catholic,

Seen in the context of a broader constitutional outline, the privatization programs become more than a mere transfer of ownership motivated by efficiency
concerns and constitute an effort aimed at a stricter definition and enforcement
of property rights. As such, privatization, while constituting a central component
of the economic reform process, also becomes part and parcel of an institution-
building strategy. In one of their first meetings the constitutional commission
addressed the need to include in the future constitution norms aimed at "reinforcing property rights" in ways that would prevent "the socialization of economic activities" as well as "excessive intervention of the state." This set of
norms comprised a corpus called "economic public order,"[6] based on the principle of subsidiarity by which the economic role of the state should be limited
to the provision of public goods.

Consequently, central components of the economic reform program
adopted constitutional status. The commission rejected the entrepreneurial state
and the constitution explicitly required a law of qualified quorum to allow the
state to engage in any entrepreneurial activity (article 19, precept 21). State roles
in sectoral policy and regulation were curtailed by a norm that impedes granting privileges or creating or imposing taxes or duties that imply any form of
discrimination among economic sectors, activities, or regions (article 19, precept 22) and by additional legislation that liberalized areas such as foreign investment and public utilities (Decree Law 600 in 1974 and article 91, Constitutional Organic Law of the Central Bank). Nontariff barriers to trade—licenses,
quotas, and permits—were prohibited (article 88, Constitutional Organic Law
of the Central Bank). The constitution also specified the "protection of economic freedom," banning the government from interfering with the exercise of
legitimate economic activities on the part of private agents (article 19, precept

---

corporatist political socialization but became a convert free-marketeer in the mid-1970s. His participation was essential in integrating the notion of protected and authoritarian democracy along
with economic liberalism in the constitutional draft. Founder of the Union Democrata Independi-
ente (UDI)—the carrier of "Pinochetism" into the democratic period—he was serving as a senator
when he was assassinated by left-wing guerrillas in 1991. For his posthumous work, see Jaime
Guzmán, *Escritos Personales* (Santiago: Zig-Zag, 1992).

6. As reported by constitutional commission member Enrique Evans de la Cuadra, *Los Derechos Constitucionales,* vol. 2 (Santiago: Editorial Jurídica de Chile, 1986), 313; a two-volume work
that summarizes five years of work in the commission. The constitution was approved in a referendum on September 11, 1980, and promulgated on October 21, 1980. See also a telling discussion
on the subject by the president of the constitutional commission Enrique Ortuzar, "La Constitución
de 1980: Razón de Ser del Régimen que ella Instaura," *Política,* especial issue (November 1983):
45–70. The following references to the constitution are from *Constitución Política de la República
de Chile 1980* (Santiago: Editorial Jurídica de Chile, 1981) and *Apéndice de la Constitución Política
de la República de Chile* (Santiago: Editorial Jurídica de Chile, 1991).

26). In stark contrast to the 1925 constitution, social security was included among the areas now open to private firms (article 19, precept 18).

The new status of private property signaled another significant departure from the 1925 constitution.[7] The 1980 constitution secures the right to property (article 19, precept 24), as did the previous constitution, but establishes, in contrast, immediate compensation and cash payment in case of expropriation (which, in turn, could only be decided by law and not by decree) and determines that qualifications derived from the social function of property cannot impose conditions, levies, or restrictions that obstruct the free exercise of private property (article 19, precept 26). For the members of the constitutional commission, "progress and development depend on the permanent existence of property rights and on that they are not exposed to circumstantial political disputes."[8] These constitutional changes were intended to establish a smaller state, though also to recover "stateness"—a series of reforms that prioritize an assertive definition of property rights and the restoration of the fiscal base, which will necessarily translate into a critical recovery of administrative capacity.

This rationale also was present in the arguments and norms that enacted central bank independence. The constitution stipulates the autonomy and technical character of the central bank and bans it from purchasing treasury bonds and financing direct government expenditures. The Constitutional Organic Law of the Central Bank (No. 18840) specified that the goal of the central bank is "to safeguard currency stability and the normal operation of internal and external payments (art. 3)." It also stipulated that the central bank was to be governed by a five-person board—to be appointed by the president and confirmed by the senate—who would serve for a period of ten years and be nonremovable during their tenure.[9]

These constitutional reforms were based on the "rules-versus-discretion" debate in monetary theory. Arguably, norms that depoliticize the policy process

---

7. *Textos Comparados de la Constitución Política de la República de Chile 1980 y Constitución Política de la República de Chile 1925* (Santiago: Instituto de Estudios Generales, 1980).

8. *Los Derechos Constitucionales,* 376. In their view, previous amendments based on the notion of social function of private property had introduced significant levels of uncertainty as to the overall normative economic framework, a tendency they saw as imperative to reverse. These amendments had, in fact, provided the legal framework that allowed the Christian Democrats in the 1964–70 term and the Socialists in the 1970–73 period to launch land reform programs that triggered intense political disputes. For this issue, see Robert Kaufman, *The Politics of Land Reform in Chile, 1950–1970* (Cambridge: Harvard University Press, 1972), especially chap. 5.

9. Articles 97 and 98 of the 1980 Constitution, and article 3, Constitutional Organic Law 18840, October 10, 1989. A debate among Chilean economists is in *Cuadernos de Economía* 77 (April 1989), special issue on central bank reforms.

shelter monetary authorities from societal demands, place barriers on politically motivated attempts to reverse macroeconomic equilibrium, and thus force governments to maintain fiscal discipline. To put an end to decades-long inflation, and in the presence of entrenched inflationary expectations among economic agents, central bank autonomy is said to be necessary to build policy consistency and bolster credibility. In this view, those expectations are associated with the past performance of politicians who, prone to manipulate monetary policy to obtain short-term electoral gains[10] or unable to finance expenditures with current earnings, are too accustomed to implement inflation-tax schemes.[11]

Given this reputation, the mere possibility that the government resorts to this type of policy manipulation is enough to trigger inflationary expectations, irrespective of the anti-inflation resolve of the authorities or the soundness of their policies. The removal of monetary policy from the control of elected officials is thus said to enhance overall credibility. Rule-based monetary policy, rather than political discretion, would resolve the reputation deficit.[12] In the Chilean policy reform process, this implied insulating monetary policy from the political process through a meta-rule; that is, a constitutional provision that stipulates central bank autonomy and a balanced budget.[13]

---

10. For the pioneering contributions on this, see Anthony Downs, *An Economic Theory of Democracy* (New York: Harper and Row, 1957); and William Nordhaus, "The Political Business Cycle," *Review of Economic Studies* 42, no. 2 (April 1975): 169–90. Significant discussions of the problem in Latin America and other developing countries are Barry Ames, *Political Survival: Politicians and Public Policy in Latin America* (Berkeley: University of California Press, 1987); John Waterbury, *Exposed to Innumerable Delusions: Public Enterprise and State Power in Egypt, India, Mexico, and Turkey* (Cambridge: Cambridge University Press, 1993); and Barbara Geddes, *Politician's Dilemma: Building State Capacity in Latin America* (Berkeley: University of California Press, 1994).

11. For early assessments of this problem, see Martin J. Bailey, "The Welfare Cost of Inflationary Finance," *Journal of Political Economy* 64, no. 2 (April 1956): 93–110; and Milton Friedman, "Government Revenue from Inflation," *Journal of Political Economy* 78, no. 4 (July–August 1971): 846–56.

12. See, for instance, Henry Simons, "Rules Versus Authorities in Monetary Policy," *Journal of Political Economy* 44, no. 1 (February 1936): 1–30; and more recently, Robert Barro and David Gordon, "Rules, Discretion, and Reputation in a Model of Monetary Policy," *Journal of Monetary Economics* 12, no. 1 (July 1983): 101–21; and Robert Barro, "Rules Versus Discretion," *NBER Working Paper* 1473 (September 1984). However, there is no consensus as to the existence of a causal link between central bank independence and low inflation. See, for instance, Adam Posen, "Why Central Bank Independence Does Not Cause Low Inflation: There Is No Institutional Fix for Politics," in Richard O'Brien, ed., *Finance and the International Economy* 7 (1993): 41–54.

13. Note Pablo Baraona's observations (minister of the economy at the time): "It is imperative to avoid the incubation of germs like inflation in the social body which initially produce a feeling of well being but later generate chaos. Only in this way will the system be preserved

An insulated monetary authority, however, is not neutral in distributional terms. Central bank independence remedies the vulnerability of monetary policy to the pressures of the inflationary, import-substituting coalitions of the past; but it locks in a different regime, one that expresses the preferences of other types of coalitions. In its institutional dimension, low inflation reallocates veto powers across economic sectors; it thus has political consequences. Inflation has distributional consequences, not unlike the exchange rate or other sectoral policy. Different levels of inflation benefit some actors at the expense of others. For example, if the government devalues its debt, there will be a redistribution from the holders of cash to the government. Unanticipated inflation, in turn, benefits debtors at the expense of creditors, a reason why the financial sector supports price stability.[14] Supporters of low inflation would thus include financiers, investors, pensioners, and others who hold wealth denominated in nominal assets.

If these considerations are correct, a coalition formed by banks, pension firms, and the contributors to the pension funds (in general, wage earners who are relatively young or recently incorporated into the labor market) would support a setting whereby fiscal balance and price stability are reinforced. To this end, one of the early goals of the economic reform program was to decentralize credit into an open capital market based on privately accumulated savings resulting from a new pension scheme. That reform was implemented in the early 1980s. With it, another crucial institutional transformation in state-society relations took place: the privatization of social security.

---

from demagoguery. These are the sources behind the idea of completely eliminating the possibility that public enterprises or the state contract debt with the Central Bank," in *Somos Realmente Independientes Gracias al Esfuerzo de Todos los Chilenos: Documento de Política Económica* (Santiago: Budget Directorate, 1978), 395. A comparative view of central bank independence illustrates that, for example, neither the Bundesbank nor the Federal Reserve have, as in Chile, the simultaneous constitutional prohibition to finance government expenditures and to purchase government bills, which together constitute a balanced budget amendment. See, on the general subject of central bank independence, John Goodman, *Monetary Sovereignty: The Politics of Central Banking in Western Europe* (Ithaca: Cornell University Press, 1992); Alex Cukierman, Steven Webb, and Bylin Neyapti, *Measuring Central Bank Independence and Its Effect on Policy Outcomes* (San Francisco: ICS Press, 1994), and for the developing world, Sylvia Maxfield, *Gatekeepers of Growth: The International Political Economy of Central Banking in the Developing World* (Princeton: Princeton University Press, 1997).

14. However, if a large proportion of the government's debt is dollar-denominated, inflation would lead to a flight to the dollar, devaluation, and thus an increase in the real value of the debt. In this context, common in Latin America after the 1980s, the government would also prefer disinflation and exchange rate stability. See Jonathan Kirshner, "Disinflation, Structural Change, and Distribution," *Review of Radical Political Economics* 30, no. 1 (winter 1998): 53–89, for a discussion along these lines.

The Marketization of the Welfare State:
Privatizing Social Security

The privatization of social security was part of a comprehensive program of reforms, the so-called seven modernizations, which also included changes in the areas of health, education, labor, public administration, and the judiciary. The logic behind these reforms had initially been espoused by *El Ladrillo* (the document that served as a foundation for the Pinochet government economic reforms) and later reinforced by Miguel Kast in the Planning Ministry (ODEPLAN) and José Piñera from the pages of his magazine *Economía y Sociedad*.[15] In a nutshell, these reforms envisioned the extension of market principles to social policies and integrative roles traditionally reserved for the government, and they anticipated an institutional design that would preempt and/or deflect demands on fiscal resources. For Kast, Piñera, and others, well-organized groups in Chilean society, demanding an ever-increasing share of state resources, had overloaded the capacity of governments to respond. Echoing ungovernability debates in the advanced industrial world, they postulated that the marketization of social provisions was an effective solution to this condition.[16]

Allegedly, this political situation manifested itself most prominently in the area of social security. The pay-as-you-go system was propitious for pressure groups to demand (and often obtain) increases in current retirement benefits, financed through money creation or through borrowing—and, thus, by exacting future generations.[17] The creation of an individually funded and privately administered system would lessen pressure from the fiscal sector, insulate benefits and assets from the political process, and generate incentives for maintaining an

---

15. For Piñera, see "Hacia un Nuevo Modelo Político," *Economía y Sociedad* 3 (May/June 1978): 2–8; and "Institucionalidad Económica," *Economía y Sociedad* 4 (July/August 1978). For Kast, "Política Económica y Desarrollo Social en Chile," and "Relaciones de la Política Económica con la Administración del Estado de Chile: El Estado Empresario y el Principio de Subsidiariedad," *Estudios Públicos* 13 (summer 1984): 199–209 and 211–29, respectively. Kast was among the first to advocate the elimination of universal social programs and the adoption of social policy targeted to the poorest sectors of society.

16. In a neoconservative tone, an important ideologue of the government argues that "the totalitarian danger . . . also attacks in the form of tendencies to egalitarianism and the Welfare State. In fact, as such tendencies intensify and cause the paralysis of liberty, economic development enfeebles and . . . social tensions grow, to the point of leading to the ethical, and later political, collapse of democracy." Arturo Fontaine Aldunate, "Más Allá del Leviatán," *Estudios Públicos* 1 (December 1980): 136.

17. Specifically on social security, see Guido Tabellini, "The Politics of Intergenerational Redistribution," *Journal of Political Economy* 99, no. 2 (April 1991): 335–57. For a more general treatment of the conflicts associated with intergenerational transfers, see Knight, *Institutions and Social Conflict,* 164–70.

adequate macroeconomic regime, one that would be necessary for the stability of the new system and the profitability of the contributors. Piñera was appointed labor and social security minister in December 1978, and his goal was to launch the institutional transformations associated with the modernizations, especially to undertake the transition to a new pension system.

The privatization of social security took place by Decree Laws No. 3500 and No. 3501 of November 4, 1980. The new system was consistent with the overall approach of the economic model: to avoid distributing resources along class or sectoral lines—so as to prevent corporatist modes of organization—and to introduce economic incentives to undermine the capacity for collective action on the part of the working class.[18] To this end, it was explicitly conceived as one territorially, rather than sectorally, based. The core of the reform, in effect today, consists of a mandatory scheme of private and competitive administrators of individual savings. Workers contribute with 10 percent of their monthly income toward a savings account administered by firms known as Pension Funds Administrators (AFPs). Each AFP manages a single fund, allocates returns to individual accounts, and charges a commission for the service. Contributors are free to select any AFP and switch among them. When eligible for benefits, workers can opt between phased withdrawals and a real annuity. In addition, all beneficiaries enjoy a guaranteed minimum pension, which is not indexed but adjusted by the government occasionally.

In the initial regulatory guidelines, the AFPs had a very limited menu of options. Investment in equity or in foreign instruments was not allowed. Most resources were thus distributed between corporate bonds and bank debt (given their interlocking directorates, when the main banks were placed on receivership during the 1983 crisis, the state also took control of the pension funds). In January 1985, however, Decree Laws No. 18398 and No. 18401 relaxed previous restrictions on the AFPs' portfolios and authorized them to invest in stock and required them to purchase central bank bonds. In mid-1985 the ministry of finance initiated the reprivatization of the banks and firms taken over during the 1982–83 crisis, and it announced a schedule for the privatization of large, and traditionally considered strategic, SOEs in the tradable and public utility sectors (with the exception of the copper holding CODELCO).

The decision to allow diversification in the investment options of the pension funds provided the resources needed for the last phase of privatization, avoiding, unlike in the 1974–78 period, the overindebtedness of the private

---

18. Piñera explicitly highlighted this issue in his announcement of the social security reform on November 6, 1980. A reprint of that speech and his own account of the reform process is in his *El Cascabel al Gato: La Batalla por la Reforma Previsional* (Santiago: Zig-Zag, 1991).

sector. Privatization received a most significant impetus through this method without negative macroeconomic effects or price distortions, to the extent that the initial scheme, which specified divestiture operations of around 30 to 50 percent of the stock of these firms, was revised repeatedly in order to privatize the natural monopolies in full.[19] By 1988 the private social security system had committed 7 percent of its portfolio to corporate stocks, and by 1990 about 25 percent of the stock of the firms privatized between 1985 and 1989 was owned by the pension funds administered by the AFPs. This is why this program was called "indirect popular capitalism."

These rapidly growing pension funds, seeking additional investment opportunities, have had a significant impact on capital markets. First, in combination with the privatization of the large SOEs between 1985 and 1990—whose proceeds amounted to $1.5 billion—the pension funds became an important source of demand for shares traded in the Santiago Stock Exchange. By 1992, 28 percent of the pension funds were invested in equity, which represented 9.6 percent of the total Chilean corporate stock. Second, the increasing volume of funds prompted the government to reinforce regulatory mechanisms, which resulted in parallel institutional development—a positive externality for the economy as a whole. Third, this trend constituted a compelling stimulus for the government to allow for financial innovation, specialization, and the diversification of instruments. The democratic government continued innovation. In 1992 the Aylwin administration relaxed the regime even more, allowing AFPs, under the supervision of the Superintendence of AFPs, to invest overseas.

By 1995 five million Chileans had a pension fund account under the privatized social security system. Since the AFPs started operation in 1981, the funds have produced an annual return of 13 percent on average—over twice the annual average GDP growth of the last decade—amounting to an equivalent of 40 percent of the GDP. The country's savings rate has increased to 27 percent of the GDP.[20] By the year 2000 the pension funds represented 56 percent of the GDP. The political ramifications are no less important than the central role of the private pension funds for macroeconomic stability and microeconomic efficiency. The privatization of social security redefined property rights, bolstered

---

19. The resources from the privatization of the SOEs were partly used to finance the old system, which, given massive transfers of workers to the AFPs and the obligation of new workers to enter the new system, had lost contributions while remaining liable of pensions. See José P. Arellano, *Políticas Sociales y Desarrollo: Chile 1924–84* (Santiago: CIEPLAN, 1986), chap. 3; and Peter Diamond and Salvador Valdés Prieto, "Social Security Reforms," in Barry P. Bosworth, Rudiger Dornbusch, and Raúl Labán, eds., *The Chilean Economy* (Washington, D.C.: Brookings, 1994).

20. Sergio Baeza, *Quince Años Después: Una Mirada al Sistema Privado de Pensiones* (Santiago: CEP, 1995).

the overall process of privatization, and widened the constituency with a vested interest in low inflation. In the words of the architect of the reforms, "pension savings accounts now represent real and visible property rights . . . a typical Chilean worker is not indifferent to the behavior of the stock market or interest rates. Intuitively, he knows that a bad minister of finance can reduce the value of his pension rights."[21]

Misión Cumplida: Restored Stateness, "Protected" Democracy

The military government wielded unprecedented levels of discretionary power and Pinochet enjoyed more concentration of authority in his office than any other leader in Chilean history and any of his contemporary South American dictators. This does not mean, however, that the regime was a personalistic dictatorship. To a great degree, Pinochet was constrained by the very institutions that gave him power. The institutional blueprint fixed in place by the military government constitutes a major state-building effort, to the extent that it included a formula and a schedule that would steer the very termination of military rule. In this the Pinochet experiment is also unique. In fact, rarely do autocratic regimes establish norms that specify, well in advance and with great detail, when and how the regime would abandon power.

In this sense, the 1980 constitution called for a general referendum in 1988, to decide either the continuation of General Pinochet as president for another eight years or a democratic transition through national elections in 1989. The opposition parties of the center-left, clustered together under the label *Concertación,* prevailed in the plebiscite of October 1988 and prepared for the election of December 1989. In the months between the plebiscite and the election, and to reverse what the leaders of the Concertación had referred to as "authoritarian enclaves," a process of intense negotiation took place between the leadership of political parties and the military government in order to introduce revisions to the 1980 constitution and ensure a smooth transition toward civilian rule. Reforms were negotiated during early 1989 and approved in another referendum, held on July 30 of that year. These reforms amended a wide variety of strictly political components of the 1980 constitution—broad aspects of the electoral regime, the functioning of congress, and the length of the presidential

---

21. José Piñera, "Empowering Workers: The Privatization of Social Security in Chile," *Cato Journal* 15, no. 2–3 (fall/winter 1995/96): 155–66. This statement is consistent with the views of several middle-level officials of CORFO when the agency was steering the privatization program. In interviews with this author, they repeatedly highlighted that the main goal behind the privatization of social security was to force workers to become "true capitalists."

period, among others. None of the norms that form the "economic public order" was subject to revisions.[22]

By that time the main economists of the opposition, grouped at CIEPLAN (Corporation for Latin American Economic Research), had openly recognized that the Chilean economy was strong and stable, and while they emphasized the need to reduce poverty and make progress in income distribution, they highlighted that those goals should be pursued within the parameters of the existing economic model: fiscal discipline, export orientation, and a dynamic private sector.[23]

The Concertación coalition won the December 1989 election, and the government of Patricio Aylwin was inaugurated on March 11, 1990. On March 12, 1990, most Chilean public servants found paper pads on their desks. Those pads had an illustration, La Moneda (the presidential palace), and an inscription, *Misión Cumplida,* literally, "mission accomplished." The pads were left by officials of the outgoing military government. The message was obvious: despite the electoral defeat, the transition process had taken place within the guidelines of the 1980 constitution. When the military government and its civilian allies refused to revise the economic principles and policies that had obtained constitutional status, they made sure that the reforms would survive the government; they locked them in the constitution.

These so-called authoritarian enclaves in the 1980 constitution played a role in reassuring conservative parties, business elites, and military officers. Some sectors of the Concertación, however, were convinced that, in the long run, the effec-

---

22. Moreover, important addenda to the constitution, such as the Constitutional Organic Law of the Central Bank, and legislation that accelerates the privatization of SOEs were actually passed after the plebiscite of October 5, 1988. The most successful negotiation for the Concertación on the economic terrain was the composition of the board of the central bank, which allowed for the appointment of Andrés Bianchi, an independent economist, as president. Another area where the constitutional provisions remained largely intact was that which secures vast institutional prerogatives for the military. The 1989 process of constitutional reform is documented in detail by Francisco Geisse and José Antonio Ramirez Arrayas, *La Reforma Constitucional* (Santiago: CESOC, 1989). For an analysis of economic legislation after the plebiscite, see Gustavo Marín and Patricio Rozas, "Privatizaciones en Chile: De la Normalización del "Area Rara" a la Ley del Estado-Empresario," *PRIES-Cono Sur Documento de Trabajo* 24 (September 1989). For military prerogatives, see Alfred Stepan, *Rethinking Military Politics* (Princeton: Princeton University Press, 1988); and Brian Loveman, "Mision Cumplida? Civil Military Relations and the Chilean Political Transition," *Journal of Interamerican Studies and World Affairs* 33 (fall 1991): 35–74.

23. CIEPLAN had produced the most articulate criticism of the economic policies throughout the Pinochet government. The recognition of positive attributes of the economic reform policies of the military government in an open letter signed by twelve CIEPLAN economists on the eve of the plebiscite signaled the beginning of a period of broad economic policy consensus. See "El Consenso económico-social es posible," *La Época,* August 28, 1988.

tiveness and legitimacy of the democratic government would be jeopardized by the constitution.[24] By 1992, proposals for constitutional reforms were presented in congress. Even if none of those proposals affected economic aspects of the constitution, business leaders and other sectors formerly linked to the Pinochet regime unequivocally endorsed the need to maintain the stability of the institutional framework and categorically rejected the idea of implementing constitutional changes.[25] A process of negotiation only allowed the government to pass some reforms, such as the replacement of mayors appointed by Pinochet with elected ones and the composition of the National Television Council.

The Concertación program also had emphasized a commitment to a prudent macroeconomic management. In this context, officials of the democratic government frequently highlighted the need to avoid "economic populism." Initially, this emphasis may have been interpreted as a message directed to curb the mistrust of the business community, or as an ex-post rationalization of economic reforms that were, by most accounts, a fait accompli. Seen in retrospect, however, the 1980 constitution appears to be a "blessing in disguise" for the democratic government as well.[26] Aware of the hyperinflationary episodes and the resulting political crises that had shaken the democratic transitions in neighboring Latin American nations, the maintenance of macroeconomic equilibrium became *the* central priority of the Concertación government. Thus, the 1980 constitution provided leaders, now democratic ones, with mechanisms to deflect sectoral demands on fiscal resources. The new constitution also resolved embedded instabilities of the previous institutional order, removing the long-standing problem of executives elected with a minority and—by requiring majorities in congress to pass legislation[27]—reinforcing centripetal tendencies.

---

24. The issue of constitutional reform was in the Concertación electoral platform. "Programa de Gobierno de la Concertación de Partidos por la Democracia," *El Diario,* July 6, 1989, 9–17.

25. For example, Carlos Cáceres (former minister of finance and the interior during the military government), "Reformar la Constitución Afecta la Estabilidad Económica," *El Diario,* June 24, 1992, 10; Juan Antonio Guzmán (President of business peak association CPC), "CPC Respaldó Crítica a Reformas Constitucionales," *Estrategia,* June 12, 1992, 3.

26. The phrase belongs to Timothy Scully, "The Political Underpinnings of Economic Liberalization in Chile," in Leslie Armijo, ed., *Conversations About Democratization and Economic Reform: Working Papers of the Southern California Seminar,* 1995, 198.

27. The mechanisms for implementing constitutional reforms have made it virtually impossible for the Concertación government to introduce modifications without an agreement with conservative sectors, previously supporters of the military regime. Different quorums were established, ranging from two-thirds and three-fifths, to five-sevenths of both houses of congress. For example, for modifications of Constitutional Organic Laws (such as the central bank one), five-sevenths is required.

This is why Alejandro Foxley, minister of finance between 1990 and 1995 and, subsequently, president of the Christian Democratic party and senator, recognized early in the first democratic government that the constitutional rules left by Pinochet had "somewhat ironically fostered a more democratic system," for they forced major actors into compromise rather than confrontation and, by "avoiding populism," they thus allowed for "economic governability."[28]

The oft-preached protected democracy thus came together based, first and foremost, on the economic reform program of the Pinochet government and on its consolidation in institutional instruments. As a whole, this institutional configuration fixed in place a new political economy arrangement, a form of state that locks in an open, market-oriented strategy of development. The inviolability of private property, strict limits on state intervention in the economy, the independence of the central bank (with a balanced budget amendment), and private ownership of social security and public utility services, among other attributes, are the constitutional boundaries within which post-Pinochet economic policy has had to take place. This way, the idea of a protected democracy is also one that, rooted in an assertive definition of property rights, the reconstruction of the fiscal foundation of the state, the centralization of executive authority, and the insulation of vital policy-making domains from contingent political disputes, restores stateness and resolves decades-long credibility problems.[29]

---

28. Foxley made this statement in a talk delivered at the University of Notre Dame, on September 13, 1991. A few weeks later, in Santiago, I followed up on this in several discussions with Foxley and other members of his policy-making team. For a reprint of Foxley's presentation, see "Surprises and Challenges for a Democratic Chile," in *Global Peace and Development: Prospects for the Future,* The Helen Kellogg Institute for International Studies, University of Notre Dame, September 1991, 5–8.

29. Yet some of these policy-making domains were more permeable to the distributive pressures of the military. For example, the constitution stipulates that the military budget may never fall below the amount spent in real terms by the last year of the Pinochet government, that the army is entitled to 10 percent of copper sales (which is a main reason behind the decision to maintain state ownership of CODELCO), and that elected officials cannot intervene in the preparation of the military budget or the purchase of armaments. These attributes, however, have contributed to centralizing tendencies within the coercive apparatus, which, however antidemocratic, one may also interpret as state formation activities. Samuel Valenzuela has used the term "perverse institutionalization" to characterize these features in his "Democratic Consolidation in Post-transitional Settings: Notion, Process, and Facilitating Conditions," in Scott Mainwaring, Guillermo O'Donnell, and J. Samuel Valenzuela, eds., *Issues in Democratic Consolidation: The New South American Democracies in Comparative Perspective* (Notre Dame: University of Notre Dame Press, 1992), 57–104.

Conclusion

This chapter has shown that much of the success of market reform depends on the degree to which those policies are accompanied by vast processes of institutional innovation. The very dynamic of marketization translates the policy process into an institution-building effort. Even at the risk of sounding functionalist, one conclusion is that the reform package "demands" certain institutional changes for its completion and consolidation into a "new economic order," as Chilean constitutionalists put it. Some policies themselves, privatization among them, become processes of institution building. As the program advances and institutional changes are made, a reorganization of political power takes place and authority tends to concentrate in the hands of the executive. Economic reform processes in authoritarian contexts speak to this phenomenon—Chile most notably, as discussed. Yet even in polyarchical settings, as I examine in the following chapters, the executive accumulates a vast amount of power and centralizes unprecedented decision-making power in transitional (Argentina, Hungary) as well as consolidated (Britain) democracies.

As discussed in this chapter, the logic of market reforms is driven by the need to change the rules by which the economy functions. Reformers thus strive to establish independent central banks, balance the budget, and privatize goods and services among others. In the process, new institutional arrangements are designed: innovative legislation or reformed public agencies. This is why the economic reform process becomes an exercise of institution building. Policymakers privatize public enterprise and recommodify social provisions; they thus seek to reform public administration. However, they also "re-form" the state as the dynamics of privatization redefine property rights and redesign revenue-collecting procedures.

In the next few chapters I examine these issues comparatively, focusing on the British, Mexican, Argentine, and Hungarian market reform and privatization experiments in that order. I extend the discussion to these cases to elaborate more broadly on the extent to which these processes of market reform are conducive to specifying property rights, designing revenue production systems, and centralizing administrative and political resources. If this is so, one important conclusion would be that privatization and market reform become episodes of state formation across region, regime type, and politico-economic system.

PART 3

Privatization as Coalition Building and State Formation

Comparative Perspectives on Economic Reform

Chapter 5

Great Britain

From Keynesianism to Thatcherism and Beyond

This chapter shifts the analysis from market reform carried out in a developing, import-substituting economy under a repressive authoritarian regime to an examination of privatization in a Keynesian, advanced industrialized society under a well-established democratic political order. Despite these differences, through comprehensive privatization programs these reforms had consequential coalitional implications in both countries. As reviewed previously, in Chile a small distributional coalition formed by financial elites captured key policy-making positions and became the main beneficiary of the reform policies by taking over the divested assets. In Britain, no comparable capture of policy arenas took place. By and large, privatization was based on the initiative of the Conservative government, though to a great extent in order to make inroads among the working-class electorate and alter the character of political competition in the long term.

This chapter is organized consistently with the narrative I adopted for the case of Chile. First, I discuss the historical political economy context that preceded Margaret Thatcher's privatization program. In doing so, I review the British case in its "natural" context; that is, the decline of the Keynesian macroeconomic approach, as experienced by most West European political economies. As discussed in the first chapter, I combine a method of analysis based on different contexts and similar outcomes with a method by which roughly analogous cases may exhibit variance in outcome. Second, I examine the policy reform program and the collective action implications of this experiment, focusing in particular on the coalitional ramifications associated with the privatization of council housing and the wider share ownership program—Britain's own "people's capitalism."

Finally, I focus on the long-term effects of the political economy of the Thatcher decade on established institutional domains. The privatization and state reform program redefined property rights, redesigned extractive systems, and reorganized decision-making procedures and routines. I focus explicitly on the reorganization of the civil service, changes in the provision of social welfare, and the concentration of power in the central government (largely at the expense of council authorities) particularly in the office of the prime minister (to an extent, at the expense of cabinet). I thus spell out how this institutional redesign process is necessary to understand not only eighteen years of Conservative rule but also the transformation from "old" to "new" Labour. On this basis, and similarly to the other cases examined in this book, I conclude that the privatization experiment constituted a significant chapter in the history of British state formation.

The Keynesian Context

The Keynesian approach emphasizes the role of government spending in determining the level of economic activity. By maintaining a steady increase in spending, the government stimulates consumption and investment. By regulating the level of spending, governments control the rate of inflation. Even though the supply of money has some influence, the most effective way of regulating spending is by adjusting the relationship between government spending and revenues; that is, by means of fiscal policy. As applied to the British economy, this view on the role of fiscal policy signaled a different approach to the role of government in the economy, largely brought about by the experience of the 1930s. The so-called postwar consensus was based on the expectation that the government should provide a series of basic goods and services. These included welfare goods—health, housing, and social security, among others—as well as public services—energy, communications, and water supply.

While the provision of the first type of goods was largely financed through taxation, the provision of the latter involved the creation of public corporations financed by revenue from sales and government subsidies. This, in turn, opened a debate on whether public ownership should be extended into tradables and other activities not necessarily in the area of natural monopolies, and the extent to which the government should intervene to manage the restructuring of important industrial sectors. The state-owned enterprise sector was enlarged through nationalization policies, which included public utilities such as gas, electricity, coal, and the railways. Welfare provisions were extended, largely as a result of the Beveridge report of 1942, which recommended a universal system of social security and the creation of a national health service. Public housing programs were expanded and state education restructured. Last but not least, the government began to perform new planning roles.

The postwar consensus did not crystallize until the 1950s, when Keynesianism became the mainstream policy approach. During the 1940s the Labour party had focused more on nationalization than on class compromise and demand management, and the key policy-making agencies had opposed inflationary policies. In the 1950s, however, Labour reshaped its identity around full employment and the welfare state, that is, around Keynes and Beveridge. Simultaneously, the Treasury became more permeable to the Keynesian approach.[1] The left thus supported a type of capitalism under which the goals of socialism could be achieved.[2] And the right saw in Keynesianism a barrier against nationalization and a formula for preserving Conservative power.[3] The basics of the Keynesian "middle way" were thus established. British politics entered the "collectivist age."[4]

Conservatives supported full employment to the same extent Labour did. Full employment had become an entrenched concern during the war and a central policy goal for the postwar period. With regard to the welfare state, Conservatives argued against the universal provision of benefits and in general favored selectivity. They did not question, however, that the provision of education, housing, health, and social security was a legitimate right of the population and a responsibility of the government. Conservatives did not share Labour's view about the importance of the nationalized sector. With the notable exception of iron and steel, which they privatized upon coming into office in 1951, the Conservative party approached the question of ownership in pragmatic terms. With similar pragmatism, in fact, Conservatives expressed a strong commitment to full employment with demand management as the instrument to achieve it.

In the 1950s and early 1960s the postwar consensus seemed established; those were the years when the Keynesian approach was relatively successful. In that period, coinciding with the years of Bretton Woods, the pound was tied to the dollar at a fixed exchange rate, which worked well with fairly conservative fiscal policies in the United States. The main problem of demand management, however, was that when spending increased too rapidly, foreign goods were driven into the country, creating trade deficits and balance-of-payment constraints. In those sit-

---

1. See, among others, Margaret Weir, "Ideas and Politics: The Acceptance of Keynesianism in Britain and the United States," in Peter Hall, ed., *The Political Power of Economic Ideas: Keynesianism Across Nations* (Princeton: Princeton University Press, 1989); and Kerry Schott, "The Rise of Keynesian Economics: Britain 1940–64," *Economy and Society* 11, no. 3 (1982): 292–316.

2. The landmark statement of this position is Anthony Crossland, *The Future of Socialism* (London: Jonathan Cape, 1956).

3. Robert Skidelsky, *The End of the Keynesian Era: Essays on the Disintegration of the Keynesian Political Economy* (New York: Holmes & Meier, 1977).

4. Samuel Beer, *British Politics in the Collectivist Age* (New York: Knopf, 1967).

uations, governments had to resort to deflation, mostly by reducing spending and increasing interest rates. Given the declining competitiveness of British industry—and thus the decrease in exports—these cycles tended to reproduce themselves more frequently over time: expansions were immediately, and almost inevitably, followed by trade deficits, foreign exchange shortages, and balance-of-payment problems. Keynesianism had developed into a stop-go cycle.

The other big problem of demand management was inflation. In the 1950s, as a result of increasing spending, productivity grew faster than money wages; the result was higher output and employment. By the 1960s, money wages began to rise faster than productivity; the outcome was thus inflation. When unemployment was relatively high, increased spending resulted in higher output and employment. But in the 1960s unemployment was relatively low and thus the outcome was inflation. The type of trade-off that was acceptable between inflation and unemployment became a subject of controversy and heated conflict in the 1960s and 1970s. As a result, governments began to use income policies as an anti-inflationary device. This led to the establishment of arenas for corporatist bargaining, a concomitant ramification of the Keynesian approach and common to other West European nations.[5] As of 1961 successive governments in Britain, both Conservative and Labour, created different institutions and opened several forums for negotiating prices and wages. They all had limited success.[6]

The main economic problems—inflation, foreign exchange shortages, and recurring balance-of-payment crises—were often seen as the consequence of the continuing poor performance of industry caused by structural deficiencies. Keynesian techniques did not suffice to produce sustained growth, analysts and politicians argued, because, while demand management may be effective in reemploying underutilized resources, it is not appropriate for overcoming deficiencies in the structure of those resources—that is, in the way supply constraints affect price formation.[7] The attention of policymakers turned to industrial policy and planning.

---

5. For a landmark comparative analysis, see John Goldthorpe, ed., *Order and Conflict in Contemporary Capitalism* (New York: Oxford University Press, 1985). For an extension of the discussion on corporatism, updated to the 1990s, see Herbert Kitschelt et al., eds., *Continuity and Change in Contemporary Capitalism* (Cambridge and New York: Cambridge University Press, 1999).

6. For different assessments of this, see Keith Middlemas, *Politics in Industrial Society: The Experience of the British System Since 1911* (London: André Deutsch, 1979); and Leo Panitch, *Social Democracy and Industrial Militancy: The Labour Party, The Trade Unions, and Incomes Policy, 1945–1974* (Cambridge: Cambridge University Press, 1976).

7. See Stuart Holland, "State Entrepreneurship and State Intervention," in Holland, ed., *The State as Entrepreneur* (London: Weidenfeld & Nicolson, 1972), 5–44. Note the similarities of this interpretation with the approach of the Latin American structuralist school, which always emphasized supply bottlenecks.

Thus, in 1962, the National Economic Development Council (NEDC) was created. It consisted of a tripartite forum for interest intermediation among the government, industry, and labor that, in combination with the National Economic Development Office (NEDO), was designed to be the central planning agency for the British economy. Other agencies for selective intervention were created by subsequent Labour (1964–70 and 1974–79) and Conservative (1970–74) administrations. The Department of Economic Affairs (DEA) and the Ministry of Technology were created in 1964 and had alternative responsibility for the formulation of industrial policy. In 1966 the state-holding Industrial Reorganization Corporation (IRC) was created, following similar experiences in other West European nations.[8] It was later disbanded by the Heath government, but the idea was revived in 1975 by the Wilson administration, which erected the National Enterprise Board (NEB).[9] The Keynesian approach thus evolved into the mixed economy due to industrial policy rather than ideological considerations.

The Monetarist Turn

In the aftermath of the oil shock of 1973–74, the Labour government had initially decided to reflate the economy by increasing social spending and public sector wages. Consumption rose and the economy began to grow again but at the cost of a heavy burden for industry, given that it had to absorb the oil increase, and a rate of inflation of 25 percent in the spring of 1975, which in turn had a negative impact on investment levels. As inflation replaced full employment as the main priority of the government's economy policy, the seeds of a profound sea change were thus established in British political economy.

To the extent that inflation proved persistent, the Wilson–Callaghan administration enacted the Social Contract, the Labour government attempt to reach wage restraint agreements. The Contract failed for the same reasons previous income negotiations had failed: divisions between the Trade Union Congress (TUC) and the Labour party, the incapacity of the TUC to bind individual unions to negotiated agreements, and the inability of union leaders to force rank-and-file compliance.

---

8. Holland, "Adoption and Adaptation of the IRI Formula," in Holland, ed., ibid., 242–65. This formula also gave impetus to the creation of the Chilean state holding CORFO as early as in 1938.

9. See Wyn Grant, *The Political Economy of Industrial Policy* (Cambridge: Butterworth, 1982), chap. 5. See, also, Daniel Kramer, *State Capital and Private Enterprise: The Case of the UK National Enterprise Board* (London: Routledge, 1988).

By 1976 public expenditure and borrowing were out of control and unemployment was on the rise. In July there was a run on the pound and a balance-of-payment crisis more severe than earlier ones. The government resorted to an unprecedented solution: to apply for a loan to the International Monetary Fund (IMF). An agreement was reached in December. All other credit was exhausted, and the British economy was placed under technical supervision. The concern with inflation and the commitment to the IMF forced the Labour government to focus on the control of the money supply. Demand management was abandoned, unemployment rose, and dissatisfaction grew. The government did not have many options. The goal was deflation and the method available was monetarism.[10] All these negative trends combined in even more dramatic ways during the "winter of discontent," a series of strikes in the first weeks of 1979 that, as a commentator observed, "put the finishing touches to the destruction of the Post-war Settlement."[11]

While the conditions associated with the stabilization program were hard to accept by the rank and file of the TUC, the very idea of an IMF loan to Britain was alarming for the financial elites of the city. Across the board distress created an appropriate context for early advocates of monetarism and critics of the post-war consensus approach. This was the case of Sir Keith Joseph, former member of the Heath government, founder of the think tank Center of Policy Studies (CPS) in 1974, and close ally of Margaret Thatcher. Since the early 1970s Sir Keith had been a fervent advocate of sound money and a harsh critic of "the illusory middle ground," which he dubbed as "a concession to socialism."[12]

The election of Margaret Thatcher to the party leadership catapulted these policy views to a position of dominance. Ongoing economic difficulties and an increasing sense of ungovernability[13] soon transformed Sir Keith's ideas into

10. See David Coates, *Labour in Power? A Study of the Labour Government, 1974–1979* (London and New York: Longman, 1980); and, more recently, Peter Hall, "The Movement from Keynesianism to Monetarism: Institutional Analysis and British Economic Policy in the 1970s," in Steinmo, Thelen, and Longstreth, eds., *Structuring Politics*, 90–113. It is worth highlighting that demand management was facing structural constraints throughout Western Europe. The example of the expansionary program of the Mitterrand administration in France in the 1980s, leading to serious balance-of-payment problems later followed by a devaluation, fiscal adjustment, and privatization, constitutes an early example of left-leaning parties adopting orthodox macroeconomic policies and microeconomic liberalization. See Peter Hall, *Governing the Economy* (New York: Oxford University Press, 1986), chap. 8; and Ezra Suleiman, "The Politics of Privatization in Britain and France," in Suleiman and John Waterbury, eds., *The Political Economy of Public Sector Reform and Privatization* (Boulder: Westview, 1991).

11. Peter Jenkins, *Mrs. Thatcher's Revolution: The End of the Socialist Era* (Cambridge, Mass.: Harvard University Press, 1987), 19.

12. *Stranded on the Middle Ground* (London: Centre for Policy Studies, 1976).

13. For examples of this perception, see Robert Moss, *The Collapse of Democracy* (London: Temple Smith, 1975); Anthony King, ed., *Why Is Britain Becoming Harder to Govern?* (London:

the official platform of the Conservative party. As of 1976, virtually all party documents on economic policy exhibited an uncompromising endorsement of a deregulated market economy, and by 1978 they began to include explicit proposals for the privatization of the nationalized industries.[14] The conditions for what later came to be known as "Thatcherism" were thus created. The winter of discontent would take care of bringing it to power.[15]

The Thatcher Experiment

The Conservatives came to office in 1979 with a clear mandate: to reverse economic policy based on demand management and to place emphasis on the supply-side of the economy. The government eliminated controls over prices, capital movements, and incomes, and reformed entrenched labor laws in order to reduce the monopoly power of unions over income policies. On the macroeconomic side, the emphasis was placed on hard monetary controls, reductions in government spending, and the removal of full employment policies.

These instruments, which came together under the rubric "medium-term financial strategy" (MTFS), soon proved insufficient. The goal of the MTFS was a reduction of the inflation rate by declining targets of monetary growth and budgetary deficits over a period of four years. However, the government had difficulty in bringing the rate of growth of the money supply within its target, which led to large increases of interest rates. Capital inflows increased, which, added to the North Sea oil boom, depressed the exchange rate, putting additional hardships on the manufacturing sector. This made the budgetary goals more difficult to accomplish. Large cuts in education, housing, and the Civil Service were offset by increases in defense and social security (the consequence of higher unemployment) and by decreases in tax revenues (the consequence of recession).[16]

After 1981 the government began to abandon the monetarist approach and turned to a supply-side one. Monetary targets were revised and the focus

---

BBC, 1976); and "Overload: Problems of Governing in the 1970s," *Political Studies* 23, no. 2/3 (1975): 284–96; James Douglas, "The Overloaded Crown," *British Journal of Political Science* 6, no. 4 (1976): 493–505.

   14. For example, *The Right Approach: A Statement of Conservative Aims,* Conservative Central Office, 1976; the report of the Conservative Party's Policy Group on the Nationalized Industries, known as the Ridley Report and made public by *The Economist,* May 27, 1978, 21–22; and the 1979 Conservative Electoral Manifesto.

   15. Peter Ridell, *The Thatcher Government* (Oxford: Basil Blackwell, 1985), 21–40.

   16. For this period, see Geoffrey Maynard, *The Economy Under Mrs Thatcher* (Oxford: Basil Blackwell, 1988), 30–43; and Alan Walters, *Britain's Economic Renaissance: Margaret Thatcher's Reforms, 1979–1984* (New York and Oxford: Oxford University Press, 1986).

was placed on how to reinvigorate the economy by restoring entrepreneurial incentives in order to foster growth and employment.[17] A selective reduction of taxes was meant to produce incentives for reinvestment. In the 1979 budget the basic rate of income tax had been cut from 33 to 30 percent and the top rate had been cut from 83 to 60 percent. They were cut again in 1984 and later in 1988, to get to the basic rate of 25 percent and a top rate of 40 percent.[18]

Increases in employment were expected to follow the deregulation of labor markets. To that end, and justified in supply-side terms, the 1980, 1982, 1984, and 1988 Acts pursued the weakening of union power. These Acts withdrew some legal immunities (especially for secondary strikes and picketing), made union officials more accountable (by secret ballots), weakened the closed shop, and put union funds at stake in case of violations of the law. Highly contested, the "critical test" for this new legislation came with the miners' strike of 1984–85. The Thatcher government proved inflexible and a strike that appeared as little more than another manifestation of British long-term deficit of governability was turned into crucial political victory of the prime minister.[19]

The most significant and successful policy course within the supply-side approach, however, was the privatization of public utilities and the nationalized sector. Whereas the original targets for public expenditure and the money supply were not achieved, the divestiture process went farther and faster than it was initially projected. To a great extent the privatization of SOEs became an effective way to achieve the fiscal goals that the MTFS was not capable of accomplishing by itself. The argument of this chapter, however, is that the privatization program went farther and faster than expected not only because of its fiscal impact but also for its anticipated political effects. As in the other cases examined in this book, to the extent that the redefinition of property rights affects coalition building and electoral politics, and to the extent that it undertakes the reorganization of administrative procedures and the centralization of political ones, market reform programs serve as instruments through which political order is generated and political power distributed. In other words, the state is "re-formed" through privatization, in authoritarian and democratic political regimes as well.

---

17. John Burton, "Picking Losers . . .?" *IEA Hobart Papers* 99 (1983); and Patrick Minford, *The Supply Side Revolution in Britain* (London: Institute of Economic Affairs, 1991).

18. "Margaret Thatcher's Ten Years," *The Economist,* April 29, 1989, 19–22. For a view from inside the Treasury, see Leo Pliatzky, *The Treasury Under Mrs Thatcher* (Oxford: Basil Blackwell, 1989).

19. Arthur Shenfield, "Mrs Thatcher: Hammer and Reformer of the Unions," in Madsen Pirie, ed., *A Decade of Revolution: The Thatcher Years* (London: Adam Smith Institute, 1989), 19–32.

Privatization

In 1979 the nationalized industries in the United Kingdom accounted for about 10.5 percent of GDP. They employed 2 million people and dominated key segments of the transport, energy, communications, steel, and shipbuilding sectors. Yet their performance had been considered disappointing in terms of their total return on capital employed; their record on prices, productivity, and manpower costs; and the low level of customer satisfaction.

Privatization had initially involved a modest divestiture in the tradable sector, but it expanded after 1983, when it began to be seen as an industrial policy, as a macroeconomic instrument, and as an ideological tool for the overall Thatcherite project.[20] The transfer of SOEs to the private sector was thus meant to promote competition and improve efficiency, but it was mostly pursued to alleviate the borrowing requirement of the public sector and use receipts from privatization to bring the government budget strategy within target.[21] As in various experiences of privatization, these goals worked against each other; and the British government prioritized the latter. For this reason, key utility companies—such as British Gas and British Telecom—were sold for the most part intact, while the regulatory offices were not granted enough powers to supervise these newly privatized monopolies. The breakup of these firms and the design of tighter regulation would have increased efficiency in the long run but decreased the sale value of the companies and raised less revenue in the short run.[22] Constrained by macroeconomic imbalances and the political-business cycle, the Thatcher government targeted the fiscal benefits of privatization over gains in efficiency and competition to, first, stabilize the PSBR and, later, seek electoral gains on the basis of tax cuts.[23]

---

20. For comprehensive analyses of the ideological dimension involved in the Thatcherite project, see, by conservative think tanks, Ralph Harris and Arthur Seldon, eds., *The Emerging Consensus . . .?* (London: IEA, Hobart Paperback 14, 1981); Nigel Lawson, "The New Britain: The Tide of Ideas from Atlee to Thatcher," *CPS Winter Address,* Centre for Policy Studies, February 1988; Masden Pirie, ed., *A Decade of Revolution: The Thatcher Years* (London: Adam Smith Institute, 1989). By critics from the left, see Stuart Hall, *The Hard Road to Renewal: Thatcherism and the Crisis of the Left* (London: Verso, 1988); and Bob Jessop et al., *Thatcherism: A Tale of Two Nations* (Cambridge: Polity Press, 1988).

21. See, for example, John Moore, "Why Privatise?" speech delivered on November 1, 1983; reprinted in *Privatisation in the United Kingdom: Background Briefing* (London: HM Treasury, 1990).

22. See Cento Veljanovski, *Selling the State: Privatisation in Britain* (London: Weidenfeld and Nicolson, 1988), chap. 7; and Veljanovski, ed., *Privatisation & Competition: A Market Prospectus* (London: Institute of Economic Affairs, 1989).

23. For an emphasis on revenue collection as the main motive behind privatization, see Vincent Wright, "Industrial Privatization in Western Europe: Pressures, Problems, and Paradoxes," in Wright, ed., *Privatization in Western Europe* (London: Pinter, 1994), 1–43.

Other factors contributed to prevent the breakup of the natural monopolies. One was the decision to implement the "wider share ownership program," also known as people's capitalism. In the mid-1980s the government began to focus on the potential effect of the distribution of shares upon getting popular support for the privatization program as a whole and for the Conservative party in future elections, as well as making renationalization unlikely. Tendering the companies undivided could boost the price during the flotation process and increase profits for popular capitalists.[24] A second factor was related to the need to speed the program itself, constrained by the electoral calendar. Since it was easier and faster to privatize those firms as monopolies, even those who favored restructuring the firms before selling them accepted this suboptimal form in order to avoid the risk of losing office and abort the overall privatization program.[25]

By all accounts, the privatization experiment constitutes a watershed period in British political economy. By the end of the third Thatcher government in 1991, the state's share of GDP had been reduced to 5 percent; twenty-nine major companies and their subsidiaries had been privatized; a number of social services had begun to be provided through contracts with private firms; a large number of council houses had been sold; and 800,000 jobs had been transferred to the private sector.

The SOEs: Phases of the Program

The first phase of privatization (1979–83) involved industries typically found in the private sector, although with some special characteristics that predisposed them to public ownership, for example Amersham International, Britoil, and British Petroleum. These early sales raised comparatively small sums of money for the Treasury at a time when monetary policy was very tight and tax revenue under pressure due to the recession. The transfer of ownership was politically expedient and administratively simple. This phase was rather ad hoc since there was no specific and established privatization program on the part of the government. There was, however, a clear orientation toward the sale of council housing, which, especially in the early phases of the divestiture effort, constituted the single most important item in terms of its fiscal impact.

The sale of 51 percent of British Telecom (BT) signaled the beginning of the second phase (1984–89). The election of 1983 marked a shift in the policy

24. Interview Cento Veljanovski, former Research and Editorial Director of the Institute of Economic Affairs, expert on regulation.

25. See Ray Rees, "Economic Aspects of Privatization in Britain," in Wright, ed., *Privatization in Western Europe,* 44–56.

priorities of the government, with a greater emphasis on share ownership and its redistributive goals. The decision to privatize the natural monopolies as units simplified the management of the wider share ownership program, which gave a strong impetus to privatization. BT shares received more than two million applications and British Gas received four million. By 1989 the program consisted of nine million individual shareholders.

The third phase (1989–91) began with the Water Act of 1989, which provided for a change in the operation of the water industry in England and Wales, and the privatization of the nine regional water authorities. In the same year, the Electricity Act provided for the restructuring and privatization of the electricity industry in England and Wales, and of the separate industry in Scotland, with the exception of nuclear power plants that remained in the public sector. The flotation of water shares took place in November 1989. Demand for shares was large, to the extent that they were more than five times oversubscribed. The Treasury raised £5.3 billion—minus previous debt write-off and other expenses. The flotation of shares of the electricity distribution companies took place in December 1990. Proceeds from this sale amounted to £5.2. billion.[26] Table 4 provides a schematic description of the phases and proceeds of privatization.

As table 4 shows, the privatization program began with small operations but gained momentum in the mid-1980s when, as a consequence of the deficiencies of the MTFS, the government adopted a supply-side approach. Privatization was convenient to balance the budget, initially by increasing revenue and later on by decreasing the borrowing requirements. There was some anti-inflationary logic in its implementation. As the policy priorities moved from controlling inflation to creating incentives for investment, privatization received a further impetus. When it became apparent that the proposed modernization of BT would require Treasury financing, the tide of opinion within the government fluctuated decidedly in favor of full-fledged privatization.

In political terms, privatization was used first in negative terms, namely, as an instrument to curtail the public sector, deactivate unions in a sector formerly 100 percent unionized, and weaken the electoral capabilities of the Labour party. Thereafter, the government used privatization as a positive instrument, that is, a political device to generate consensus, build coalitions, and redraw entrenched institutional boundaries of the British state. As the packaging of the program turned from denationalization to encouraging ownership of homes and extending ownership of shares among low-income groups, key polity arenas were restructured. As in Latin America and Eastern Europe, market-friendly policies became

---

26. The flotation of the generation companies took place in February 1992.

TABLE 4.   Phases and Main Proceeds of Privatization in Britain, 1979–90 (£ million)

Company	1979–83	1984–88	1989–90
Amersham Int.	64		
Assoc. British Ports	46	51	
British Aerospace	43	347	
British Petroleum	284	543	
British Sugar	44		
Britoil	334	719	
Cable and Wireless	181	840	
NEB Holdings	122	232	
National Freight	5		
British Telecom		4,701	
British Gas		6,133	400
British Airways		854	
Enterprise Oil		384	
Rolls-Royce		1,031	
British Airport Authority		1,223	
British Steel		1,138	1,280
Water plcs (first issue)			5,300
ESI (electricity, first issue)			5,200
Miscellaneous	412	163	
Total	1,535	18,359	12,180

Source: Privatisation in the United Kingdom: Background Briefing (London: HMSO, 1990); Department of Trade and Industry, *Sources on Information on Privatisation,* January 1991; and Jane Roberts, David Elliot, and Trevor Houghton, *Privatising Electricity: The Politics of Power* (London: Belhaven Press, 1991).

hegemonic (witness new Labour), unusual coalitions were put together, new electoral patterns developed, and critical changes took place in the institutional arena, as the redefinition of property rights was accompanied by the alteration of administrative processes within the state apparatus and the centralization of authority in the executive.

A Property-Owning Democracy

For the Conservative party, a property-owning democracy was considered to be the most potent bulwark against a reappearance of the collectivist and socialist trends of the past. Two specific procedures were undertaken in order to alter the preferences of the electorate and thus reorganize the coalition-building process: the privatization of public housing—"a nation of homeowners"—and the distribution of shares of the privatized public utilities—"a nation of shareholders."

Margaret Thatcher had anticipated in the electoral campaign the "Right to Buy" issue. The Housing Act of 1980 set the framework for the privatization of council housing. It included discounts of 33 to 50 percent on the market value

TABLE 5. Sales of Dwellings by Local Authorities in Britain, 1960–89

Year	Sales	Total of Decade
1960–69		50,510
1970–79		202,145
1980	81,483	
1981	102,720	
1982	202,045	
1983	141,457	
1984	103,177	
1985	92,294	
1986	88,718	
1987	105,107	
1988	155,556	
1989	170,691	
1980–89		1,243,248

Source: Department of the Environment, *Housing and Construction Statistics, 1979 to 1989* (London: HMSO, 1990); and Ray Forrest and Alan Murrie, *Selling the Welfare State: The Privatisation of Public Housing* (London: Routledge, 1988).

and the legal right to a mortgage. In 1984 the Housing and Building Control Act established a maximum discount to 60 percent of the value and in 1986 the Housing and Planning Act increased it once again to a maximum of 60 percent for houses and 70 percent for apartments. Those subsidies made the purchasing of homes very attractive. House sales increased twenty-five times vis-à-vis the 1960s and more than six times that of sales in the 1970s. As a consequence, the percentage of owner-occupiers among all households rose from 52 to 66 percent in the period of 1979–1989. Table 5 describes this evolution.

The privatization of public housing was also significant in terms of its fiscal impact. Throughout the 1980s, in fact, the sales of council dwellings represented the single most important item of the entire privatization program. By the end of the 1988–89 fiscal year capital proceeds from the privatization of SOEs amounted to £24.5 billion for the decade. Capital proceeds from the housing program amounted to £17.6 billion for the same period. Generally cashed by the local authorities, this revenue was often used by the central government to discount the regions' Public Sector Borrowing Requirement (PSBR).

The sale of shares of public enterprises among the public, in turn, began with the inauguration of the program in 1979 and included twenty-nine large corporations. The real breakthrough of popular capitalism, however, began with the sale of BT in 1984 when approximately one million of the successful applications, 50 percent of the total, were from first-time buyers of shares. Additional privatizations—of British Aerospace, Britoil, and Cable and Wireless in 1985, and British Gas and the flotation of the Trustee Savings Bank in 1986—provided further impetus to the wider share ownership program.[27] As a result, the number of individual shareholders tripled between 1984 and 1987 alone. By 1987, 24 percent of the British population owned shares compared with the 7 percent of 1979. About fifteen million people were involved at different points in time in the purchase of shares of the privatized industries and at the beginning of 1990, and despite the large number of investors who had sold their shares for short-term profit, almost nine million people still owned shares in the privatized companies (see table 6).

The Electoral Impact

Conventional theories on voting behavior in the United Kingdom used to emphasize the class-based nature of its electoral system. Several studies showed the singular correlation between occupational roles and voting over time. Influential analyses, elaborated to explain this unusual regularity, viewed party identification as coming primarily from socialization in the family and later modified at work. Other dimensions—patterns of consumption, education, or income—were discarded as explanatory variables in their own right and seen merely as indicators of class.[28] Yet Britain began to vote differently in the 1970s and 1980s. Class-party identification ceased to be the single most important predictor of voting behavior. As class cleavages lost their electoral weight, demonstrated by the decline of the working-class Labour vote, specialists began to look for explanations of a "decade of dealignment" that put "British democracy at the crossroads."[29]

One way of explaining the electoral dealignment was to look at changes in the social structure and working-class attitudes. Social and economic changes of the 1950s and 1960s indicated that the working class as a whole had become more penetrable to practices and values from outside its own political and cultural traditions. A working class that was owning cars, televisions, and even following the professional class on vacation was not likely to

27. *A Nation of Shareholders: Report of the CBI Wider Share Ownership Task Force* (London: CBI, 1990).

28. For this, see David Butler and Donald Stokes, *Political Change in Britain: The Evolution of Electoral Choice,* 2d ed. (London: Macmillan, 1974).

29. Bo Särlvik and Ivor Crewe, *Decade of Dealignment: The Conservative Victory of 1979 and Electoral Trends in the 1970s* (Cambridge: Cambridge University Press, 1983); Patrick Dunleavy and Christopher Husbands, *British Democracy at the Crossroads: Voting and Party Competition in the 1980s* (London: George Allen & Unwin, 1985).

TABLE 6.   Number of Shareholders in Selected Companies in Britain, at Date of Main Sale and in 1990 (in thousands)

Company	At Privatization	In 1990
Amersham (1981)	63.7	5.9
British Ports (1981)	37.2	12.2
British Telecom (1984)	2,051.3	1,236.8
Enterprise Oil (1984)	13.6	9.6
Jaguar (1984)	125.0	42.9
British Aerospace (1985)	157.8	136.5
Cable and Wireless (1985)	151.7	173.6
Britoil (1985)	37.2	245.5
British Airways (1986)	1,100.0	347.8
British Gas (1986)	4,407.0	2,780.3
Rolls-Royce (1987)	2,000.0	924.9
British Airports (1987)	1,980.0	1,064.8
British Steel (1988)	650.0	336.8
Water plcs (1989)	2,705.1	1,318.3
Total	15,479.6	8,635.9

Source: Privatisation in the United Kingdom: Background Briefing (London: HM Treasury, March 1991). For British Steel and Water plcs in 1990: *Labour Research,* March 1991, 23.

behave in ways that could reproduce class consciousness, at least not in the terms it was understood in the postwar. "From the 1950s onwards," as Gareth Stedman Jones observed, "the automatic equation between trade unionism, Labour voting and a cluster of labour movement loyalties became increasingly hard to make."[30]

This highlighted the significance of those other, previously underestimated, factors like consumption or housing tenure in shaping electoral behavior. At times, the notion of social class may not produce valid and direct empirical referents through which to assess electoral behavior. Divisions grounded in more concrete conflicts of material interest have a more immediate impact than cleavages based on a notion of class that often refers to a mere set of cultural contrasts. One of the most significant of those tangible divisions is that of ownership versus nonownership of housing. Its importance became noticeable in the late 1970s[31] and crucial in the 1980s, as the Thatcher policy experiment displayed how self-aware and relatively cohesive an interest group homeowners had become.

30. *Language of Class: Studies in English Working Class History, 1832–1982* (Cambridge: Cambridge University Press, 1983), 250.

31. Särlvik and Crewe, *Decade of Dealignment,* 102, noticed that 61 percent of outright owners and 53 percent of mortgagees voted conservative against 28 percent of council tenants in the 1979 election.

Tenure also reflects class position to a considerable degree, for access to owner-occupation has generally depended on a relatively secure and well-paid job. Yet, even when class is controlled for, electoral studies report that housing crosscuts class and that working-class homeowners are more likely to vote Conservative than are working-class council tenants. Whether it is home ownership that leads to conservatism or conservatism that induces the move into home ownership—something on which there is no concluding evidence—is less relevant than the fact that available data show a strong association between property owning and Conservative voting.

Whether it was a constituency of new homeowners or one of shareholders, the extension of popular capitalism had an impact on electoral behavior. By the end of 1982 almost four hundred thousand families had been able to purchase their homes and one hundred thousand individuals had bought shares in the privatized industries. By the end of 1986 those figures had increased to eight hundred thousand families becoming homeowners and to almost 2 million individuals becoming shareholders, and by 1990 they had increased again to 1.2 million homeowners and 8 million shareholders. It is possible, then, to infer that the actual electoral impact of the preferences of each group of owners was decisive for the 1983 and 1987 general elections. In fact, 44 percent of working-class homeowners voted Conservative in 1987, and 32 percent voted Labour in the 1987 election. Among working-class council tenants 57 percent voted Labour and 25 percent, Conservative.[32]

The impact of privatization is thus significant for the coalitional preferences of low-income groups subject to different programs. The British example of the privatization of council housing and the distribution of shares among the population is particularly pertinent to show how, as social groups alter their material interests—whether they become homeowners, stockholders, or both—they also shift their electoral behavior in a more conservative direction. The Conservative party has benefited greatly from that; its main leaders openly recognized the electoral objectives of those programs. A nation of shareholders and a property-owning democracy were factors that contributed to the four consecutive electoral victories of the Conservative party.

Technically, however, to the extent that these new coalitions were organized on the basis of the distribution of existing wealth, rather than on account of expanding existing output, they qualify as distributional ones. In contrast to

---

32. David Butler and Dennis Kavanagh, *The British General Election of 1987* (New York: St. Martin's Press, 1988), 276. See also Anthony Heath et al., *Understanding Political Change: The British Voter, 1964–1987* (Oxford: Pergamon Press, 1991); and Geoffry Garrett, "The Political Consequences of Thatcherism," *Political Behavior* 14, no. 4 (1992): 361–82 for similar data.

much of the privatization experience in Latin America and Eastern Europe, where the behavior of well-connected interest groups provided the most significant impetus to their programs, in the United Kingdom the Thatcher government took the initiative and launched privatization. Catered to investment groups, but also to low-income groups in a larger proportion than in the other cases examined in this study, the divestiture program was designed with explicit electoral goals.

This does not mean that a Conservative victory could be guaranteed. It was widely accepted that the very narrow victory of John Major in the 1992 election was partly the consequence of the impact of increasing interest rates on homeowners accustomed to paying very low mortgages. It is equally certain, however, that the very nature of political competition has deeply changed. As I argue later, it was not until the emergence of "new" Labour, and Tony Blair's victory and government, that the real, long-term impact of Thatcherism could be assessed. To understand the nature of new Labour, however, it is necessary to first examine the process of institutional redesign that accompanied Margaret Thatcher's privatization program.

The Institutional Consequences of Thatcherism

At the outset of her government, Margaret Thatcher made explicit that her reform program would not only encompass the economy, it would also aim at transforming significant areas of the state apparatus. To the extent that the size of the public sector (in the nationalized industries and administration as well) was viewed as the main cause of the long-term decline of British economy, policy shifts necessarily translated into major transformations of established institutional routines and realms. Accordingly, ambitious reforms in the direction of marketization took place in the civil service and in the structure of local government. The concentration of authority in the office of the prime minister, in turn, altered the fundamentals of cabinet government. Put together, these changes represent state formation strategies aimed at resolving decades of ungovernability.

The 1979 Conservative Manifesto had, in fact, promised to reduce "waste, bureaucracy, and over-government." Rolling back the state implied breaking away from the economic, social, and political consensus of the postwar period—namely, privatizing public companies but also curbing the power of organized labor, especially in the public sector, formerly fully unionized. Combined with Thatcher's dislike of Whitehall, this approach led to an ambitious reformist zeal vis-à-vis the civil service. Accordingly, by November 1979, the Downing Street

Policy Unit, led by Sir John Hoskyns, produced a document that proposed to "deprivilege the civil service."[33] Portraying himself as an outsider, Hoskyns's proposal tried to turn the bureaucratic machinery on its head, though it lacked a clear reform strategy.[34] His initiative, however, did signal the beginning of staff cuts.[35]

Simultaneously with the Hoskyns initiative, the government set up the "Efficiency Unit" under the leadership of Sir Derek Rayner, a top executive of Marks and Spencer brought into government as a part-time adviser to the prime minister. The goal of the Efficiency Unit was to reduce costs and increase the efficiency of the central government administration. The implementation of "efficiency scrutinies" and the "Financial Management Initiative"—both cost-reduction and streamlining procedures—led to the coinage of the term "Raynerism," alluding to the introduction of managerial reforms and cost-effective procedures in the routines of public administration.[36]

Critics of Raynerism emphasized the narrowness of its cost-cutting approach. One of those criticisms came from inside Whitehall. In the spring of 1987, a report assessing the impact of the Rayner years was presented to the prime minister. Initially known as the Ibbs Report (after Sir Robin Ibbs, Rayner's successor in the Efficiency Unit), the document highlighted that few financial and management improvements had taken place, and it charged the "intrusiveness of the Treasury and Cabinet," and the "prevailing Whitehall culture of caution" for the lack of change.[37]

The report did not have practical consequences until February 1988, when the prime minister launched a radical program of public sector rehash: "The Next Steps Initiative." The Ibbs Report had argued that the functions of government were too disparate and the civil service too big and too diverse to be treated as a single entity, and that Whitehall should be treated as a collection of

---

33. Peter Hennessy, *Whitehall* (London: Fontana, 1989), 628. Hoskyns had been a prominent member of the Centre for Policy Studies, a think tank founded by Sir Keith Joseph in the 1970s.

34. Sir John Hoskyns, "Whitehall and Westminster: An Outsider's View," *Parliamentary Affairs* 36 (1983): 137–47.

35. Disproportionately concentrated on the blue-collar industrial civil service—a hundred thousand posts in the three Thatcher administrations versus sixty thousand in the white-collar sector—staff cuts led to a 20 percent decline in civil service manpower. Kevin Theakston, *The Civil Service Since 1945* (Oxford and Cambridge: Blackwell, 1995), chap. 5.

36. As David Walker, public administration correspondent of *The Times,* summarized the spirit of the reforms: "those who are about to be privatized, let them first adopt the manner of the private sector," in "The Civil Service," Masden Pirie, ed., *A Decade of Revolution: The Thatcher Years* (London: Adam Smith Institute, 1989), 36. For a detailed discussion of the Efficiency Unit, see Les Metcalf and Sue Richards, *Improving Public Managment,* 2d ed. (London: Sage, 1990).

37. Peter Hennessy, *Whitehall,* 620–27.

separate businesses. The main goal stated in the report of the Efficiency Unit was to establish a clear-cut separation between a core civil service of ministerial policy advisers and a range of executive agencies engaged in operational tasks. The initiative thus gave agency status to large parts of the staff in departments as varied as Employment, Trade and Industry, Social Security, and the Cabinet office. Several administrative functions were abolished, privatized, subcontracted, or transferred to a public agency run like a private sector firm. As a result, the structure of the civil service was fundamentally altered. The number of civil servants employed in agencies grew rapidly: from 7,700 in 1989 to 80,000 in 1990, 183,000 in 1991, and 290,000 (half the total) in 1992. The agency program was completed in 1995 (under John Major), covering 71 percent of the total public servants and reducing the core civil service to only 50,000.[38]

The reforms associated with the Next Steps led to decentralization in the implementation of public policy and to more managerial autonomy. The logic applied to the privatization of SOEs permeated the initiative from scratch: agencies should move toward the private sector firm model. Within departmentally determined guidelines, heads of agencies acquired greater control over service quality, recruitment, organization, and pay of their staff. Notions such as government by contract, delegation, cost-effectiveness, and targeting, among others, were brought into the Whitehall routines. Agencies began to measure their performance in terms of "customer satisfaction" and market research began to be used as a means to evaluate them. An overall business-like environment was introduced in the Civil Service.

The counterpart to this decentralizing tendency, however, was a centralization of decision-making power at the highest levels of public administration and a concentration of political initiative in the office of the prime minister. What on the surface appeared as a decentralization approach, constituted, in fact, a set of reforms leading to a large centralization of power at the top decision-making level of the executive by establishing a clearly differentiated two-tier officialdom and by insulating policymakers from career public servants. By reinforcing the boundaries between policy and administration, the Next Steps resulted in the depoliticization of the civil service while increasing the government's political control over policy-making. One significant example is the changing approach of the Treasury vis-à-vis these reforms. Initially hostile toward the Next Steps, for fear of losing control over public spending and seeing its power diminished, it soon provided vital support when it became clear that it would re-

---

38. Theakston, *The Civil Service Since 1945,* 134.

tain a central role in organizing and launching individual agencies, determining their overall guidelines with their parent departments, setting their financial targets, and monitoring their performance. The Treasury's institutional role actually increased, as key decision-making procedures became more centralized.[39]

Even when these reforms did not lead to the "end of civil service," they did alter important patterns of power distribution inside the government, highlighting entrenched conflicts between the executive and public bureaucracies, between those who rule and those who administer. As in the other cases examined in this book, conflicts between the logic of authority and the logic of administration are often exacerbated by liberalization programs, as reform-minded elites see career civil servants as part of the problem they are determined to resolve: too large deficits and oversized public sectors that affect resource allocation as much as the capacity of the executive to govern. This is why during the implementation of privatization policies, one finds a permanent tension between the government proper and civil servants, public managers, and public sector unions. This problem, which appears to cut across regime type,[40] also helps explain why in its quest for centralized decision-making capacity, economic reform experiments translate into strategies of institutional change.[41]

The conflicts between central and local government during much of the Thatcher government can be seen under this light as well. Historically, the enlargement of local government had been a responsibility of both Labour and Conservative administrations. In *The Right Approach*,[42] however, the Conservative party displayed concerns with the disproportionate growth of local government spending and employment relative to those of the central government. The whole effort at reforming local government during the Thatcher years was concentrated on the marketization of services historically supplied by councils.

---

39. Patricia Greer, *Transforming Central Government: The Next Steps Initiative* (Buckingham: Open University Press, 1994), 48–51; and David Richards, *The Civil Service Under the Conservatives, 1979–1997* (Brighton: Sussex Academic Press, 1997), chap. 3.

40. Not unlike similar downsizing of public sector employment in Latin America, the Next Steps initiative was carried out largely through executive action and with relatively little parliamentary debate. See Greer, *Transforming Central Government*, chaps. 4 and 6.

41. One can also argue that the ongoing conflicts between Margaret Thatcher and the cabinet—for some analysts only an exaggerated version of a protractred problem of British constitutional structure, though for others an unprecedented antagonism inside the executive—were part of this centralizing drive. Important as those conflicts were, since they did not result in institutional changes that affected future administrations, they are not treated as part of the state formation strategies discussed in this study. For this issue, see Anthony King, ed., *The British Prime Minister,* 2d ed. (London: Macmillan, 1985). For a detailed account on the way these conflicts over time eroded the party's support for Thatcher, see Alan Clark, *Diaries* (London: Weidenfeld and Nicholson, 1993).

42. *The Right Approach: A Statement of Conservative Aims* (London: Conservative Central Office, 1976).

The aim was to fragment public institutions and foster private sector alternatives or, at least, to condition public provision to market or quasi-market incentives. The implementation of competitive tendering in services such as garbage collection, cleaning, and catering, among others, had been in effect since the mid-1980s. The same applies to a requirement to offer the National Health Service (NHS) catering and laundry services to competitive tender.[43]

The central government also curtailed the power of local authorities by introducing market options in education and housing. This last one signaled an alteration in the pattern of socialization of a large number of families. As was discussed previously, about 1.2 million families bought their homes, which had favorable electoral consequences for the Conservative party. The sale of council houses also modified the relationship between local governments and citizens as it removed one of the central provisions of local governments. The financial repercussions were also significant, since the privatization of housing also implied the elimination of one of the sources of revenue for local governments.

This tendency, in turn, was further endorsed by legislation giving unprecedented prerogatives to the central government over the control of revenue and spending policies of the councils. As the old Rate Support Grant was replaced by a New Block Grant, the spending plan of local authorities was thus determined by the central government. Local governments resorted to raising the rates of local taxes, which in turn was met by a legislative response by the central government. The Rates Act of 1984, in turn, gave the Secretary of State for the Environment the power to rate-cap local authorities.

After a few initiatives of varied success, including the unpopular poll tax, the Local Government and Housing Act of 1989 gave the central government powers to limit all transactions involving credit allocation and to compel local authorities to charge for particular services and to set down the rates to be charged. With this Act, only one quarter of the revenues of local authorities can be raised from a locally determined tax, and their capital spending is placed under tight central control. The financial autonomy of local government was, thus, dramatically reduced.[44]

The growing power of central government at the expense of local authorities, the decentralization of civil service, and the marketization of service

43. Kate Ascher, *The Politics of Privatisation: Contracting Out Public Services* (London: Macmillan, 1987).

44. See, among a wealth of research on the subject, Arthur Midwinter and Claire Monaghan, *From Rates to the Poll Tax: Local Government Finance in the Thatcher Era* (Edinburgh: Edinburgh University Press, 1993); and Hugh Butcher et al., *Local Government and Thatcherism* (London: Routledge, 1990).

provisions account, if not for the demise of the welfare state, at least for its political reorganization and programmatic retrenchment. The issue is important, due to the fact that research on the subject has emphasized the "resilience of the welfare state," largely based on the fact that social expenditures remained stable throughout the Conservative period.[45] An argument focused exclusively on the budgetary dimensions of the welfare state, however, overlooks more important transformations of the welfare state taking place in ideological[46] and organizational terms.[47]

In summary, the Conservative project aggressively favored a movement away from bureaucratic decision making toward decentralized, market-based allocation. The project inexorably involved a shift of power, opening up markets by bringing in competition and challenging the monopolistic position of public agencies. Doing so, however, entailed a relentless centralization of political authority, in part deemed necessary to revamp the strategy of development in its fundamentals but also to launch an ambitious program of institutional redesign, one that qualified as a state formation project.

From Thatcherism to New Labour

In line with the main propositions of this study, one important conclusion to the British case is the observation, evident to most analysts, that Thatcherism is essential to understand New Labour. As the center of gravity of the political spectrum moved to the right, the Labour party was forced to move in that direction, becoming, according to some interpretations, little more than a party of the center.[48] These shifts were partly the result of ideological factors—a persistent free-market rhetoric on the part of the Conservative party for almost two decades, which changed the very nature of the political debate—but also essentially political ones—institutional legacies meant to alter the rules by which allocation is conducted, political order generated, and power distributed. It is in Tony Blair's government, more than in John Major's, where the highly consequen-

---

45. For example, Paul Pierson, *Dismantling the Welfare State?* (New York Cambridge University Press, 1994), and "The New Politics of the Welfare State," *World Politics* 48 (January 1996); and Geoffry Garrett, *Partisan Politics in the Global Economy* (New York: Cambridge University Press, 1998).

46. As suggested, early on, by Joel Krieger, *Reagan, Thatcher, and the Politics of Decline* (Oxford: Oxford University Press, 1986).

47. Recently highlighted by Richard Clayton and Jonas Pontusson, "Welfare State Retrenchment Revisited," *World Politics* 51, no. 1 (October 1998): 67–98.

48. See *The Independent,* "A Triumph of Conservatism," April 14, 1996, 20.

tial nature of the ideological and institutional trends initiated by the Thatcher government can best be seen and evaluated.

Early on during the campaign, Tony Blair emphasized that "New Labour would not dismantle Thatcherism," for trying to do so would lead to the failure of his government.[49] From the outset, his agenda was coated in Conservative language and his policy proposals have preempted Conservative criticisms by explicitly addressing classic Thatcherite themes: entrepreneurship, wealth creation, and business incentives, among others. It is suggestive that, in what appeared to be an effort to reassure the business community by signaling a commitment to macroeconomic stability, Blair's first act of government was, going even beyond Thatcher, to increase the independence of the Bank of England by granting it full control of interest rate policy. The decision took the entire political establishment by surprise and generated the first and significant conflict between "new" and "old" Labour.[50] The issue had not been in the party's manifesto and, moreover, was announced just before the first debate in the House of Commons and prior to any cabinet meeting. When Gordon Brown, Chancellor of the Exchequer, addressed the CBI's national conference in November 1997, he justified that decision as necessary for stability, low inflation, and, unprecedentedly for a Labour party chancellor, the depoliticization of monetary policy.[51]

The Bank of England issue is relevant because it constitutes the first source of tension in a government otherwise oriented toward deepening democracy, devolution, and constitutional reform. Similar tensions may arise with welfare-related issues, an arena in which the centralization-decentralization dynamic manifested itself most conspicuously. By marketizing welfare provisions, the Conservative administrations have taken financial and organizational resources away from local governments along with increasing decision-making power at the center. Simultaneously, they have distrib-

---

49. See, for example, *New York Times,* "Labour Won't Try to Undo Thatcherism, Chief Says," April 3, 1996, 3. See also the illuminating piece by Samuel Beer, "The Roots of New Labour," in *The Economist* 346, February 7, 1998, 23–25.

50. See, for example, James Blitz, "Furious Left Wing Shatters Illusion of Unity," *Financial Times,* May 7, 1997, 11.

51. "Our decision on our first Tuesday of government to make the Bank of England independent, and to set in place a more open and accountable system of monetary decision-making, not only implemented one of the CBI's own proposals, but it has in my view already given consistency, confidence, and credibility to monetary policy making. I believe we are agreed it is right to take these decisions out of politics, and to free them from short-term political pressures. Our aim, business' aim: in place of stop-go, long-term stability." HM Treasury, "Chancellor's Speech at the CBI National Conference," November 10, 1997, 138–97.

uted responsibilities for the provision and regulation of services among a vast number (420, across the country) of quasi-autonomous nongovernmental organizations—quangos—that enjoy discretionary powers, are independent from local authorities, and are managed by unelected officials selected on a highly partisan basis. At the time, problems of accountability and increasing opportunities for patronage generated by the quango expansion were highlighted in political and scholarly debates.[52]

By 1996, however, Britain's transition from the "Keynesian welfare state" to a "Schumpeterian workfare state," was openly and fully embraced by the Labour party.[53] Accordingly, its social policy agenda centered on education, training, and a form of solidarity removed from universalism (away from welfare dependency toward jobs, and emphasizing liberty over equality) and best captured by the idea of a stakeholding society.[54] Yet, despite the much-debated issue of reversal of the quango phenomenon, the most democratic aspect of this situation, it has been reported, was a gradual but widespread replacement of Tory placemen with Labour placepeople.[55]

In sum, and paraphrasing Samuel Beer, "British collectivist age" is definitely over. Privatization has had a lot to do with it, for both its economic and political implications. Redrawing property rights through expanding share and home ownership became a strategy of coalition building, redefining working-class electoral preferences. Reorganizing welfare favored administrative decentralization but centralization of decision making, leading to the reassertion of state power. This way, two key traditional components of the conservative agenda were revamped: working-class vote and state authority. Together, they led to a distinctive chapter in state formation. The newness of New Labour, then, and its biggest challenge, appears to be to develop a meaningful political project within this radically different, and extremely unfamiliar, form of state, itself the legacy of Thatcherite institutional redesign.

---

52. As reflected in, for example, Simon Jenkins, *Accountable to None: The Tory Nationalization of Britain* (London and New York: H. Hamilton, 1995); and F. F. Ridley and David Wilson, eds., "The Quango Debate," special issue of *Parliamentary Affairs* 48, no. 2 (April 1995).

53. See Bob Jessop, "The Transition to Post-Fordism and the Schumpeterian Workfare State," in Roger Burrows and Brian Loader, eds., *Towards a Post-Fordist Welfare State?* (London: Routledge, 1994), 13–37; and Nick Ellison, "From Welfare State to Post-Welfare Society?" in Brian Brivati and Tim Bale, eds., *New Labour in Power* (London: Routledge, 1997), 34–61.

54. See, for example, by Labour MP Frank Field, *Stakeholder Welfare* (London: IEA Health and Welfare Unit, 1996). It is not trivial that the essay was published by the free-market think tank Institute of Economic Affairs. Blair appointed Field Minister of State with responsibility for welfare state reform.

55. *The Independent,* "A Different Approach to Patronage," July 22, 1998, 3.

Conclusion

Sustained economic reform and privatization reshape coalitions, although in different ways. The cases studied here vary in a number of political and economic dimensions, thus allowing for a comparison of the coalitional implications of privatization in different contexts and introducing nuances to the main argument. Unlike the other cases examined in this book, the British divestiture experiment was not the result of collusion between political and economic power, and the capture of policy-making arenas. The Thatcher government initiated the program in a rather independent fashion, inspired by a staunch belief in the superiority of decentralized private-based allocation over state ownership and regulation. Yet this policy also pursued explicit political goals: to introduce material incentives in order to alter the preferences of a segment of the electorate traditionally identified with the Labour party and, thus, to modify the nature of political competition.

The sales of council houses to tenants and the distribution of shares among wage earners constituted the main components of the privatization program. Ownership would, and to an extent did, organize a new coalition of supporters of the Conservative party. In the process, however, and to the extent that it was put together on the basis of the redistribution of existing wealth among its members, rather than on the basis of expanding output, this coalition qualifies as a distributional one. Seen under this Olsonian framework, we can shed new light on the "nation of homeowners" and the "nation of shareholders."

The second claim of this book addresses the institutional effects of marketization and highlights the state-building character of these policies. I have advanced this proposition based on the fact that these policies aim at restructuring property relations, collecting more revenue, and centralizing political authority, all crucial state formation activities. The British case is important because, while it can be expected that a concentration of power emerges from reform processes undertaken by autocratic regimes, the fact that similar tendencies evolved in a fully consolidated and stable democratic system provides decisive validation of this proposition. Among other institutional reforms, I have thus examined the comprehensive reorganization of the civil service, which insulated political appointees from career public servants, and legislation that curtailed the autonomy of local governments over revenue and spending policies, which tilted the balance between central and local government decidedly in the direction of the former. Despite the presence of well-established democratic procedures and institutions, and as part of a state-building effort, in Britain, too, the implementation of economic decentralization has led to an assertive centralization of political authority.

Chapter 6

Mexico and Argentina

From Import Substitution to Privatization under Postpopulism

In this book, the logic of comparison is based on a selection of cases with different contextual characteristics and similar economic reform processes, combined with a method that examines them with reference to their respective similar regional and historical political economy contexts, yet emphasizes variation in the type of institutional changes implemented and in the state formation strategies adopted. Thus, while the main comparison is a cross-regional one, in which cases are selected on the basis of the dependent variable, I complement this approach with another subset of comparisons of similar cases in order to assess variation in outcome. This way I also select cases on the basis of the independent variable. The key to this complementary perspective is the intertemporal dimension, which allows me to move from an examination of the process leading to marketization, to the analysis of the effects of similar economic reform policies on established institutional configurations.

These considerations come together in this chapter on Mexico and Argentina. The previous chapter recognized Britain as being different from all other cases examined in this book, yet as being similar to other West European cases also exposed to the failure of Keynesian macroeconomic policies over time. In the same vein, this chapter sees Mexico and Argentina as different from each other, especially in regard to their respective political regimes, but similar in terms of the general problems of import-substituting industrialization (ISI) that Latin America as a whole experienced. In line with the main theoretical propositions of this book, in this chapter I assess the impact of distributional coalition building on the nature of marketization policies in Mexico and Argentina. Subsequently, I hold privatization constant and examine differences in the institutional changes implemented and the state formation strategies adopted in both cases.

The main argument of this chapter is that despite differences in the types of political regime observed in all three Latin American cases (military in Chile, dominant party in Mexico, competitive democratizing in Argentina), similar rent-seeking behavior on the part of financial-industrial groups accounts for the pace and content of market reform. This is largely the result of the fact that, as inflation and balance-of-payment crises worsened during the terminal crisis of ISI, firms with political clout no longer sought to extract rents from fiscal resources and focused, instead, on public utilities and banks. Once under way, privatization facilitated the centralization of administrative and political resources and, thus, increases in discretionary executive authority.

The state-building strategies pursued, however, were different. While, as in Chile, Mexico pursued the consolidation of economic reform by passing amendments to the "economic chapter" of the previous (1917) constitution, in Argentina the constitutional reform of 1994 was instrumental in the reelection of the incumbent president and in increasing executive power even further but did not include any significant reference to the status of the economic reforms implemented by the Menem government. Thus, in Latin America similar economic crises associated with ISI and similar collective action patterns account for the mix and timing of policy reforms. State formation strategies followed the implementation of market reforms, though important variation in these strategies is highlighted in this chapter.

Mexico

Between 1983 and 1993 the Mexican government privatized about one thousand firms. The process started slowly under De la Madrid (1982–88), with a small number of firms privatized and with proceeds of about $2.6 billion. The program received a significant impetus under the Salinas de Gortari administration (1988–94), when large SOEs (including two major airlines), several public utilities, and eighteen banks nationalized during the debt crisis of 1982 were offered for sale. To steer the privatization program, the government created the Disincorporation Unit in October 1990. This way, by the end of 1994, the number of SOEs had been reduced from more than one thousand to eighty, and fiscal proceeds in the 1989–94 period mounted to $20 billion. In the following, privatization is seen as part of the overall liberalization experiment and is discussed within the context of the country's changing historical political economy.

Sustainable Development and the "Bankers' Alliance"

Historical attributes of the economy and structural changes over time explain the creation of a proliberalization coalition in Mexico in the 1980s and its patterns of collective action. For most of the century, and especially if compared with other ISI economies in the region, Mexico had had a relatively open financial system. Financial adaptation was a common practice among economic elites, especially when political events threatened their property rights, such as immediately after the revolution and during implementation of the land reform program in the 1930s. Because of this, early on governments had to create attractive conditions at home so as to neutralize capital flight. They generally maintained free capital and currency markets and, for the most part, allowed fully convertible dollar-denominated accounts while setting high barriers of entry to limit the activities of foreign banks.

These policies sustained the "bankers' alliance," an arrangement based on a close relationship among the Finance Ministry, the Bank of Mexico, and the largest private banks.[1] The bankers became the main link between the government and the business community as a whole. An explicit trade-off was established: the government would safeguard an auspicious, yet protected, financial environment and a prudent macroeconomic regime, and business elites would refrain from intervening in politics. A moderate public deficit was financed through domestic and international financial capital markets and the private sector was willing to mobilize rapidly growing domestic savings. Governments managed to redirect investment toward the manufacturing sector and finance ISI, avoiding the macroeconomic distortions commonly seen in other Latin American nations. A period of low inflation, exchange rate stability, and rapid growth, "stabilizing development," followed in the 1950s and 1960s.[2]

This cooperative relationship was strained in the 1970s, however. At that time growth had exacerbated sectoral, regional, and income inequalities; private investment began to fall; and external balances deteriorated. As stabilizing development showed its own internal limits, the Echeverría administration (1970–76) responded with active macroeconomic policies. Thus, overly expansionary fiscal and monetary policies led to a typical Latin American cycle of inflation and current account deficit—which, unlike Argentina, Chile, and Brazil, Mexico had managed to avoid—concluding with a stabilization pack-

---

1. The term belongs to Sylvia Maxfield, *Governing Capital: International Finance and Mexican Politics* (Ithaca: Cornell University Press, 1990). See also Norah Hamilton, *The Limits of State Autonomy: Postrevolutionary Mexico* (Princeton: Princeton University Press, 1982).

2. By the main architect, which includes an analysis of the main problems of stabilizing development, see Antonio Ortiz Mena, "Desarrollo Estabilizador: Una Década de Estrategia Económica en México," *El Trimestre Económico* 37, no. 146 (April/June 1970): 417– 49.

age and a 59 percent devaluation in August 1976, ending twenty-two years of exchange rate stability.[3]

These events would not go unnoticed by the business community. As of that moment, private sector elites began to express their discontent through individual as well as coordinated activities. Increased levels of capital flight exemplify the former, while the latter type was best expressed by the growing politicization of business groups, as reflected by their involvement with the opposition PAN (National Action Party) and the creation of new institutions. In May 1975 the CCE (*Consejo Coordinador Empresarial*) was founded with the explicit goal of influencing policy-making on the verge of a change of sexenio. Conceived as an "organization of organizations," the design of its decision-making structure was disproportionately tilted in favor of liquid asset sectors. Few firms grouped in associations of finance, insurance, and brokerage houses, plus the elite CMHN (Mexican Council of Businessmen), which includes thirty-eight conglomerates with pivotal financial interests, often outvote thousands of firms clustered under the traditional associations of industry (CONCAMIN), employers (COPARMEX), commerce (CONCANACO), and agriculture (CNA). Given this internal distribution of power, the CCE early on became a militant advocate of economic liberalism and a critic of state intervention.[4]

The López Portillo administration (1976–82) initially eased tensions thanks to the country's vast oil reserves (and positive price shocks) and the abundance of foreign credit. The government used oil as a collateral and borrowed heavily to increase state intervention. Highly liquid international financial markets allowed the government to increase its financial and political autonomy vis-à-vis business elites, but it had also provided private firms with more funding options and financial adaptation instruments. Private sector access to foreign credit facilitated a process of concentration and conglomeration among firms that participated in this process, as it allowed them to finance the purchase of new assets by contracting debt on behalf of firms while simultaneously protecting their

3. See Carlos Bazdresch and Santiago Levi, "Populism and Economic Policy in Mexico: 1970–1982," in Rudiger Dornbusch and Sebastian Edwards, eds., *The Macroeconomics of Populism in Latin America* (Chicago: University of Chicago Press, 1991), 223–62.

4. See, for example, Ricardo Tirado and Matilde Luna, "La Politización de los Empresarios Mexicanos (1970–1982)," in Julio Labastida, ed., *Grupos Económicos y Organizaciones Empresariales en México* (Mexico DF: Alianza/UNAM, 1986), 411–45; Cristina Puga and Ricardo Tirado, "El Consejo Coordinador Empresarial: Una Radiografía," in *Cuadernos del Proyecto Organizaciones Empresariales en México,* No. 1, Facultad de Ciencias Políticas y Sociales-Instituto de Investigaciones Sociales de la Universidad Nacional Autónoma de México, 1992; Cristina Puga, *México: Empresarios y Poder* (Mexico DF: UNAM-Porrua, 1993).

capital by sending it abroad.[5] When in the 1980s the price of oil declined and interest rates rose, the government tried to control capital flight by limiting currency movements and imposing exchange controls. After defaulting from debt service payments in August 1982, and in a paramount instance of state autonomy aimed at reasserting the power of the presidency, López Portillo nationalized the banks in September of that year.[6] As a result, criticism turned into outright confrontation. The bankers' alliance broke down.

From the Debt Crisis to the Making of a New Alliance

Unprecedented levels of capital flight and inflation forced the De la Madrid administration (1982–88) to execute a veritable policy U-turn in order to restore private sector confidence, especially among financial and large manufacturing firms. The interruption of the once-fluid communication between the PRI and business elites persuaded the government that major decisions would have to take account of private sector preferences. The first signal was, in this sense, a political one: to centralize economic policy-making on a technocratic elite linked to public financial agencies—mostly the central bank and the ministry of budget and planning—renowned for their economic orthodoxy.[7] Soon thereafter the government provided generous compensation to the expropriated bankers, returned their nonbanking assets (industrial-commercial firms, brokerage houses, etc.), allowed private investors to repurchase up to 33 percent of the nationalized banking sector, and launched FICORCA—a program that bailed out firms with large foreign obligations.[8]

Bank nationalization had prompted private financiers to transfer their resources from the banks to other financial concerns, mainly brokerage houses. Forced to raise credit domestically (due to the drying up of foreign flows) and curb capital flight, the government issued treasury bonds (CETES) as the main instrument and granted exclusive trading rights to those brokerage houses. The

5. See Jorge Basave, *Los Grupos de Capital Financiero en México (1974–1995)* (Mexico DF: UNAM/El Caballito, 1994); especially chap. 3.

6. For this interpretation, see Carlos Tello, central bank director at the time, *La Nacionalización de la Banca en México* (México DF: Siglo XXI, 1984).

7. For a journalistic investigation, see *Sucesión Pactada: La Ingeniería Política del Salinismo* (Mexico DF: Plaza y Valdés, 1993). For academic references of this process, see Miguel Angel Centeno and Sylvia Maxfield, "The Marriage of Finance and Order: Changes in the Mexican Political Elite," *Journal of Latin American Studies* 24 (February 1992): 57–85; and Miguel Angel Centeno, *Democracy Within Reason: Technocratic Revolution in Mexico* (University Park, Pa.: Penn State University Press, 1994).

8. Ernesto Zedillo, the head of FICORCA between 1983 and 1987, was elected president in 1994.

trading of CETES led to a stock exchange boom and a colossal expansion of the brokers, not merely as traders but as suppliers of larger financial services. As a result, from 1982 to 1990 the participation of brokerage houses in the overall flow of funds increased 587 percent while that of the (nationalized) banking system decreased 40 percent. In the process, this sector not only grew but also restructured itself. The highest rates of expansion were not experienced by the ex-bankers but were instead enjoyed by relatively newer firms owned by younger and more innovative financiers who took advantage of the volatility of the 1980s.[9]

In the mid-1980s, the collapse of the price of oil reduced the country's main source of revenue, enhancing the leverage of creditors, mobile-asset holders, and exporters. The government responded by initiating a program of trade liberalization. Licenses, quotas, and reference prices were all abolished, and tariffs, which had reached 100 percent in the early 1980s, were lowered to a maximum of 20 percent toward the end of 1987. Foreign exchange constraints forced the government to reinforce the competitiveness of export-capable firms—provided that, depending on the import content of their products, their demand for hard currency was mitigated. Export-promotion programs were implemented along with import liberalization, targeting large firms already engaged in exports. These firms received significant concessions on inputs, high levels of protection for their final products, and preferential lines of credit. As a result, exports grew, concentrated in the automobile, glass, steel, cement, and electricity sectors.[10]

In the last quarter of 1987, with a sizable fiscal deficit and inflation reaching 160 percent, the government outlined a stabilization strategy that included deeper structural reforms and the adoption of a nominal exchange rate anchor. This new approach, along with concerted income and price controls, came together under the Economic Solidarity Pact (PASE), signed in December of that year.[11] As in the southern cone nations in the 1970s, by conceiving and

9. See the following chapters in Esthela Gutiérrez Garza, ed., *Testimonios de la Crisis IV: Los Saldos del Sexenio (1982–1988)* (Mexico DF: Siglo XXI, 1990): Cristina Puga and Constanzo de la Vega, "Modernización Capitalista y Política Empresarial," 237–60; and Alejandro Dávila Flores, "La Bolsa Mexicana de Valores: Alternativa Para el Financiamiento de la Inversión Productiva?" 109–38.

10. For an overview, see Blanca Heredia, "Contested State: The Politics of Trade Reform in Mexico" (Ph.D. diss., Columbia University, 1995); and Jaime Ros, "La Reforma Comercial en México Durante los Años Ochenta: Sus Efectos Económicos y Dimensiones Políticas," *UN-ECLA Series Reformas de Política Pública* 4 (1993).

11. For the PASE, see Robert Kaufman, Carlos Bazdresch, and Blanca Heredia, "Mexico: Radical Reform in a Dominant Party System," in Stephan Haggard and Steven Webb, eds., *Voting for Reform* (New York: World Bank/Oxford University Press, 1994), 360–410; and by the pact's architect, Pedro Aspe, *El Camino Mexicano de la Transformación Económica* (Mexico DF: FCE, 1993).

portraying trade opening as a price-stabilizing device, protectionism in Mexico was now linked to inflation, prompting the government to seek broader societal support for liberalization. As trade policy became a central macroeconomic concern, it was placed in the hands of public financial agencies. As a result, SECOFI, the main industrial policy agency, was ostracized, leaving import substituters without input on the policy process and unable to generate coordinated action against liberalization.[12]

Consequently, the proliberalization coalition gained momentum. Given the capacity of the bigger establishments to control key prices, the government gave primacy to direct consultation with large industrial and commercial firms, circumventing sectoral chambers and associations, especially those opposed to liberalization. This strategy enhanced the position of the elite CCE, making it the government's main interlocutor throughout the design and implementation phases of the PASE.[13] This alliance proved politically pivotal after March 1988, when the exchange rate was fixed and the increasing exposure of domestic industry augmented grievances from import substituters.[14] Only large firms could absorb the costs of simultaneous trade opening and appreciation, while at the same time expect to extract tangible market reserves for their support, whether as subsidies to export promotion, which they were already enjoying, or as privatization, which they were demanding. Given the size and multisectoral character of those firms, the CCE was their most effective organizational tool.

---

12. Heredia, "Contested State," chap. 5.

13. On paper the pact was a typical tripartite concertation, but the most important accords were made with big business. Agustín Legorreta, former banker and then-president of the CCE, confirmed that "the pact was an agreement between the president and a very comfortable little group of three hundred people who make the economically important decisions in Mexico. We gave the government a deadline to fix its finances. It has met that goal earlier. The government has even fulfilled the verbal promises which were not part of the pact's text, such as the liquidation and dissolution of nationally significant firms like Aeroméxico and Cananea." See *Unomásuno*, May 18, 1988, 1, 14. In a follow-up to this statement the weekly *Proceso* 607, June 20, 1988, 10–19, reports increasing pressures for privatization on the part of the CCE. See especially, "Legorreta usa toda su capacidad de presión para que se privatice la economia," pp. 10–11. Reportedly, the other organized influence over policy-making came from the Monterrey-based industrial elite who had regular meetings with President De la Madrid and his economic cabinet. See María de Lourdes Melgar Palacios, "Economic Development in Monterrey: Competing Ideas and Strategies in Mexico" (Ph.D. diss., MIT, 1992).

14. Until 1988, currency devaluations were used to partially offset trade opening. With the PASE, the adoption of a fixed exchange rate led to a decline in effective protection in the manufacturing sector, from an average 34.8 percent in 1988 to 13.8 percent in 1991. Data from Fernando Sánchez Ugarte et. al., *La Política Industrial ante la Apertura* (México DF: SECOFI/FCE, 1994), 127. For exchange rate management, see Adriaan Ten Kate, "Trade Liberalization and Economic Stabilization in Mexico: Lessons of Experience," *World Development* 20, no. 5 (May 1992): 659–72.

During Salinas de Gortari's term (1988–94) the ties between the PRI and large private investors strengthened, bolstering the overall program of reform. A number of factors account for this. First, by mid-1988 and after a few revisions, the PASE had begun to yield positive results in the area of stabilization. Second, the strong performance of the center-left Democratic Current (which opposed economic liberalization) in the August 1988 election turned out to be a blessing in disguise for Salinas, for it convinced the business community that the safest strategy was to close ranks behind the PRI even further.[15] Third, the new president's approach toward business groups differed from De la Madrid's. De la Madrid had sought to create conditions conducive to curb the distrust of the private sector and, at best, to restore the arrangement of stabilizing development. Salinas, instead, pursued more explicit political accords with business elites and made no secret of his alignment with the largest firms since the electoral campaign; in fact, he met with them in every state he visited.[16]

In just the second week of his term, and in a decision that reversed an entrenched postrevolutionary tradition that had excluded businessmen from public office, Salinas appointed Claudio X. Gonzalez (director of Kimberly Clark, stockbroker, and president of the CCE between 1985 and 1986) as presidential adviser for foreign investment. With that, the collaboration between policymakers and large investors took a new direction. For large private firms, access to top executive offices became frequent and transparent, at the expense of sectoral associations that were often vilified as mere protectionist lobbies and therefore ignored.[17] This context was conducive to deeper reforms in the financial and parastatal sector: further opening of the capital account and, satisfying a long-postponed demand of the private sector, the privatization of the large SOEs and the banks. Both reforms were also essential to attract the capital needed to finance the growing trade deficit and sustain the exchange-rate-based stabilization program.

Desincorporación, the buzzword for privatization, was a key mechanism for reshaping private economic groups, strengthening traditional groups adapted to a new environment and facilitating the emergence of new industrial-financial conglomerates. It also put the finishing touches to the new PRI-private sector alliance. The divestiture process had started under De la Madrid, but under Salinas the nationalized commercial banks and the natural monopolies were

---

15. For this interpretation, see Francisco Valdés Ugalde, *Autonomía y Legitimidad: Los Empresarios, la Política, y el Estado en México* (México DF: Siglo XXI/UNAM, 1997), 219–21.

16. Carlos Elizondo, "Privatizing the PRI? Shifts in the Business-PRI Relationship" (Manuscript, CIDE, México DF: March 1994).

17. See Puga, *México: Empresarios y Poder,* 181–204.

transferred to the private sector—93 percent of them to domestic firms—generating proceeds of $20 billion.[18] Most enterprises were sold through auctions. To participate, private firms had to meet technical, financial, and operational standards: for the most part, only large firms were able to do so. In some cases the capital contribution by the buyers involved an asset swap from domestic public debt paper to real assets of the public firms. In other cases, fiscal incentives were given to Mexicans who were willing to repatriate capital in order to purchase stock of the privatized companies.

The most important means of financing the purchase operations, however, has been through the organization of financial packages based on the procurement of funds on domestic and international financial markets. Domestic groups thus took over firms, providing, in many cases, a minority contribution of capital and gaining control of large amounts of capital from other investors. Even if foreign capital played a crucial role in the process, its participation was indirect; that is why 93 percent of the privatized firms passed into the hands of Mexican businesses.

Since it involved players of different arenas, this method provided a most decisive impetus to privatization. The most notorious of these operations took place in the telecommunications sector, when in December 1990 TELMEX was purchased as a monopoly for $1.76 billion by the CARSO group in association with France Telecom and Southwestern Bell. CARSO, originally a stockbrokerage firm that diversified into other activities, pursued an aggressive strategy of procurement of funds for the TELMEX operation, taking advantage of the issue of nonvoting shares on the international market. In this way, CARSO took over the control of the company by purchasing only 20.4 percent of the stock, while simultaneously assuming control of 25 percent of the market capitalization of the Mexican stock exchange. The example of TELMEX also illustrates another distinctive feature of the Mexican privatization program: the increasing sectoral diversification of firms involved in the process and, subsequently, the integration of large financial and industrial companies into private economic conglomerates.[19]

The main conduit for the consolidation of these groups was their participation in the bank divestiture operations that took place between June 1991 and July 1992. Most of the shares of the eighteen privatized banks ($12.5 bil-

---

18. See Jacques Rogozinski, head of the "Disincorporation Unit," *La Privatización de Empresas Paraestatales* (México DF: FCE, 1993).

19. Basave, *Los Grupos de Capital Financiero,* chap. 5; and Celso Garrido, "National Private Groups in Mexico," *CEPAL Review* 53 (August 1994): 159–75.

lion) was distributed among stockbrokerage houses in combination with large manufacturing firms that sought to expand their activities into the financial sphere, such as in the cases of Banamex-Accival, Comermex, and Somex—respectively the first, fourth, and fifth largest cases of privatization. Similarly, and further reinforcing sectoral integration and concentration, ownership is shared between stockbrokers and large exporting concerns in the manufacturing sector in the cases of Bancomer and Serfin—the second and third operation in magnitude—purchased respectively by the Monterrey-based Visa and Vitro conglomerates.[20]

Financial backlog caused by the crisis and the nationalization phase, and a less regulated domestic environment increased the expected profits of the postprivatization period. These factors, added to the fact that the process was conducted through secret auctions, created an incentive for bidding high. On average, the banks were sold at 3.5 times their book value. Early profits disclosed by the banks soon indicated the existence of hidden profits and explained the decision to bid high. By 1992, the profits of twelve banks were 35 percent higher in real terms than the previous year. In the same period Banamex, the biggest bank, increased its profits by 45 percent. The newly private banks have benefited from promising market conditions, from legislation that specifies stricter property rights, and from a regulatory framework that included high differentials between active and passive rates in a liberalized domestic capital market but combined with high barriers of entry to foreign banks.[21]

The economic power distributed through the reform process can hardly be exaggerated: it cemented a new political relationship between the PRI and the large financial and industrial conglomerates. This alliance did not emerge spontaneously as a consequence of liberalization. On the contrary, the coalition was built piece by piece ex-ante, largely on the basis of benefits distributed selectively among firms and sectors throughout the liberalization experiment. The strategic quality of this alliance became explicit in February 1993, when at a

20. See Rebecca Hovey, "The Mexican Commercial Bank Privatizations: Market Reform, Economic Power, and the Transformation of Public and Private Interests" (Ph.D. diss., Cornell University, 1996); and, by the head of the Bank Disincorporation Unit, Guillermo Ortiz Martínez, *La Reforma Financiera y la Desincorporación Bancaria* (México DF: FCE, 1994).

21. Under NAFTA, Mexican bankers managed to negotiate a gradual opening that restricted the operation of foreign banks to no more than 15 percent of the market in the first six years of the agreement (a process accelerated after the currency crisis of December 1994). See Carlos Elizondo, "The Making of a New Alliance: The Privatization of the Banks in Mexico," *CIDE Documento de Trabajo* 5 (1993).

dinner with twenty-seven of the country's wealthiest men (most of them beneficiaries of privatization), Salinas asked each of them to donate $25 million for
the 1994 electoral campaign. At this point, it became evident that this distributional coalition—a plutocracy, in the words of one observer[22]—had sustained
a decade of economic policy reform.

Institutional Reform and Centralization of Power

For Jacques Rogozinski, head of the Mexican privatization agency, the link-
age between reducing the size of the state and increasing its capacity is un-
equivocal: "We do not need a state that administers more but one that governs
better."[23] A series of state formation strategies became key factors contributing to consolidate the economic reform process and stabilize relations between
the government and its core coalition of support. Over time, those strategies
facilitated the centralization of executive authority and the definitive recovery of the political initiative the official party had lost in the wake of the 1982
crisis.

The economic reform process involved constitutional and legal reforms of
unprecedented nature. The Mexican legal system had regulated corporate activity on the basis of two different principles: either as an activity granted to
private individuals and firms as a concession, or as an activity pertaining to the
private sector and subject, under specific regulatory requirements, to the authorization of the state. The distinction is critical in terms of the specificity of
property rights. Banking, for example, had historically been considered a "public service," even before the revolution. As a public service, however, the legislation had facilitated the formation of powerful and expanding financial groups
but had generated ambiguities, especially with respect to whether the activity
was conducted under "concession" or as pertaining to the private sector. This
had implications over the real status of property rights of private banks. Banking legislation passed in 1941 appeared to have been even more vague, while

---

22. Lucy Conger, "Power to the Plutocrats," *Institutional Investor* (International Edition) 20,
no. 2 (February 1995): 28–37. For the dinner, see *Proceso* 853, March 8, 1993, 6–19. Reportedly,
business groups were involved in the PRI campaign since 1988, through the so-called Comisión de
Financiamiento y Consolidación Patrimonial del PRI. See Carlos Alba Vega, "Los Empresarios y
el Estado Durante el Salinismo," *Foro Internacional* 36, no. 1–2 (January/June 1996): 31–79. More
on these links was revealed during the Fobaproa scandal, a $65 billion bailout of several of the pri-
vatized banks in 1998. Guillermo Ortiz Martínez, for instance, revealed the existence of political
favoritism in the privatization and bailouts of the banks. See *El Financiero* "Fórmense, vamos a
repartir los bancos, dijo Salinas," July 20, 1998, 68–69.

23. *La Privatización de Empresas Paraestatales,* 37.

financial reforms passed in 1967 specified the character of banking as a concession granted by the state.[24]

Because of these ambiguities, considered to be at the roots of the nationalization of the banks in 1982, the first state formation strategy associated with the economic reform program consisted of a process of constitutional reform, deemed necessary to prepare the legal terrain for privatization. During the De la Madrid administration, reforms to the so-called Economic Chapter of the 1917 constitution (articles 16, 25, 26, 27, 28, 73) sought to increase the legal status of private initiative, placing it at an equal level with the role of the state in the economy. This way, areas previously considered strategic, and thus belonging to the exclusive domain of the state, could be subject to modification. Under Salinas, with the acceleration of the privatization and structural reform programs, the scope of legal and constitutional change widened. For example, legislation passed in June 1990 amended articles 28 and 123 of the constitution in order to redefine the concept of banking as an activity of public "interest" (as opposed to public "service"), thus allowing for the privatization of financial institutions. As discussed, the divestiture process took place between June 1991 and July 1992, and the banks were all transferred to private owners.[25]

Similarly, reforms of article 27 in 1992 introduced unprecedented changes in the common land system (*ejido*), one of the most important institutions of postrevolutionary Mexico. The initiative, passed by Congress in January 1992, granted property rights to occupants of ejidos, ending social ownership of land in an effort to generate the conditions for further commercialization of agriculture. This amendment changed the nature of land tenure. Until the reform of article 27, peasant beneficiaries of land reform only enjoyed rights of use of the

---

24. Revealing evidence of this ambiguity is that two experts on banking legislation, former central bank director Carlos Tello and fomer head of the Bank Divestiture Committee and former minister of finance Guillermo Ortiz Martínez have contradictory interpretations. For the former the law regulates a concession while for the latter it provides authorization. For Tello, see footnote 6, and for Ortiz, footnote 20, both above.

25. Article 25 of the constitution still maintains the "guidance (*rectoría*) of the state in national development." Because of this, Carlos Elizondo, "Constitutionalism and State Reform in Mexico," in Mónica Serrano and Victor Bulmer-Thomas, eds., *Rebuilding the State: Mexico After Salinas* (London: University of London, Institute of Latin American Studies, 1996), 41–58, has argued that the juridical principles that had made possible the nationalization of the banks in 1982 remain intact. For a contrasting argument, see Augusto Bolívar Espinoza and Luis Antonio Bonifaz Moreno, "Las Reformas Constitucionales," *El Cotidiano* 8, no. 50 (September/October 1992): 36–43; and Francisco Gil Villegas Montiel, "Cambio Constitucional en México Durante el Sexenio de Carlos Salinas de Gortari," *Foro Internacional* 36, no. 1–2 (Enero/Junio 1996): 158–87, who claims that the legislature elected in 1991 became a de facto constitutional assembly. For a rather official view on the reforms, see Javier López Moreno, *Reformas Constitucionales para la Modernización* (México DF: Fondo de Cultura Económica, 1993).

land, as the state retained the title of the land. For the authorities, a trend toward a stricter specification of property rights in the countryside was deemed necessary for increasing investment and dismantling a pervasive system of patronage, both of which had allegedly accounted for the historically low productivity of the country's agricultural sector.[26]

Later, in May 1993, and consistently with the previous privatization of the banking sector, another initiative of the executive, amendments to constitutional articles 28, 73, and 123, sanctioned the autonomy of the central bank. The reforms stipulated that the bank's fundamental objective is to maintain the purchasing power of the currency. In line with the idea that rules resolve the credibility problems previously created by discretion over monetary policy, the new law gives the central bank control over monetary policy and severely limits the credit it can extend to the federal government. This was intended to ensure that government budget deficits do not lead to an expansion in the monetary base and a rise in inflation.[27]

A second strategy was based on a gradual bypass, if not an altogether obliteration, of corporatism, the traditional formula of governance in postrevolutionary Mexico. Designed by the party-state in the 1930s, the corporatist structure of interest intermediation was effective at a time in which the dominant strategy of development, ISI, was relatively successful and required a minimum of macroeconomic coordination. The corporatist structure also allowed the PRI to exercise political control of subordinate groups. As the model of development showed signs of strain in the 1970s, however, corporatist control and coordination began to fail.[28] By the 1980s, on top of its political failure, corporatism had become incompatible with the economic liberalization program. The removal of policy areas from the political process significantly limited the viability of the corporatist arrangement. To the extent that market reforms seek to relieve fiscal resources from the pressures

---

26. The reform of article 27 has also introduced significant modifications in the power structure of a number of rural communities, magnifying center-periphery tensions. For an overview, see Wayne A. Cornelius and David Myhre, eds., *The Transformation of Rural Mexico: Reforming the Ejido Sector* (La Jolla: Center for U.S.-Mexican Studies, University of California, San Diego, 1998); and for center-periphery changes, see Blanca Heredia, "Clientelism in Flux: Democratization and Interest Intermediation in Contemporary Mexico," *CIDE Documento de Trabajo* 31 (1997).

27. Central bank independence, however, should be taken with a grain of salt. During 1994, an electoral year, the money supply grew by about 20 percent. See Interamerican Development Bank, *Latin America After a Decade of Reforms* (Washington, D.C.: IDB and Johns Hopkins University Press, 1997), statistical appendix.

28. See Ilán Bizberg, "La Crisis del Corporativismo Mexicano," *Foro Internacional* 30, no. 4 (April/June 1990): 695–735.

of sectoral demands and aim at increasing the primacy of the market as the main mechanism of allocation, reform-minded elites—in Mexico and elsewhere—will, at a minimum, prefer to avoid corporatist structures. At a maximum, these reformers often picture the very idea of interest intermediation as the institutionalization of the rent-seeking practices their reforms are, allegedly, about to eliminate.[29]

"Desectorialization," the repudiation of the corporatist design, was the official term produced at the party's Fourteenth National Assembly in September 1990.[30] Along with this new approach to its mass organizations, the party leadership adopted a twofold strategy of control and participation in order to supersede corporatism. At the level of the popular sectors, and under direct supervision of the presidency, the government implemented PRONASOL, a program of social assistance targeted to the poorest, unorganized segments of the population. Used as an electoral machine as much as a system of patronage, PRONASOL displaced the PRI's structure from these traditional roles, to a point of seriously straining relations between the presidency and the party by giving increasing prerogatives to the economic reform team.[31] At the level of business interests, desectorialization meant to bypass the traditional sectoral associations and forge unprecedentedly close—even transparent—relations between the Salinas government and the large industrial and financial groups, for the most part beneficiaries of the privatization program. As discussed earlier, under the CMHN and the CCE, Mexico's wealthiest businessmen had secured direct access to Los Pinos (the presidential palace) at the expense of the once-powerful sectoral associations of industry and commerce. These interests often participated in the PRI's electoral committees, known as *Células Empresariales,*

29. For strong anticorporatist statements by policymakers and ideologues across reform countries, see José Piñera, *La Revolución Laboral en Chile* (Santiago: Zig-Zag, 1991); Eammonn Butler, Madsen Pirie, and Peter Young, *The Omega File* (London: Adam Smith Institute, 1985),113–30; Pedro Aspe, *El Camino Mexicano de la Tranformación Económica,* and Jorge Bustamante, *La República Corporativa* (Buenos Aires: EMECE, 1989).

30. John Bailey, Denise Dresser, and Leopoldo Gómez, "XIV Asamblea del PRI: Balance Preliminar," *La Jornada,* September 26, 1990.

31. The head of PRONASOL was Donaldo Colossio. Nominated, according to the tradition, by the outgoing president, Colossio was assassinated during the campaign in March 1994. Seasoned observers of Mexican politics interpreted his assassination as a clear sign of the growing conflict between a weakening party apparatus and the Salinas reform clique. See, for example, Miguel Angel Granados Chapa, *Escuche, Carlos Salinas* (México DF: Océano, 1996). For Pronasol, see Wayne Cornelius, Ann Craig, and Jonathan Fox, eds., *Transforming State-Society Relations in Mexico: The National Solidarity Strategy* (San Diego: Center for US-Mexican Studies, University of California, San Diego, 1994); and Kathleen Bruhn, "Social Spending and Political Support: The 'Lessons' of the National Solidarity Program in Mexico," *Comparative Politics* 28 (January 1996).

whose main goal was to mobilize financial and political resources in support of the official candidates.[32]

The third state formation strategy consisted of the insertion of new institutional designs and strategies into the nation's foreign economic policy agenda. The decision to join the North American Free-Trade Agreement (NAFTA), and earlier GATT, appears as an effort to signal economic agents about the government's genuine commitment to sustain liberalization over time.[33] Given the capacity and propensity of the dominant party to tinker with domestic institutions (including property rights, as the fresh memories of the 1982 nationalization constantly reminded private entrepreneurs), not even the constitutional changes were seen as sufficient proof of the inalterability of the normative order emerging from the economic reform process. Thus, the Mexican government attempted to resolve its long-standing reputation deficit by resorting to an international, institutional straitjacket on future attempts to reverse the fundamentals of an open market economy. In other words, by abdicating from national policy autonomy through explicit international commitments, the Salinas government sought to enhance credibility and "lock in" domestic economic reform.

In sum, the economic reform process in Mexico became an instrument to carry out unprecedented institutional changes. For some analysts, the nationalization of the banks in 1982 had been driven by the goal of recovering the power of the presidency, which had been weakened by the confrontation with the private sector since the 1970s. It was only by rebuilding strategic ties with large industrial and financial elites, however, that that recovery was made possible. First with De la Madrid and later with Salinas, the transformation of the state's role in the economy was accomplished through the creation of new bases of political support. In the process, the centralization of authority allowed a decaying political system—the dominant party regime—to survive the dramatic loss of legitimacy of the 1980s, and its central political institution—the presidency— to recover a political initiative that empowered the PRI to continue to be a viable option well into the 1990s.[34]

---

32. See footnote 22, above, and also Andrés Oppenheimer, *Bordering on Chaos: Guerrillas, Stockbrokers, Politicians, and Mexico's Road to Prosperity* (Boston: Little, Brown, 1996), for an investigation on the *células*.

33. See Aaron Tornell and Gerardo Esquivel, "The Political Economy of Mexico's Entry to NAFTA," *National Bureau of Economic Research Working Paper* 5322, no. 28 (October 1995).

34. A slightly different view is offered by Lorenzo Meyer, who argues that after 1994 the presidency began to decay again. See his "La Crisis del Presidencialismo Mexicano: Recuperación Espectacular y Recaída Estructural," *Foro Internacional* 36, no. 1–2 (January/June 1996): 11–30.

Argentina

The Argentine privatization program was triggered by the deep macroeconomic crisis of the late 1980s. During the 1980s, financing requirements for state-owned enterprises had surpassed 50 percent of the total nonfinancial public sector deficit, and necessary investments in public utilities were long overdue. By the time Carlos Menem was inaugurated in July 1989, the experience of hyperinflation had created a widespread sense of the need of massive reforms, and unexpected popular support for privatization.[35] The government swiftly passed legislation to initiate the reform program. In August 1989 the State Reform Law established that publicly owned companies were eligible for privatization, and the Economic Emergency Law of September 1989 gave the executive extraordinary powers to expedite the process. The macroeconomic situation and these two pieces of legislation explain the sweeping character of privatization and the haste and resolve of the policymakers. The main goals of the program were, first, to improve the macroeconomic situation by divesting large public companies and, second, to facilitate the modernization of those companies through the participation of the private sector while relieving the government budget from future expenditures. Thus, between 1989 and 1995, 121 firms were privatized for $9.7 billion in cash and $13.4 billion in debt-reduction instruments.

The Long and Contradictory Path to Economic Reform

In contrast to the rather cumulative trajectory exhibited by the reform experiments previously examined, the Argentine liberalization experience displays a series of discontinuous, and often contradictory, policy episodes. The first of those episodes took place under the military government that came to power in March 1976 as a consequence of the deepest political crisis in the country's history. In orthodox economic circles, that crisis was seen as the straightforward consequence of protracted ISI. Allegedly, protectionism in the manufacturing sector had swollen domestic industry and, thus, artificially strengthened unions, which, in the process, radicalized their demands. José Martínez de Hoz, a promi-

---

35. For a comparative study, see Kurt Weyland, "Swallowing the Bitter Pill: Sources of Popular Support for Neoliberal Reform in Latin America," *Comparative Political Studies* 31, no. 5 (October 1998): 539–68. See, also, Carlos Gervasoni, "La Sustentabilidad Electoral de los Programas de Estabilización y Reforma Estructural: Los Casos de Argentina y Peru" (paper presented at the Twentieth International Congress, Latin American Studies Association, Guadalajara, Mexico, April 17–19, 1997); and Edward Gibson and Ernesto Calvo, "Electoral Coalitions and Market Reforms: The Case of Argentina" (paper presented at the Twentieth International Congress, Latin American Studies Association, Guadalajara, Mexico, April 17–19, 1997).

nent member of the agro-export and financial elite who persuaded top military leaders of this connection, became minister of the economy.[36] His approach was appealing to the armed forces: liberalization would seek not just to allocate resources more efficiently, but also to discipline hypermobilized organized groups, decompose the social base of populism, and restore order.[37]

Accordingly, by April 1976 the authorities had devalued the currency, liberalized prices, frozen wages, and reduced export taxes and import tariffs. In June 1977 additional measures deregulated the banking industry by easing the entry of new financial institutions, reducing reserve requirements, freeing interest rates, and redirecting public sector borrowing toward private credit markets. As a result, real interest rates became positive, leading to a considerable slowdown in 1978. Despite the recession, inflation had remained stuck around 150 percent, prompting the economic authorities to deepen stabilization policies and accelerate the course of liberalization. The government thus launched "The 20th of December 1978 Program," the cornerstone of which was an exchange rate policy based on an active crawling peg.[38] The *tablita,* as it came to be known, consisted of a series of preannounced devaluations based on a declining rate of inflation. With the tablita came the elimination of restrictions on trade and capital accounts. Through these measures, the government expected to bring the economy more in line with international prices and induce a process of reallocation according to Argentina's comparative advantages.[39]

The preannounced exchange rate, set at levels below the rate of inflation to reduce inflationary expectations, increased real appreciation. With trade and financial liberalization, this new competitive environment put pressure on manufacturing firms, especially those in the consumer-oriented ISI sector. Domestic real interest rates higher than international ones and the exchange rate risk

---

36. At the time, Martínez de Hoz was the president of the Argentine Economic Council (CEA), an elite organization that grouped the most traditional firms in extractive, manufacturing, and financial activities, renowned for their free-market stance. His economic team included a group of orthodox economists highly reputed in financial circles.

37. Adolfo Canitrot, "La Disciplina como Objetivo de la Política Económica: Un ensayo sobre el Programa Económico del Gobierno Argentino desde 1976," *Estudios CEDES* 2, no. 6 (1979).

38. Carlos Rodríguez, "El Plan Argentino de Estabilización del 20 de Diciembre," *CEMA Documento de Trabajo* 5 (1979).

39. Exchange-rate-based stabilization was pioneered by Argentina, Chile, and Uruguay in the 1970s. In the early 1980s, these countries also experienced similar balance-of-payment crises associated with real appreciation and current account balances unsustainable in the medium term, which produced runs on the currency and drainage of central bank reserves. This issue became a highly debated one in the 1990s, as across the board capital account liberalization contributed to analogous crises in Mexico in 1994, Asia in 1997, Russia in 1998, and Brazil in 1999.

offset by the tablita generated massive inflows of capital and drove firms into dollar-denominated debt, either to keep their operations afloat or to engage in arbitrage. Characteristic of exchange-rate-based stabilization programs, appreciation and the oversupply of foreign credit financed a consumption boom of imports, which was instrumental in gathering support among otherwise castigated middle sectors, precisely during the most coercive phase of the military regime. As a result, private external debt increased from $4 billion in 1978 to $9 billion in 1979, leading to a threefold increase in total (private and public) debt between 1978 and 1981. Most private debt was concentrated in large firms and banks, one-third of it among ten banks and ten industrial firms.[40] Argentines thus made up the term *patria financiera* (financial motherland)[41] to refer to the main beneficiary of the liberalization process.

As in Chile at the time, and in Mexico in the late 1980s, the liberalization of cross-border capital flows opened an entirely new chapter in Argentina's political economy. While under ISI, appreciation generally led to foreign exchange crises due to the accumulation of trade deficits over time, from 1978 on, attacks on the currency through transactions on the capital account could deplete international reserves suddenly. This occurred after 1979, when the deterioration of the balance of payments conveyed the limits of the predetermined exchange rate, leading to massive outflows of capital in anticipation of a future devaluation.[42]

This inherently vulnerable macroeconomic context was further compounded by changes in the nature of the country's distributional conflict. Under ISI, income struggles among sectors had been based on the distribution of the agrarian surplus, but as commodity prices began to decline in the second half of the 1970s (eventually collapsing in the mid-1980s), economic groups increasingly began to direct demands toward the welfare-with-producer state. The military government responded to these pressures in three ways. First, it revitalized an existing program of sectoral incentives, called "regime of industrial promotion," and combined it with tax exemptions for firms relocating in

40. A. Humberto Petrei and James Tybout, "Microeconomic Adjustments in Argentina during 1976–1981: The Importance of Changing Levels of Financial Subsidies," *World Development* 13, no. 8 (August 1985): 949–67.

41. In the early 1970s, disputes within the Peronist movement developed between factions who advocated either a "patria socialista" or a "patria peronista." Later on, and as a consequence of the influence accumulated by labor leaders during the 1973–76 Peronist government, the public made references to the "patria sindical." In the late 1970s and early 1980s, allusions to the "patria financiera" conveyed that power was now located in the financial sector.

42. The ensuing banking crisis prompted the government to take over fifty-nine financial institutions between March 1980 and December 1981 alone. See Luis Giorgio and Silvia Sagari, "Argentina's Financial Crises and Restructuring in the 1980s," in Andrew Sheng, ed., *Bank Restructuring: Lessons from the 1980s* (Washington, D.C.: World Bank, 1996), 161–73.

frontier provinces (due to security concerns of the military). Second, it increased public investment in infrastructure, petrochemicals, and the military-industrial complex, generating opportunities for contractors and suppliers of the state who took advantage of old legislation that gave priority to nationally owned firms in public auctions. And, third, in 1981–82, the central bank enacted a program by which private debtors could transfer their foreign obligations to the state. This scheme of multiple subsidies generated larger deficits that, when monetized in the context of an open capital account with a fixed exchange rate, also contributed to wipe out foreign exchange reserves rapidly, leading to sharp devaluations and explosive cycles of ever-increasing inflation.[43]

Paradoxically, a military-sponsored liberalization experiment institutionalized Argentina's secular distributional conflict at the level of the fiscal sector. More than ever before, influence over the destination of state resources was the main way to resolve inter- and intrasector rivalries and, thus, the way alliances among economic groups were built. By the turn of the decade, severe fiscal constraints limited the government's largess in the overall distribution of subsidies, forcing firms to pursue economies of scale in rent seeking, and increased the selectivity of the process, generating incentives for favoritism, overinvoicing, and misappropriation, among other practices. Thus, by the early 1980s a few private groups had accumulated vast amounts of wealth while the economy as a whole was verging on the brink of collapse. In the manufacturing sector, for example, firms able to access industrial promotion and public contracts expanded significantly during the 1976–83 period, while the sector as a whole declined by about 12 percent. These beneficiaries, in turn, were virtually the same ones who were responsible for 79 percent of the total private external debt that was transferred to the state, but who represented only 5 percent of all private debtors.[44] At this point a new distributional coalition was

---

43. For a full treatment of this, see Eugenio Díaz-Bonilla and Hector E. Schamis, "From Redistribution to Stability: Exchange Rate Policies in Argentina, 1950–98," in Jeffry Frieden and Ernesto Stein, eds., *The Currency Game: Exchange Rate Politics in Latin America* (Baltimore: Johns Hopkins University Press, 2001).

44. Data from Jorge Schvarzer, "Estrategia Industrial y Grandes Empresas: El Caso Argentino," *Desarrollo Económico* 18, no. 71 (October/December 1978): 307–51; and "Cambios en el liderazgo Industrial Argentino en el período de Martínez de Hoz," *Desarrollo Económico* 23, no. 91 (October/December 1983): 395–422; Mario Damill and José María Fanelli, "Decisiones de Cartera y Transferencias de Riqueza en un Período de Inestabilidad Macroeconómica," *Documento CEDES* 12 (1988); Daniel Aspiazu, Eduardo Basualdo, and Miguel Khavisse, *El Nuevo Poder Económico en la Argentina de los Años Ochenta* (Buenos Aires: Legasa, 1986); Eduardo Basualdo, *Deuda Externa y Poder Económico en la Argentina* (Buenos Aires: Nueva América, 1987); Eduardo Basualdo and Daniel Aspiazu, *Cara y Contracara de los Grupos Económicos: Estado y Promoción Industrial en la Argentina* (Buenos Aires: Cántaro, 1991).

formed. Nicknamed *patria contratista* (contractor motherland) by the public, but self-identified as "the captains of industry," the success of this group was based on their capacity to access the wielders of political power and their effective control of (mostly family-owned and originally import-substituting) diversified economic conglomerates through highly centralized decision-making structures.[45]

Checked by domestic discontent and internationally isolated after the Falklands-Malvinas war, the military had to execute a quick withdrawal from office, leaving behind a truncated liberalization experiment, a high concentration of economic power, and a vacuum of political power. The democratic administration of Raúl Alfonsín (1983–89) tried to fill the political vacuum by creating a "third historic movement," namely, by absorbing the labor movement (largely Peronist) into a new permanent electoral majority.[46] An extensive "deperonization" of the working class, however, depended not only on prolonging the initial success of the "Austral Plan," the stabilization program launched in mid-1985, but also on the availability of resources to distribute material rewards and divide the labor leadership. Given these coalition-building priorities, the Radical government sought to retain discretionary control over the key macroeconomic variables, thus avoiding structural reforms deemed necessary to make disinflation durable.

Conflicting objectives also characterized the approach vis-à-vis business. On the one hand, the government emphasized the need to increase the overall competitiveness of the economy (via deregulation, export promotion, etc.) to put a definitive end to inflation. On the other hand, the capacity of the leading financial and industrial firms to set key prices of the economy compelled the authorities to involve the captains of industry more formally into the policy-making process.[47] This political alliance translated into a more orthodox macroeconomic management (money supply reductions, spending cuts, interest rate increases) but combined with a microeconomic approach that maintained a rather closed trade regime and selective subsidies for firms in the manufacturing sector. The micro soon affected the macro. By 1987–88, outlays for public contracts and the regime of industrial promotion represented 2 percent of GDP

---

45. For detailed studies, see Pierre Ostiguy, *Los Capitanes de la Industria: Grandes Empresarios, Política y Economía en la Argentina de los Años 80* (Buenos Aires: Legasa, 1990); and Luis Majul, *Los Dueños de la Argentina* (Buenos Aires: Sudamericana, 1992).

46. See Luis Aznar et al., *Alfonsín: Discursos sobre el Discurso* (Buenos Aires: EUDEBA/ FUCADE, 1986).

47. See Ostiguy, *Los Capitanes de la Industria,* 328–38; and William Smith, "Democracy, Distributional Conflict, and Macroeconomic Policymaking in Argentina, 1983–89," *Journal of Interamerican Studies and World Affairs* 32, no. 2 (summer 1990): 1–42.

and more than half of the nonfinancial fiscal deficit.[48] With a fiscal position already compromised by debt service payments and the collapse of commodity prices, high inflation resumed.

A Peronist landslide in the September 1987 congressional and gubernatorial elections further impaired the Alfonsín administration's capacity for economic management. A last attempt to recover stability was made in August 1988 through yet another package, the *Plan Primavera* (Spring Plan).[49] Like the Mexican PASE signed in December 1987, the program was based on a series of price agreements with the peak associations of industry (UIA) and commerce (CAC), tighter monetary and fiscal policies, and the adoption of a fixed exchange rate. Yet Argentina's political and macroeconomic context at the time was far more precarious than Mexico's. The government's capacity to enforce compliance across society was thus remarkably lower: agricultural interests exhibited zero tolerance to currency appreciation and labor rejected wage restraint.

By the end of 1988 the credibility deficit of the Plan Primavera was widespread. As long as the government was determined to maintain the nominal anchor and the capital account remained open, the central bank was forced to intervene in currency markets, eroding its reserves. This process accelerated as of January 1989, when the realization that the macroeconomic imbalances were unsustainable led to runs against the currency, flight from money, and other forms of financial adaptation. In early February the situation deteriorated dramatically. Central bank authorities suspended foreign exchange auctions, unexpectedly ending their commitment to exchange rate stability. The largest corporations responded to this unforeseen decision with a concerted flight to the dollar that virtually collapsed the price system in domestic currency. At that point, the attack on the currency had become a political gesture, to the extent that financial media described it as a "market coup."[50]

Privatization: From the Politics of State Contracts
to the Politics of State Assets

February 1989 signaled a new chapter in Argentina's historical political economy. Delivered against the Alfonsin government, the alleged market coup was also a warning to the Peronist candidate Carlos Menem, front-runner in the May

48. World Bank, "Argentina: Public Finance Review, From Insolvency to Growth," February 11, 1993, Report 10827-Ar.

49. By the central bank president during most of this period, see José Luis Machinea, "Stabilization under Alfonsin's Government: A Frustrated Attempt," *Documento CEDES* 42 (1990).

50. *Ambito Financiero*, December 15, 1989, 1, 2.

1989 election.[51] Menem acknowledged the message. The populist rhetoric of his campaign—"productive revolution" and massive wage increases (*salariazo*)—was abandoned as soon as he was elected and embraced an agenda defined as "popular liberalism." Menem's sudden conversion, it was said, was a "hyperrealist" and "hyperpragmatic" response to hyperinflation. He reportedly had no option but to "strike a deal" with the captains of industry.[52] In fact, when Menem was inaugurated in July, central bank reserves equaled $500 million and the monthly inflation rate was 190 percent. The new government needed to prioritize the reconstruction of the fiscal base. The distribution of rents through subsidies and public contracts could not continue, but at the time no government could afford the opposition of the large economic conglomerates, the corporate culture of which had been forged more in the political arena than in the marketplace.

Accordingly, Menem delivered an unambiguous political signal by filling the key economic policy-making positions with top executives of Bunge y Born (Argentina's oldest conglomerate and a staunch adversary of Peronism) and leaders of the Ucede political party (the earliest and most articulate advocate of economic liberalization).[53] With this support, Menem pursued the centralization of authority in his office, a task he deemed essential to overcome what, by all accounts, constituted the deepest economic crisis in the country's history, and to launch a reform program. On the president's initiative, Congress approved the "State Reform Law" in August, which made virtually all public companies eligible for privatization, and the "Economic Emergency Law" in September, which gave extraordinary powers to the executive to expedite the process. This legal framework set the stage for the elimination of industrial subsidies, the reduction of import restrictions (with some significant sectoral exceptions), cuts in public expenditures and employment, and increases in tax collection.

The announcement of the privatization of politically sensitive SOEs such as the telephone and airline companies, television channels and radio stations, and some railroads signaled the initiation of the Menem privatization experiment. This way the government reinforced its free-market commitment in order

---

51. In author interviews with members of the Bank Association (ADEBA) and representatives of large industrial conglomerates held between May and August 1989, several of them admitted that by February 1989 there was a widespread feeling that "something drastic had to be done" to make politicians understand, "once and for all," that the business class would not tolerate unpredictability any further.

52. Author interviews with top economists of the Justicialista Party, later officials in the economy and foreign ministries, June 1989, Buenos Aires, and December 1989, Washington, D.C.

53. For this unprecedented alliance, see Edward Gibson, *Class and Conservative Parties: Argentina in Comparative Perspective* (Baltimore: Johns Hopkins University Press, 1997), chap. 6.

to convince business elites that the Peronist ideological "conversion" was neither temporary nor instrumental. Aside from a handful of cases, and beyond explicit political effects, the pace of the divestiture process was slow, largely due to resilient inflation that even produced two more hyperinflationary episodes, in August 1990 and February 1991.

The appointment of Domingo Cavallo as minister of the economy in March 1991 signaled a qualitative change in the overall program of reform and gave a decisive impetus to the privatization process. Cavallo's first task was to launch a new anti-inflation strategy, the "Convertibility Program," which was discussed and approved in Congress. Still in effect by 2001, the program pegged the peso one-to-one to the dollar, determined the full convertibility of domestic currency, and transformed the monetary and exchange rate functions of the central bank into a quasi currency board by which the monetary base has to equal liquid international reserves. The program had immediate positive effects, bringing inflation down to one digit in just three months.

Price and exchange rate stability, and what appeared as a commitment to rules, rather than discretion, were considered necessary conditions for a full-fledged privatization, especially given the increase in private sector demand for credit to finance the purchases. After 1991 divestiture operations involved power, gas, water and sewerage, steel, and petroleum, among others, and by 1994, the privatization program extended to the social security area, following a Chilean-style reform program in combination with a public pillar. Since, in general, the divestiture process outlined a payment method that included foreign debt paper, purchasing consortia often included a creditor bank, an international firm operating in the area to be privatized, and a large domestic firm belonging to one of the main economic groups. The case of the telephone system is illustrative: the public monopoly was privatized as a duopoly, which included Citibank, Telefónica de España, and the local Techint group as one half, and Morgan Bank, France Telecom, and the Pérez Companc group as the other.[54]

Since the government maximized speed and fiscal proceeds, companies were generally tendered undivided and with monopoly rights, and with less-than-optimal regulation in place.[55] As a consequence, contractors and suppliers

---

54. See Claudia Herrera, "The Privatization of the Argentine Telephone System," *CEPAL Review* 47 (August 1992): 149–61.

55. This was especially the case in the telephone industry. On the multiple problems of regulation, see Andrea López et al., "Nuevas relaciones entre el Estado y los usuarios de servicios públicos en la post-privatización," INAP, Dirección Nacional de Estudios y Documentación, 1997; Alice Hill and Manuel Abdala, "Argentina: The Sequencing of Privatization and Regulation," in Brian Levy and Pablo Spiller, eds., *Regulations, Institutions and Commitment: Comparative*

that specialized in certain areas took advantage of their information, experience, and effective access to those organizations and took over energy, water, petroleum, railroads, and highways, for the most part in association with foreign banks and international operators.[56] The result was a pattern of concentration in ownership and in capital markets along with horizontal diversification by which domestic firms participate in ownership of various privatized companies. This context was conducive to rapid gains in the productive efficiency of the privatized firms, the result of tariff increases, the preservation of protected markets, and regulatory flaws.[57] This occurred not just in the public utility sector, where monopolies tend to prevail due to economies of scale and high barriers of entry, but also in tradables and areas subject to competition, such as oil refineries, air transport, and international telecommunications.

For the Menem government, reversing the traditional economic policy tenets of Peronism and building unprecedented ties with economic elites entailed to refashion power relations between the Peronist party (PJ) and organized labor—the so-called backbone of the Peronist movement, its traditional, though increasingly alienated, societal basis of support. To this end, the government adopted two distinctive approaches. One was the classic divide-and-conquer strategy, in order to propel pro-reform union leaders to positions of power. At the very least, proprivatization leaders generally counted on the explicit support of the presidency in their union careers. In other cases, such leaders were rewarded with greater political payoffs, as in the case of the leader of the telephone union, who was appointed undersecretary of telecommunications, and in the case of top leaders of the powerful oil union, who were appointed to the board of directors of the oil company.

The second strategy involved the distribution of material payoffs. Similarly to different varieties of employee-share ownership programs implemented in Chile, Britain, and Hungary, among others, the Menem privatization program adopted the so-called Participatory Property Program (PPP). This program consisted of keeping a percentage of the privatized assets in order to distribute stock

---

Studies in Telecommunications (Cambridge: Cambridge University Press, 1996); and Ben Alfa Petrazzini, "Telephone Privatization in a Hurry: Argentina," in Ravi Ramamurti, ed., *Privatizing Monopolies* (Baltimore: Johns Hopkins University Press, 1996).

56. For a detailed account on the active participation of future beneficiaries in various stages of the legal design of the divestiture process, see Ana Margheritis, "Implementing Structural Adjustment in Argentina: The Politics of Privatization" (Ph.D. diss., University of Toronto, 1997).

57. See Pablo Gerchunoff and Guillermo Cánovas, "Privatización en un Contexto de Emergencia Económica," *Desarrollo Económico* 34, no. 136 (January/March 1995): 483–512; and "Privatization: The Argentine Experience," in William Glade, ed., *Bigger Economies, Smaller Governments* (Boulder: Westview Press, 1996), 191–218.

among workers, but under administration of the union. In contrast to other versions of people's capitalism, Argentina's PPP was an extremely selective one: unions had to secure and mobilize political support in order to have access to the shares. And even more selectivity, in fact, was displayed in the privatization of social security, as friendly unions were allowed to open their "privately owned" pension fund, as in the cases of commerce, electricity, automobile, and restaurant unions.[58]

Seen in retrospect, therefore, privatization constituted the very political instrument of Menem's reform program. While it allowed the government to navigate the turbulent waters of internal party politics and reshuffle organized labor politics, it was also conducive to finally securing a lasting deal with the captains of industry. The central bank replenished state coffers and the contractors made up for lost rents. In fact, the domestic groups involved in the largest privatization operations—Macri, Techint, Bridas, Pérez Companc, Astra, Soldati, Roggio[59]—were also the main beneficiaries of public contracts and the regime of industrial promotion in the 1970s and 1980s, and also among the largest private debtors who transferred their foreign obligations to the state through the subsidy implemented in 1981–82. In sum, throughout the 1990s the captains of industry consolidated their economic leadership and, by constituting themselves in the dominant distributional coalition, thus reaffirmed a political centrality that no government could afford to ignore.

Fencing-in the State and Concentrating Executive Authority:
The Institutional Dimension of Menem's Liberalization Program

The Argentine economic crisis of the late 1980s, whose most visible symptom was hyperinflation, opened a "window for reform."[60] In the market, the crisis had enhanced the structural power of the large industrial conglomerates and

58. For a detailed account, see María Victoria Murillo, "Union Politics, Market-Oriented Reforms, and the Reshaping of Argentine Corporatism," in Douglas Chalmers et al., eds., *The New Politics of Inequality in Latin America* (New York and London: Oxford University Press, 1997); and *Labor Unions, Partisan Coalitions, and Market Reforms in Latin America* (Cambridge: Cambridge University Press, 2001).

59. Data from INDEC, *Anuario Estadístico de la República Argentina* (Buenos Aires: Ministerio de Economía y Obras y Servicios Públicos, 1997), 480–98.

60. The term is borrowed from John Kingdon, *Agendas, Alternatives, and Public Policies* (New York: HarperCollins, 1984), chap. 7; and John Keeler, "Opening the Window for Reform: Mandates, Crises, and Extraordinary Policy-Making," *Comparative Politics Studies* 25, no. 4 (January 1993): 433–86. Keeler focuses on the effects of deep economic crises in triggering reforms in a number of cases across regions, an argument consistent with Albert Hirschman, "Reflections on the Latin American Experience," in Leon Lindbergh and Charles Maier, eds., *The Politics of*

mobile asset sectors. In the political arena, in turn, coping with that crisis opened a period of "extraordinary policy-making," one that gave the newly elected president an unprecedented opportunity for centralizing authority in his office.[61] Major economic reform processes are often carried out in a rather centralized decision-making fashion, leading to a concentration of power in the executive. In authoritarian polities (military, as in Chile, or civilian, as in Mexico) there is no apparent tension between the need to reform and the tendency toward centralization. In established polyarchies (U.K.) and in transitional polities (Argentina, Hungary), however, extraordinary policy-making may affect the "democraticness" of the system, as the centralization of decision-making authority contradicts fundamental consultation and power-sharing mechanisms. Rightly so, observers have highlighted the autocratic quality of this type of process.[62] They have not emphasized enough, however, the effectiveness of this expanded and concentrated executive authority in cementing new distributional coalitions forged in the policy arena, and in specifying and enforcing property rights, altering revenue collection mechanisms, and rebuilding administrative capacities.[63]

As Domingo Cavallo, architect of Argentina's stabilization-cum-liberalization program from 1991 to 1996, has repeatedly argued, his economic program's main goal was "to reconstruct the state."[64] Far from thinking in terms of retreating or shrinking, Cavallo emphasized the need to increase the strength and assertiveness of the state. If centralization conveys strength, Cavallo's goal was accomplished during Menem's decade in power. Especially during his first term, from 1989 to 1995, Menem's period in office exacerbated the centripetal

Inflation and Economic Stagnation (Washington, D.C.: Brookings, 1985); and Allan Drazen and Vittorio Grilli, "The Benefits of Crises for Economic Reforms," *American Economic Review* 83, no. 3 (June 1993): 598–607, among others. For a criticism of this argument on grounds of being tautological, see Dani Rodrik, "Understanding Economic Policy Reform," *Journal of Economic Literature* 34, no. 1 (March 1996): 9–41.

61. As chief of the Executive, it is paradoxical that Menem (and Alfonsin before him) enjoyed far higher centralization than any of the four military presidents who preceded them. In fact, given that the 1976–83 military regime had distributed major decision-making positions in three thirds among officers of the army, navy, and air force, the military ruled in a rather decentralized fashion, even characterized by increasing interservice conflict.

62. For example, Guillermo O'Donnell, "Delegative Democracy," Working Paper 172, Kellogg Institute, University of Notre Dame, 1992; and Stephan Haggard and Robert R. Kaufman, *The Political Economy of Democratic Transitions,* chap. 10.

63. Consider, however, how this tension is seen even in economic reform programs of a social-democratic nature. For example, the political success associated with the New Deal set a centralizing and quasi-authoritarian trend that included three reelections and the (failed) packing of the Supreme Court in 1937. See William Edward Leuchtenburg, *Franklin D. Roosevelt and the New Deal, 1932–1940* (New York: Harper & Row, 1963). I return to these issues in the concluding chapter.

64. See, for example, his *Volver a Crecer* (Buenos Aires: Sudamericana Planeta, 1984); and *Economía en Tiempos de Crisis* (Buenos Aires: Sudamericana, 1989).

tendency of a strong presidential system, using virtually all available constitutional resources and some paraconstitutional ones. As previously mentioned, the first two presidential initiatives sent to Congress were the State Reform Law (Law 23696, technically called the Administrative Emergency Law) and the Economic Emergency Law (Law 23697) by which the Legislature delegated broad decisional power to the Executive.[65]

Upon extracting these two crucial prerogatives from the opposition-controlled Congress, Menem sought greater influence over the Supreme Court. The executive presented a bill to Congress to increase the number of justices from five to nine. This packing strategy paid off. In September 1989 the Senate passed Menem's bill and sent it to the Lower House. In April 1990, and in a procedure allegedly plagued with irregularities, the Chamber of Deputies approved Law 23744, which increased the members of the Supreme Court from five to nine. Since two justices resigned during the process, the president was able, with the acquiescence of the Senate, to appoint six out of the nine members of the Court between April and May 1990.[66]

With a broad delegation of authority granted by Congress immediately after taking office in July 1989, control of both Houses of Congress as of December 1989, and a packed Supreme Court since May 1990, Menem began to exercise what numerous analysts termed "rule by decree," *decretazo* in Spanish (literally, "coup de decret"). In addition to a large number of decrees contemplated by the constitution, the Executive widely used a paraconstitutional initiative called "Decrees of Need and Urgency." These decrees were combined with the presidential prerogatives granted by the Economic Emergency laws; together they became the main instruments to implement the economic reform program. This way the executive passed laws circumventing Congress's law-making authority and usually presenting policy proposals as fait accomplis, often even failing to inform the Legislature.[67]

---

65. Taking office five months in advance due to the hyperinflationary crisis (a recession that made the period reminiscent of the interval between the election and the inauguration of Roosevelt between November 1932 and March 1933), Menem demanded from the Radical-controlled Congress the approval of these two laws as requisite to swearing in in July.

66. See Horacio Verbitsky, *Hacer La Corte: La Construcción de un Poder Absoluto sin Justicia ni Control* (Buenos Aires: Planeta, 1993); and for a request for impeachment of the Court members, see Raúl Baglini et al., *Juicio a la corte: texto y fundamentos del pedido de juicio político promovido a los jueces de la Corte Suprema de Justicia de la Nación por Diputados Nacionales de la Unión Cívica Radical* (Buenos Aires: R. Baglini, A. D'Ambrosio, 1993).

67. An account from inside on the absence of information provided to Congress, especially by Cavallo and the members of his economic cabinet, is in Alberto Natale, then vice president of the Parliamentary Commission on State Reform, *Privatizaciones en Privado* (Buenos Aires: Planeta, 1993).

The numbers speak for themselves: between 1853 and July 1989, twenty-five decrees of need and urgency were issued. Between July 1989 and August 1994 (date of promulgation of the new constitution, which made the decree of need and urgency constitutional), 366 of these decrees were issued by the Menem government, covering areas such as taxation, deregulation, privatization, suspension of the right to litigate against the state, and suspension of payments to public contractors, among others. The result of this strategy was an increase of presidential discretion and, as a way of restoring the macroeconomic position, an explicit fencing-in of the state, one that was made impervious to opposition, demands, or even legal claims against it.[68]

These decrees were often complemented by the use of veto powers and veto threats. The executive expanded the veto capacities of the president to levels unknown during democratic periods. Between July 1989 until 1993, the president issued thirty-seven full vetoes and forty-one partial vetoes, systematically using partial promulgation. With the new constitution in 1994, extended presidential veto powers consolidated this tendency.[69]

The appointment of Domingo Cavallo as minister of the economy in early 1991 constituted a landmark in this trend. Although Cavallo had initially favored and managed to get the Convertibility Program approved by Congress, he also emphasized that speed and decisiveness were essential for the success of the reform program. In fact, his appointment led to the suppression of several secretariats and undersecretariats, the creation of several new ones directly under the command of the president and the minister of the economy (himself) and, as in Chile during the height of the reform process, the transformation of the ministry of public works into an undersecretariat of the ministry of the economy. With increasing decision-making capacity in his hands, the minister became a very active political operative, often mediating between the government and interest groups, and taking part in congressional debates in order to curb possible parliamentary dissent prior to a crucial vote. Presidential decrees increased from sixty-three in 1990 to eighty-five in 1991 and sixty-nine in 1992, receding afterward as the reform program neared completion.

---

68. The Economic Emergency Law was often invoked to issue special decrees that suspended the right to litigate against the state. See Delia Ferreira Rubio and Mateo Goretti, "Cuando el Presidente Gobierna Solo: Menem y los Decretos de Necesidad y Urgencia Hasta la Reforma Constitucional," *Desarrollo Económico* 36, no. 141 (April/June 1996): 443–74.

69. On veto powers, see Ana María Mustapic and Natalia Ferreti, "El Veto Presidencial Bajo los Gobiernos de Alfonsín y Menem (1983–1993)," *Universidad Torcuato Di Tella, Working Paper* 14 (March 1995).

In sum, by colluding with the largest segments of Argentina's business groups, Menem cemented a minimum winning coalition that benefited from the economic reform program and provided key political support. By distributing selective incentives among potential opponents, he divided and disarticulated rivals. By redrawing property relations through privatization, his government hardened property rights. By recomposing the fiscal base of the state through the divestiture of public assets, among other forms, his government reorganized extractive methods and reshuffled revenue collection capacities. The combination of these factors, in turn, allowed the president to reconcentrate authority in the executive and centralize decision-making power. As Cavallo had foreseen, these activities associated with economic reform and privatization entailed state building, not state shrinking or retreat.

Conclusion

This chapter has examined evidence from two important reform programs in Latin America—those of Mexico and Argentina—which support the main arguments of this book. As these two countries began to experience high inflation, economic elites shifted their rent-seeking efforts from fiscal resources (subsidies and regulations) in the direction of state assets. Macroeconomic instability and balance-of-payment crises magnified the structural power of large and diversified industrial conglomerates and liquid asset groups and diminished the capacity of the government to disregard their preferences and resist their pressure. If, during the heyday of ISI, firms with political clout tried to secure market reserves through protectionism and state intervention, in the 1980s and 1990s they sought market reserves by taking over natural monopolies and banks. Privatization thus consolidated new winning coalitions and, consequently, gave rise to significant changes in crucial institutional configurations. As I have shown, market reform triggers broad state-building strategies. The increasing centralization of authority discussed should be seen as a typical, recurrent characteristic of state formation.

Despite differences in the types of political regime observed in Chile (military), Mexico (dominant party), and Argentina (competitive democracy) during their deep reform phases, similar collective action patterns developed between the Chilean *grupos,* the Mexican *conglomerateurs,* the Argentine *capitanes,* and their respective governments account for the mix and timing of policy changes. In Chile (similar to Hungary) this pattern adopted the form of overt collusion between leaders of the military government and business elites, while in Argentina and Mexico it was the result of the strategic behavior of financial-industrial firms and their capacity of access to policy-making arenas. These similarities across a range of different contexts come in support of the proposition that liberalization does not necessarily dismantle rents but merely restructures them and, thus, that the behavior of distributional coalitions constitutes a primary, and often-neglected, explanatory factor of market reform programs.

The approach to comparison undertaken in this book, however, also entails analyzing each case in its "natural" context; that is, examining variance in outcome among roughly analogous cases. Seen in this light, all three Latin American cases examined in this study experienced similar economic difficulties associated with ISI: accelerating inflation, mounting indebtedness, and worsening balance-of-payment disequilibria over time. As in Chile, comprehensive market reform programs were implemented in Mexico and Argentina only when these long-simmering economic difficulties had translated into severe political crises. Once under way, however, different state formation strategies emerged. While all three countries achieved significant levels of centralization of power in the executive and undertook constitutional reform processes, only in Chile and Mexico did the constitutional process pursue amendments of an explicit economic nature. Articles related to budgetary procedures, social security administration, central bank management, and the nature of private property rights are now part and parcel of the Mexican and, especially, the Chilean constitutions.

In Argentina, in contrast, the constitutional reform process is suspected of having been no more than an instrument necessary for Menem's reelection. Thus, Argentina's institutional changes fell short of a state formation process *stricto senso*—as had been the case in Chile and Mexico through their constitutional process, and in the United Kingdom through its comprehensive reform of the civil service. In Argentina, instead, those changes appear more as a series of decisions geared in the direction of consolidating presidential discretion, such as the sanction of the decrees of need and urgency as constitutional. Ultimately, Menem himself admitted to this point: "how I would have liked to have had Pinochet's power in order to transform Argentina."[70]

---

70. Extemporaneous remarks to a group of U.S. academics at Olivos, presidential residence, June 20, 1997.

Chapter 7

Hungary

From State Socialism
to Democratic Capitalism

Previous chapters have examined cases that were different in a number of respects, either because the analysis entails a cross-regional comparison—Britain vis-à-vis Latin America—or because there is significant variation in the intraregional comparison—for example, Chile, Mexico, and Argentina carried out their economic reform programs under three different regime types. There is also important variation in the kinds of historical political economies that were reformed—an advanced industrial and Keynesian type versus different kinds of import-substituting regimes. These cases have one important commonality, however: they have all been capitalist throughout, including Chile during its brief socialist interlude in 1970–73. By turning to the postsocialist transformation in East-Central Europe this chapter makes a dramatic turn. In fact, this book goes from one extreme, in which the privatization drive reduced the state sector merely from 11 to 7 percent of GDP (Britain), all the way to the other extreme, in which the term "privatization" means nothing less than to tear down the entire edifice of compulsory collectivization built by more than four decades of state socialism (Hungary).

At first glance, this disparity may suggest that a fundamental principle of comparative analysis is being violated; namely, that by including observations that may not belong to the same *class* of phenomena, the analysis falls into what Giovanni Sartori has termed "the traveling problem."[1] However, as I argue here, this comparison is not only fruitful but also necessary given the main propositions of this book. For example, in contrast to the neoclassical political econ-

---

1. "Concept Misformation in Comparative Politics," *American Political Science Review* 64, no. 4 (December 1970): 1033–53. This also hinges on ongoing debates on the very comparability of the Latin American and the postcommunist transitions. See, for example, Philippe Schmitter and Terry Lynn Karl, "The Conceptual Travels of Transitologists and Consolidologists: How Far to the East Should They Attempt to Go?" *Slavic Review* 53 (spring 1994): 173–85; and Valerie Bunce, "Should Transitologists Be Grounded?" *Slavic Review* 54 (spring 1995): 111–27.

omy approach and the literature on the politics of economic adjustment—which both expect marketization to dissipate rents and dissolve distributional coalitions—I have argued that impetus for reform experiments often results from collusion between political leaders and economic elites, and the preservation of rents for small distributional coalitions, even in the presence of comprehensive marketization. As I discuss in this chapter, in Hungary and other cases in East-Central Europe, the main privatization strategy consisted of the distribution of state assets among the dominant rent-seeking groups of state and reform socialism: enterprise directors and nomenklatura officials. If, despite the dramatic collapse of the system that had created them, those distributional coalitions were able to survive and readapt to the new context with relative ease, one can expect these kinds of actors to have even better prospects in cases where a capitalist economy is already in place, one in which the rules of economic interaction are not as radically altered.

In a similar vein, in contrast to a growing literature on globalization that tends to see the comprehensive penetration of market forces as the cause of a shrinking, retreating, or otherwise weakening state, this study argues, instead, that economic policy reform leads to distinctive processes of state formation. Probably nowhere is this causal connection more apparent than in the former socialist world, where a successful transformation entails the creation of the fundamental institutions of capitalism and political democracy from scratch. As I show, despite the unique and irreproducible initial conditions associated with state socialism, the strategies undertaken by Hungarian reformers to build those institutions and increase stateness in the long run appear similar to those examined in previous chapters.

I thus bring empirical evidence from Hungary and other postsocialist countries to assess my main arguments and "travel back" to the other cases so as to reinterpret and refine the previous stories. By reducing the risks of conceptual stretching, the systemic differences mentioned previously become a methodological asset, rather than a hindrance. By introducing Hungary into the comparison, I introduce even more variance in context, to evaluate the hypothesized causal relationship between distributional coalitions and economic reform. Subsequently, I hold economic reform constant across the cases and address possible variance in state-building strategies adopted and state forms emerging from similar marketization policies. With Hungary I push the comparison to the limit, but if it travels, then the generalizability and explanatory power of my main propositions are greatly enhanced.

As in previous chapters, I proceed by outlining the historical political economy setting that led to the transformation moment. I spell out the nature of the economic and political crises associated with state and reform socialism. I argue that reform socialism and the exit strategy devised by the Communist party created an appropriate milieu for the dominant distributional coalitions of the past to reinvent themselves as private entrepreneurs and take over state assets. In a nutshell, the first political effect of marketization was the empowerment of a new winning coalition. Especially after 1994, when the former communists were elected, this pattern of economic transformation allowed for a reconcentration at the center, and for the deployment of state formation strategies that stabilized the country's novel democratic capitalist system.

Forced Industrialization Under State Socialism

In the late 1940s Hungary adopted the main features of a centrally planned economy, as had been introduced in the Soviet Union in the 1930s. These included the collectivization of agriculture, the intensification of manufacturing, and the development of a mineral sector to sustain heavy industry. Trade relations were largely limited to the socialist bloc: manufacturing output was determined by exports to CMEA (Council for Mutual Economic Assistance) nations, and industrial inputs were mostly imported from those countries. By 1950 the collectivization experiment also entailed the implementation of the first five-year plan, a centralized system of control that fixed investment, production, quality, and wage levels. The five-year plans were enacted by Parliament and were broken down into yearly, quarterly, and monthly plans, as well as disaggregated into sectoral and company plans. Within this system, company autonomy was almost totally eliminated by a complex system of compulsory indicators, the most important of which was industrial production.

As Cold War tension peaked in the 1950s and military spending became the largest single item in the budget, the government began to prioritize the iron and steel sectors. High military spending aided central planning; together they were seen as an opportunity to increase the country's historically low levels of capital accumulation. The acceleration of capital formation—from 6 percent before World War II to 35 percent in the early 1950s—and the concentration of investment in heavy industry seemed to suggest, as in several Latin American nations at the exact same time, that industrial power was just "around the corner," and that the protracted struggle with backwardness could thus be won.[2]

---

2. See Ivan Berend, *Central and Eastern Europe, 1944–1993: Detour from the Periphery to the Periphery* (Cambridge: Cambridge University Press, 1996); and for a suggestive comparison, see Joseph Love, *Crafting The Third World: Theorizing Underdevelopment in Rumania and Brazil* (Stanford: Stanford University Press, 1996).

Yet the pitfalls of the command economy soon outweighed the benefits of forced industrialization. The removal of market mechanisms made companies privilege the fulfillment of quantitative goals. Concerns with technological development, productivity raises, and quality improvements were almost totally eliminated. Since targets were measured by the value of production, companies had incentives to increase value by using more and more expensive inputs. As a result, vast amounts of resources were wasted in an increasing number of unsalable products, often leading to the accumulation of superfluous stocks while the economy as a whole began to experience shortages. Party authorities attempted to reverse this trend with more administrative regulations, but to no avail. To the extent that wasting materials could help managers achieve their plan targets, unsalable stocks and resources depleted in failed investment projects became structural features of the system.[3]

By 1953 it was clear that the targets for the five-year plan were not going to be met. Compulsory collectivization resulted in unrest in the countryside, and the neglect of agriculture led to decreases in production. Drops in real wages, disruption of food supply, and a widespread sense of economic crisis became prevalent. By early 1954 the official party began to entertain ideas such as decentralization, bureaucratic rationalization, and reduction of the number of plan indicators, among others. Later, the tragic 1956 revolt added an essentially political urgency to the prospects for reform. The repressive methods used by the dominant party, compounded by Soviet military intervention, were just the expression of the magnitude of the precedent political crisis. In this context, renewal became the buzzword. In the political arena, the search for renewal brought János Kádár and a new elite in the Hungarian Socialist Workers Party (HSWP) to office. In the economic realm, in turn, in December 1956 the new leadership set up a committee of economic experts to revise the main economic policies—trade, wages, plan indicators, and prices, among others—and to devise the blueprint of a program that would combine central planning with market incentives.

It took more than a decade, however, for a significant price reform and decentralization to occur. After 1958 and during the early 1960s the government reintroduced the collectivization of agriculture, though this time allocating resources for productivity increases, introducing price incentives, and integrating production and marketing strategies among private, cooperative, and state farms. In contrast to innovations in agriculture, however, the manufacturing

---

3. For a thorough analysis, see Janos Kornai, *The Socialist System: The Political Economy of Communism* (Princeton: Princeton University Press, 1992).

sector remained under the centrally planned, import-substituting system. Typical of that strategy, the acceleration of ISI increased the import side of the trade account as demand for capital goods, energy, and intermediate inputs grew, particularly at a time in which the terms of trade were unfavorable for nonindustrialized nations. Imports from CMEA countries were less available, forcing Hungary to import from the West, which posed important constraints on the balance-of-payments with convertible-currency areas. By the late 1960s difficulties in the external sector, economic slowdown, and the specter of the 1956 crisis still lingering over Hungarian society persuaded the government that increasing domestic efficiency was imperative. In 1968 the pace of reform accelerated and a new program was launched: the New Economic Mechanism (NEM).

Reform Socialism

Though not unique in the socialist bloc—in fact, at the time price incentives were being introduced in Poland, Bulgaria, and the German Democratic Republic—the reforms under the NEM constituted the most ambitious version of "market socialism."[4] NEM restricted planning and intervention to the macroeconomic realm: basically to determine investment goals and allocate resources accordingly. On the microeconomic domain, NEM limited the role of central planning to large-investment and strategically important sectors. Targets lost their compulsory character and were relaxed and replaced by market incentives such as prices, exchange rates, credits, and taxes. Firms were able to set their own production targets and devise their own sale, financial, and investment strategies. Many controls remained, however, especially over credit, company profits, and goods considered necessary. Nonetheless, to the extent that profits became part of the indicators of company performance, managers began to care about costs, prices, and quality, among others.

Initially, the NEM yielded positive results on growth, employment, and the balance of payments; "goulash communism" appeared to be a successful formula. By the mid-1970s, however, international events combined with domes-

---

4. For a comparative view, see Tamás Bauer, "Hungarian Economic Reform in East European Perspective," *Eastern European Politics and Societies* 2, no. 3 (fall 1998): 418–32. For an overview of NEM, see Ivan Berend, *Hungarian Economic Reforms, 1953–1988* (Cambridge: Cambridge University Press, 1990); Tamás Bauer, "The Hungarian Alternative to Soviet-Type Planning," *Journal of Comparative Economics* 7, no. 3 (1983): 304–16; and Ellen Comisso and Paul Marer, "The Economics and Politics of Reform in Hungary," in Ellen Comisso and Laura D'Andrea Tyson, eds., *Power, Purpose, and Collective Choice* (Ithaca: Cornell University Press, 1986), 245–78.

tic conditions in deleterious ways. Sharp increases in energy and primary product prices deteriorated Hungary's terms of trade with Western and Eastern countries as well. Like other East European states, and some Latin American ones, Hungary responded to this unfavorable shock by reverting to autarkic, state-led industrialization. The decision to invest heavily in the manufacturing sector, however, led on the one hand to an increase in demand for imports, thus affecting the current account in the medium term, and on the other to alter domestic prices in order to insulate some industrial sectors while pursuing rapid growth, thus deviating from the basic parameters of the NEM.

Increasingly, the trade deficit began to be financed by Western credit. The introduction of a stabilization program in 1979 coincided with another oil shock and with sharp increases of interest rates in the early 1980s. Due to the composition of Hungary's debt, the balance of payments suffered additional pressure: 45 percent of total debt consisted of short-term loans and 80 percent of the hard-currency debt was composed by five-year loans.[5] A serious liquidity crisis soon followed, to a large degree compounded by the specific institutional foundation of the country's market socialist experiment. Under a traditional centrally planned economy, monetary policy has a small role as a stabilizing device; the central bank has difficulties applying monetary stringency. Under the decentralization policies of the NEM this was compounded further, for firm managers enjoyed prerogatives that they used in pursuit of their own particularistic political goals. Often this translated into a rather soft approach to wage restraint.[6]

By 1982 it was evident that the mixed formula had contributed to exacerbate macroeconomic instability, triggering arguments about the need for "reform of the reform." In March foreign exchange reserves covered less than one month of imports. Along with Poland and Rumania, that spring Western banks placed Hungary under a credit embargo.[7] Once again, policymakers had to change course in a radical way. That same year, Hungary joined the IMF and in 1983 the World Bank. Membership in Western financial institutions entailed

---

5. Comisso and Marer, "The Economics and Politics of Reform in Hungary."

6. Between 1979 and 1983, while average GDP growth was 1.9 percent and average productivity growth was 2.5 percent, the average wage growth was 7.4 percent, four times the former and three times the latter. See I. Hagelmayer, "The Causes of Inflation in Hungary and the Prospects for Its Reduction," *Acta Oeconomica* 38, no. 1–2 (1987): 5.

7. Note that this occurred even before the Latin American debt crisis initiated in August 1982. For a comparative view, see Albert Fishlow, "The East European Debt Crisis in the Latin American Mirror," and Laura D'Andrea Tyson, "The Debt Crisis and Adjustment Responses in Eastern Europe: A Comparative Perspective," both in Comisso and Tyson, eds., *Power, Purpose, and Collective Choice,* 391–99 and 63–110, respectively.

a deeper stabilization approach, basically focused on contracting investment in order to cut imports. Whatever fiscal and monetary discipline was achieved, however, it was carried out through restoring central controls on credit allocation, wages, enterprise profits, and taxes, but leaving the fundamentals for the most part untouched. To the extent that real interest rates remained negative, demand for credit on the part of state-owned firms was not affected by nominal interest rates increases. Thus, inflationary pressures continued unabated, neutralizing the effect of money supply contractions in the long run.[8] This contributed, once a moderate budget surplus was achieved in 1984, to prompt the government to resume credit expansion.

Under reform socialism, therefore, monetary and fiscal policy stricto senso had little tangible impact in terms of stabilization. Increasing autonomy on the part of firm managers (reinforced by interpenetration with a growing private sector) and the HSWP's commitment to social welfare placed continuous burdens on the budget, while credit allocation in the hands of the same officials responsible for central banking worked against the very principle of monetary stringency. By early 1987 a financial sector reform aimed at separating credit allocation from monetary policy by creating commercial financial entities, though with little macroeconomic success. Given the continued vulnerability of the National Bank, now turned into a central bank proper but also the lender of last resort for the commercial banks, pressures in favor of deficit financing remained. That year, in fact, the deficit peaked at 6 percent of GDP. In the absence of real domestic capital markets, financing options were limited to the international credit system. The result of this macroeconomic context was more inflation and more indebtedness. Hard-currency debt doubled between 1985 and 1987, mounting to $18.7 billion that year and eventually reaching $20 billion toward the end of the decade.[9] Given the declining terms of trade and the increasing interest rates during much of the 1980s, servicing the debt became

---

8. See Kornai, *The Socialist System,* 537–48; Éva Várhegyi, "The Nature of the Hungarian Credit Market: Lessons of an Empirical Investigation," *Acta Oeconomica* 42, no. 1–2 (1990): 73–86; and Márton Tardos, "The Role of Money in Hungary," *European Economic Review* 31, no. 1–2 (February/March 1987): 125–31.

9. By 1987 Hungary's situation was comparable to that of the large Latin American debtors. Its per capita debt was $1,617 (Argentina's was $1,592; Brazil's $70; Chile's $1,666; Mexico's $1,313). The ratio of debt to GNP was 74 percent (Argentina's was 76 percent; Brazil's, 39 percent; Chile's, 123 percent; Mexico's, 78 percent). The ratio of debt to exports was 155 percent (Argentina's was 673 percent; Brazil's, 436 percent; Chile's, 331 percent; Mexico's, 363 percent); and of debt service to exports was 35 percent (Argentina's was 80 percent; Brazil's, 42; Chile's, 36.5; Mexico's, 40). To Hungary's disadvantage, however, about 40 percent of exports were still ruble-based. Data from World Bank, *World Debt Tables* (Washington, D.C.: World Bank, 1989).

increasingly burdensome. Paraphrasing Ellen Comisso, the lost decade was clearly not a Latin American monopoly.[10]

Communist Decline and the Transitional Moment

The summer of 1987 became the turning point in the decades-long process of Hungarian economic transformation. In July a group of prominent economists of the independent Financial Research Institute circulated a document, "Change and Reform," in which in addition to macroeconomic stabilization and structural change, they advocated social openness and political reform. This event was not in itself unprecedented in Hungary. It could have been another one of the numerous pro-reform documents Hungarian intellectuals had published over time, had it not been that, through a panel of economic experts, the HSWP's central committee conveyed explicit support for that proposal. The party endorsed stabilization and efficiency and recognized the crucial role of prices, all of them issues of the past. Yet it also advocated further spread of ownership, what they referred to as *real* competition, and political reform. At no point do the words *capitalism* and *democracy* appear in the Central Committee's document, but those pages outline a socioeconomic system that can only be called democratic capitalism.[11] In a nutshell, it is no exaggeration to consider the "Change and Reform" debate of 1987 the foundational moment of Hungary's political and economic transition.

Three crucial decisions resulted from the "Change and Reform" debate of 1987. First, in line with the view of the economic panel, the party launched a new policy entitled "A Program of Economic and Social Development." Second, and almost simultaneously, the government signed a new standby agreement with the IMF, for the first time conceding the need to curb consumer demand, and thus reduce the population's living standards, in order to achieve stabilization. And third, the HSWP's central committee designated Károly Grósz and Miklós Németh to top responsibilities in the party's economic affairs division. This reorganization of the cadre would be of the utmost importance, for it placed pro-market reform officials in strategic positions of the party apparatus. As a result, the party congress of May 1988 called the Kádár leadership to an end, appointing Grósz as first secretary.

---

10. The original phrase was "the lost decade was clearly not a communist monopoly," in "Property Rights, Liberalism, and the Transition from 'Actually Existing' Socialism," *East European Politics and Societies* 5, no. 1 (winter 1991): 181.

11. For a reprint of these documents, see L. Antal et al., "Change and Reform," and "Stand Taken by the Economic Panel of the Central Committee of the HSWP," both in *Acta Oeconomica* 38, no. 3–4 (1987): 187–213 and 263–72, respectively.

By the late 1980s the economy was highly indebted and exposed, while foreign exchange was scarce. The polity, in turn, was becoming seriously unstable, as the dominant party was divided and the opposition active but unorganized. In this context, the HSWP's strategy was to constitute itself into the very agent of marketization, in the expectation that economic recovery would allow the new leadership to regain initiative, avert widespread defection, and control the mode and timing of political reform. Just like the Mexican PRI in the late 1980s, economic liberalization was seen as a political instrument by which the hegemonic party would give up *portions* of power to avoid risking and losing *all* the power and, thus, forestall the fragmentation of the party itself.[12]

Seen in retrospect, however, even that idea was too optimistic of a scenario. Conflict between political hard-liners and political reformers deepened within the HSWP. Whereas hard-liners grouped around Grósz and the party's central committee, reformers clustered around Németh who, more acceptable for increasingly vocal opposition groups, became prime minister in November 1988. As of that moment, however, Németh distanced himself from the party leadership on every occasion he could, favoring negotiation with the opposition, competitive elections, and ultimately leading the caretaker government after June 1989.[13] The growing estrangement between party and government prevented a controlled-from-above transition, as top party officials had expected. It also unmasked the terminal crisis of state socialism in Hungary, as one of its central pillars—the supremacy of the party over the other institutions of government—fell apart.[14]

The declining power of the HSWP and the government-party rift accelerated the process of economic transformation. In fact, if significant disagreement occurred within the communist camp as to the character of the impending po-

---

12. This interpretation is also valid for China, as Susan Shirk, *The Political Logic of Economic Reform in China* (Berkeley: University of California Press, 1993) has persuasively argued. A parallel question, beyond the scope of this study, would be to examine the conditions under which the introduction of economic liberalization policies in the context of hegemonic party rule allows the party to maintain full power (China), leads to different degrees of power sharing within a more or less competitive party system (Mexico, Hungary, Nicaragua), or results in a total erosion of the party's viability (Czechoslovakia).

13. For detailed analyses of this transition phase, see David Bartlett, *The Political Economy of Dual Transformations* (Ann Arbor: University of Michigan Press, 1997), chap. 4; and David Stark and László Bruszt, *Postsocialist Pathways* (Cambridge: Cambridge University Press, 1997), chap. 1.

14. In fact, in October 1989 the party split. The reformers founded the Hungarian Socialist Party (HSP) and the hard-liners remained in the original HSWP, while the majority of the members deserted from either party.

litical transition, more of a consensus existed among government and party officials in regard to the scope and pace of the economic transformation, even if
they had different reasons for the same preference. For Németh and his technocratic reform team—several of whom were already involved in private sector activities—full-fledged marketization was the only way to attract capital in
order to resolve the severe hard-currency crunch and improve the balance-of-
payments position. Thus, as of the second half of 1988, government ministers
announced to international investors and financial institutions that the main state
enterprises were on the block, even if they were to become fully private and
foreign-owned, and include debt-for-equity swaps.

Subsequently, in January and May 1989 the government passed two critical pieces of legislation, the Law on Economic Association and the Law on
Transformation, which set the regulatory status for foreign investment and private property, respectively. Unlike populist party leaders in Latin America and
social-democratic ones in Western Europe, who had to resort to convoluted
rhetorical formulas to legitimize reforms that reversed decades of state ownership and Keynesian-type intervention, communist leaders in Hungary felt no
obligation to justify their complete U-turn from the economic foundation of socialism.

Spontaneous- and Self-Privatization: Distributional
Coalitions in the Transition to a Market Economy

As discussed earlier, top party officials had also embraced marketization, though
they saw it as an instrument conducive to slowing down the rapid disintegration of the HSWP. This priority did not delay privatization but did lead to a different method than the one that policymakers had advocated in the financial
centers of advanced industrial nations. In a context marked by increasing levels of uncertainty as to the future of the party and the dissolution of the state-
socialist economy, the new legal framework found enterprise directors—accustomed since the NEM to operate with significant levels of autonomy from
the center—in a privileged position to become the main beneficiaries of the up-
coming changes in the nation's property regime. Through sophisticated financial
schemes, plant managers split companies by creating subsidiary firms that, organized as limited liability companies, got the fixed assets of the parent companies
in exchange for the new firms' shares. In some cases, the managers sold off the
assets of the subsidiaries to foreign or domestic buyers, cashing the proceeds or
remaining in control of the now-private enterprises. In other cases, they used
resources from the subsidiaries to repurchase the stock now held by the parent

companies. The parent companies were thus left as virtual shells, holding bonds of the subsidiaries but stripped of real assets and heavily indebted.[15]

A form of divestiture that reproduced important characteristics of the second economy developed under reform socialism, "spontaneous" privatization had, in limited and somewhat hidden form, been used since the mid-1980s. Yet the passing of the Laws on Association and Transformation, the abolition of the nomenklatura system in April 1989, the beginning of the roundtable negotiations that June, and the participation of top party bureaucrats themselves into this type of transaction gave a green light to company directors to take full advantage of their positions and accelerate the takeover process. On the verge of the Parliamentary elections of March 1990, discredited and under increasing pressure, the HSWP set up the State Property Agency (SPA), allegedly to centralize the divestiture process and avoid the excesses of the ongoing spontaneous privatization. It appeared to be too little and too late, if not merely cosmetic, to stop the process. Just between 1988 and 1990, the number of all economic units in the country grew three times, from ten thousand to almost thirty thousand. This growth was largely driven by the expansion of limited liability companies, which grew forty-five times, from four hundred in 1988 to more than eighteen thousand in 1990, representing almost two-thirds of all economic units.[16] Thus, by May 1990, when the HSWP left power and the coalition government of József Antall and the Hungarian Democratic Forum (HDF) came to office, control over a large part of state property rights had already devolved to company managers.

The legacy of communism, therefore, was not one of stable and concentrated state ownership, but one of dispersed property rights under a variety of organizational forms. Privatization, in fact, had already begun and was well under way by the time communism fell. In 1990 the path of transformation was in place, shaped by decades of reform socialism and by the exit strategy devised by the HSWP in the late 1980s, specifically, by spontaneous privatization and

---

15. David Stark, "Privatization in Hungary: From Plan to Market or from Plan to Clan?" *East European Politics and Societies* 4, no. 3 (fall 1990): 351–92; and "Recombinant Property in East European Capitalism," *American Journal of Sociology* 101, no. 4 (January 1996): 993–1027; David Bartlett, "The Political Economy of Privatization: Property Reform and Democracy in Hungary," *East European Politics and Societies* 6, no. 1 (winter 1992): 73–118; Roman Frydman and Andrzej Rapaczynski, *Privatization in Eastern Europe: Is the State Withering Away?* (Budapest: CEU Press, 1994), especially chaps. 5 and 6.

16. Furthermore, by the end of 1991 they amounted to three-quarters of all units. Data from Eva Voszka, "Spontaneous Privatization in Hungary," in John S. Earle, Roman Frydman, and Andrzej Rapaczinski, eds., *Privatization in the Transition to a Market Economy* (New York: St. Martin's Press/CEU, 1993), 89–107.

the institutional framework designed to carry it out.[17] Because of this, options such as restitution to prenationalization owners and voucher privatization—used in other former socialist countries and entertained by the Antall government[18]—proved unfeasible in Hungary.

The first measures of the new government sought to respond to public opinion demanding an end to real estate and stock deals associated with spontaneous privatization. Accordingly, and to regain control, the government replaced the head of the SPA and recentralized property rights and the supervision of the process. Ostensibly, the main goal of this decision was to prevent the retrenchment of the former communist elite in the new private sector. The Antall administration was faced with the twin contradictory goals of building a new system from scratch while simultaneously strengthening a new government in a context of extreme institutional fluidity. Thus, the ex-communists embracing private property and capitalism was auspicious for the former goal, but taking power, economic or otherwise, away from the ex-communists was favorable for the latter priority. Curbing spontaneity and refurbishing the SPA was thus conducive to the strengthening of the HDF coalition, but at the expense of bringing privatization to a standstill.

The government tried to regain momentum by announcing the privatization of small companies, which had very modest success, and the tendering of twenty large companies targeted to domestic and foreign investors, which was a total failure. The sluggishness of the process finally induced the government to introduce "self-privatization" for small- and medium-sized firms in the summer of 1991, a method that reproduced the fundamental characteristics of spontaneous privatization.[19]

Under self-privatization companies were allowed to initiate divestiture negotiations independently, with the advice of small private agencies licensed by the SPA, which officiated as brokers and consultants. This way, the managers regained control of most of the companies. To the extent that they were allowed

---

17. László Urbán, "Why Was the Hungarian Transition Exceptionally Peaceful?," in György Szoboszlai, ed., *Democracy and Political Transformation* (Budapest: Hungarian Political Science Association, 1991), 303–9.

18. Under pressure of the Independent Small Holders' Party (ISHP), an important coalition partner single-mindedly focused on land restitution. See Ellen Comisso, "Legacies of the Past or New Institutions: The Struggle over Restitution in Hungary," *Comparative Political Studies* 28, no. 2 (1995): 200–38; and Béla Greskovits, *The Political Economy of Protest and Patience* (Budapest: CEU Press, 1998), chap. 7.

19. See Péter Mihály, "Hungary: A Unique Approach to Privatisation—Past, Present and Future," and Zsigmond Járai, "10 Percent Already Sold: Privatisation in Hungary," both in István Székely and David Newbery, eds., *Hungary: An Economy in Transition* (Cambridge: Cambridge University Press, 1993).

to find outside investors themselves (often foreigners), they used their experience and inside knowledge of company operations to bargain effectively and retain part of the stock being divested. For the private agencies, most of them staffed by former officials of ministries and agencies of the economic area, the method offered attractive incentives as well, for they were entitled to a commission of 3 percent of the sale price.

Clearly, self-privatization generated increasing opportunities for collusion among managers, prospective investors, and the SPA-licensed agencies. The availability of additional financial incentives—leasing options, employee-share ownership programs,[20] and subsidized loans—provided extra impetus to the process. As a result, privatization came back to a fast track. By 1993, 255 firms had been privatized through self-privatization, and by 1994 about half of the Hungarian economy was in private hands, though only 25 percent of the proceeds from privatization was in cash. By that time 70 percent of the growing private sector elite, including those in newly founded and in privatized firms, had been directors of state-owned companies prior to 1988, while 20 percent of the last nomenklatura cadre became owners of private firms, most of them large companies.[21]

As discussed previously, macroeconomic constraints in combination with the rent-seeking behavior of financial-industrial conglomerates had shaped the pace and content of much of the Latin American economic reforms. In Britain, the electoral calendar and the goal of making inroads among the working-class electorate had, in turn, decisively accelerated Margaret Thatcher's privatization program. In Hungary and other East-Central European nations, the end of communist rule molded peculiar forms of marketization: spontaneous and self-privatization, nomenklatura privatization, and widespread management buyouts.[22] By taking

---

20. Reportedly, these programs became no more than a form of management buyout, just like in the case of the privatization of the electricity sector in Chile in the 1980s, as discussed in chapter 3. There, the initial distribution of shares along the lines of labor capitalism and administered by trusts run by the company managers themselves rapidly ended with a reconcentration in the hands of the latter, which transformed them into major shareholders.

21. For a detailed analysis of these data, see Ákos Róna-Tas, *The Great Surprise of the Small Transformation* (Ann Arbor: University of Michigan Press, 1997), chaps. 9 and 10.

22. For similar schemes throughout the region, see Jadwiga Staniszkis, "Political Capitalism and Other Patterns of Privatization," in her *The Dynamics of the Breakthrough in Eastern Europe* (Berkeley: University of California Press, 1991); Jacek Tarkowski, "Endowment of Nomenklatura or Apparatchiks Turned Entrepreneurchiks, or from Communist Ranks to Capitalist Riches," *Innovation* 1 (1990): 89–105; Jan Mladek, "The Different Paths of Privatization: Czechoslovakia, 1990–?" in Earle, Frydman, and Rapaczinski, eds., *Privatization in the Transition to a Market Economy*, 121–46; Michael Burawoy and Pavel Krotov, "The Economic Basis of Russia's Political Crisis," *New Left Review* 198 (March/April 1993): 49–70; Yudit Kiss, "Privatization Paradoxes in East Central Europe," *East European Politics and Societies* 8, no. 1 (winter 1994): 122–52; and Katherine Verdery, "The Elasticity of Land: Problems of Property Restitution in Transilvania," *Slavic Review* 53, no. 4 (winter 1994): 1071–1109.

over as property owners the companies they used to run as state managers, by colluding with party apparatchiks in the distribution of the shares, and by effectively obstructing unwanted methods of privatization, the directors transformed their vanishing political power into economic power. Rents extracted from privatization turned a decomposing political party into a proto distributional coalition.

The politics of privatization in Hungary, therefore, fell within the boundaries of an Olsonian collective action setting. For this approach, interests have incentives to organize in small groups because organization is costly and large groups are conducive to free riding. Since there is uncertainty as to how additional output will be distributed, these groups try to collude with policymaking elites to secure the redistribution of existing wealth and income among themselves. As their behavior becomes the source of deadweight losses, and their profit-maximization behavior leads to suboptimal aggregate outcomes, these groups constitute a distributional coalition.

Seen under this light, evidence from the Hungarian privatization experiment comes in support of one of the main theoretical claims of this book: that rents may continue to be available and, thus, incentives for distributional coalition-building remain, even in the presence of extensive marketization. This proposition, which calls into question the theories of the neoclassical political economy field and the expectations of most economists involved in or conducting research on reform experiments, is all the more important in light of the fact that Mancur Olson himself addressed the postcommunist transition. In a much-cited piece coauthored with Peter Murrell and published in 1991, the authors explain the collapse of Soviet-type economies as a process in which initial fast growth dwindles in the face of increasing collusion on the part of industry managers and the resulting institutional sclerosis. As these industry managers are depicted as the archetypal rent seekers of dirigisme, the article predicts, mistakenly, that they will sabotage the transition, for in a market economy rents are supposed to dissipate and distributional coalitions dismantle.[23] The uncritical reliance on Olson's earlier collective action assumptions thus left Murrell and Olson blind to the possibility that existing patterns of collusion could persist under marketization and allow managers and directors to take over the property rights of these firms, constituting one of the main impeti for privatization.

---

23. Peter Murrell and Mancur Olson, "The Devolution of Centrally Planned Economies," *Journal of Comparative Economics* 15, no. 2 (June 1991): 239–65. For a similar view, see Jan Winiecki, "Why Economic Reforms Fail in the Soviet System—A Property Rights-Based Approach," *Economic Inquiry* 28, no. 2 (April 1990): 195–221.

Given the persistence of coalition-building patterns of the past, it was perhaps a timely turn of events that it fell in the hands of a revamped socialist coalition, elected in May 1994 with an absolute majority, to complete the transformation process. The former communists had long-standing connections with the emerging private sector elite and were in control of critical institutional resources—for example, having been at the center of a closed system of collusion between management and unions under reform socialism—to bring potentially destabilizing groups within check.[24] To be sure, in addition to the initiation of privatization, by 1994 the Antall government had left in place important pieces of a functioning market economy; among others, foreign economic policies geared toward "a return to Europe," financial sector and bankruptcy legislation, and a bank reorganization and recapitalization program meant to attract foreign investment. Yet this new legislation, compounded by the absence of an effective strategy for domestic and foreign debt restructuring, by the collapse of the CMEA in 1991, and by the Russian economic crisis in 1992, led to a surge of bankruptcies during 1992–93.[25] Accumulated bad loans at home and difficulties in the external sector forced the government to bail out a number of large banks. Aside from the moral hazard problem involved, handling the financial situation in this manner translated into a macroeconomic and a balance-of-payments deterioration, larger budget deficits accompanied by negative current account balances that resulted in negative growth rates. At the end of the first democratic government, therefore, Hungary was still under the effects of a prolonged "transformational recession."[26]

Thus, the governing coalition formed by the Socialists (HSP) and the Free Democrats (AFD) inherited a precarious fiscal condition and a virtual financial meltdown. Carrying out unfinished structural reforms in the face of worsening macroeconomic and balance-of-payment disequilibria implied significant additional strain for the economy.[27] In spite of this, and after a period of inter-

---

24. For these patterns and their effects on varying levels of collective protest during the transition, see Grzegorz Ekiert and Jan Kubik, "Contentious Politics in New Democracies: East Germany, Hungary, Poland, and Slovakia, 1989–93," *World Politics* 50, no. 4 (July 1998): 547–81.

25. This should be taken with caution for, as some studies have shown, taking advantage of the property regime limbo characteristic of the postsocialist transition, bankruptcies had often been manipulated by manager-owners in combination with foreign buyers to reduce the selling price of the firms. See, for example, Michael Burawoy and János Lukács, *The Radiant Past: Ideology and Reality in Hungary's Road to Capitalism* (Chicago: University of Chicago Press, 1992); and David Stark, "Privatization in Hungary."

26. János Kornai, "Transformational Recession: A General Phenomenon Examined Through the Example of Hungary's Development," *Économie Appliquée* 46, no. 2 (1993): 181–227.

27. As the literature on sequencing of reforms had suggested on the basis of the Latin American experience. See, especially, Ronald McKinnon, *The Order of Economic Liberalization* (Baltimore:

nal conflict in the coalition, the most radical phase of Hungarian economic transformation began in March 1995. This radical phase was marked by the initiation of the most ambitious strategy of privatization, the implementation of a drastic stabilization program, the reorganization of the country's main budgetary institutions and procedures, and the consolidation of a concentrated decision-making style based on a close connection between the premier and his two key policymakers, the minister of finance and the minister of privatization. These elements together allowed the government to expand the coalition of beneficiaries of reform, to reconstruct the fiscal base of the state, and to achieve significant levels of bureaucratic centralization.

In sum, spontaneous- and self-privatization had given a good part of the former communist elite—the enterprise directors—a stake in a private-based, open market economy. The socialist landslide in the 1994 elections, in turn, was instrumental in making the other part of that elite—the party bureaucrats—commit to a multiparty, competitive polity.[28] Irony of ironies, only four years after their downfall, the former communists were back in power, though this time popularly elected and in order to accomplish the state-building tasks necessary to fix Hungarian democratic capitalism in place.

Building Capitalism, Democracy, and the State:
The Multiple Transformation

In European history the path from nation and state building to capitalism, and from capitalism to democracy, constituted a centuries-long sequence. Contrasted with this trajectory, the current postcommunist transition involves the relatively simultaneous creation of market and democratic institutions from scratch: private property rights and accountable bureaucracies, central banks and multiparty legislatures, taxation systems and independent judiciaries, among many others. On this basis, some early assessments of the downfall of communism have characterized this very simultaneity as the single most critical obstacle of the postcommunist transformation, one capable of derailing the entire process. In this view, the concurrent and swift construction of a

Johns Hopkins University Press, 1991); Sebastian Edwards, "The Order of Liberalization of the External Sector in Developing Countries," *Princeton Essays in International Finance* 156 (1984); and Dani Rodrik, "How Should Structural Adjustment Programs Be Designed," *World Development* 18 (July 1990).

28. As Valerie Bunce put it, the socialist victory in the 1994 election constituted "an investment in democracy." See her "The Return of the Left and the Future of Democracy in Central and Eastern Europe," in Birol A. Yeşilada, ed., *Comparative Political Parties and Party Elites* (Ann Arbor: University of Michigan Press, 1999).

market economy, a constitutional democracy, and, in some cases, the nation-state not only entail massive decision-making burdens but also generate mutual effects of obstruction. Moreover, the absence of an external power capable of enforcing the parameters of the reconstruction, as in postwar Western Europe, allegedly makes the future of the postcommunist world even more daunting.[29]

True, where this process included secession, as in the Soviet Union, Czechoslovakia, and Yugoslavia, the redrawing of national boundaries introduced a high degree of instability and uncertainty, for the goals of marketization and democratization were frequently overshadowed by nation-building conflicts.[30] In several of those cases the aftermath of the collapse of the ruling party—in itself enough to produce a rapid destructuration of the political center—was further compounded by state dismemberment. These "destatizing" tendencies, paraphrasing Katherine Verdery,[31] have often resulted in political fragmentation, the parcellization of sovereignty, and the primacy of regional and ethnic politics. In this type of scenario economic life has been, and can only be, dominated by multiple layers of informal activities on the part of large segments of the population, and by the most parasitic and corrupt forms of rent-seeking behavior on the part of well-positioned elites.[32] Whatever meaning and specific character state formation may adopt in these quasi-stateless political

---

29. For two prominent examples of this view, see Claus Offe, "Capitalism by Democratic Design? Democratic Theory Facing the Triple Transition in East Central Europe," *Social Research* 58, no. 4 (winter 1991): 865–92; and Jon Elster, "The Necessity and Impossibility of Simultaneous Economic and Political Reform," in Douglas Greenberg, Stanley N. Katz, Melanie Beth Oliviero, and Steven C. Wheatley, eds., *Constitutionalism and Democracy* (New York: Oxford University Press, 1993), 267–74.

30. Though one should bear in mind that it has been quite smooth in Slovenia, the Baltic Republics, and the partition of Czechoslovakia. For a comparative analysis, see Valerie Bunce, *Subversive Institutions: The Design and Destruction of Socialism and the State* (Cambridge: Cambridge University Press, 1999).

31. Katherine Verdery, *What Was Socialism and What Comes Next?* (Princeton: Princeton University Press, 1996), chap. 8.

32. As recognized by Haris Silajdzic, former prime minister of Bosnia and Herzegovina; Ithaca, September 30, 1999. See, for example, Joel Hellman, "Winners Take All: The Politics of Partial Reform in Postcommunist Transitions," *World Politics* 50 (January 1998): 203–34; Edgar L. Feige, "Underground Activity and Institutional Change: Productive, Protective, and Predatory Behavior in Transition Economies," in Joan Nelson, Charles Tilly, and Lee Walker, eds., *Transforming Post-Communist Political Economies* (Washington, D.C.: National Academy Press, 1997), 21–35; and David Woodruff, "Barter of the Bankrupt: The Politics of Demonetization in Russia's Federal State," in Michael Burawoy and Katherine Verdery, eds., *Uncertain Transition: Ethnographies of Change in the Postsocialist World* (Lanham: Rowman & Littlefield, 1999), 83–124.

economies, it will resemble the war-making, coercion-intensive path of early modern European history depicted by Charles Tilly.[33]

Seen retrospectively, however, those warnings about the risks of simultaneity seem exaggerated, as various countries in the region have succeeded in their efforts at state formation "in a hurry," including new states.[34] A different approach can, instead, be stylized on the basis of several trajectories characterized by mutually reinforcing processes of marketization and state building in postsocialism.[35] This story starts with dominant distributional coalitions, previously in control of fiscal resources, taking over state assets. As discussed above, ownership gives enterprise managers and party elites a stake in widespread marketization and, by releasing the macroeconomy from recurrent pressures, leads to a less inflationary rent equilibrium.[36] This translates into a stricter specification of property rights in the short term and a stronger fiscal base in the long one. As an institutional requisite, the transition from "soft to

---

33. Charles Tilly, *Coercion, Capital, and European States* (Cambridge and Oxford: Blackwell, 1992).

34. Even the dangers of nation building are thus overstated. Six out of the eight widely recognized "success stories" of the postcommunist transformation are recently independent states: Czech Republic, Estonia, Slovakia, Latvia, Lithuania, and Slovenia. The other two are Hungary and Poland. Some of the "old" states, in turn, appear to be stuck in an in-between situation, for example, Romania, Bulgaria, and Albania. For an evaluation of political and economic performance, see Steven Fish, "The Determinants of Economic Reform in the Post-Communist World," *East European Politics and Societies* 12, no. 1 (winter 1998): 31–78; and "Moving Backwards: The Dynamics of Democratic Erosion and Reversal in the Postcommunist World" (paper presented at the Mellon-Sawyer seminar on Democratization, Cornell University, February 22, 1999).

35. In later work, Elster and Offe come back to the alleged mutual incompatibilities of these simultaneous processes and, though conceding to the exaggerated pessimism of their initial assessments, nonetheless link the problem of simultaneity to the "unfinished" and "unconsolidated" character of the project. Given the nature of the transformation from state socialism to democratic capitalism, and considering that the process has been going on for only ten years, it goes without saying that the institution-building tasks ahead continue to be monumental. The choice of words, however, may suggest an additional problem: to assume, in some teleological way, that the process under study—which this book sees as state formation—can, and at some point will, be "finished." See Jon Elster, Claus Offe, and Ulrich K. Preuss, *Institutional Design in Post-communist Societies* (Cambridge: Cambridge University Press, 1998).

36. On the basis of the stabilization program of 1995, Daniel Treisman, "Fighting Inflation in a Transitional Regime: Russia's Anomalous Stabilization," *World Politics* 50 (January 1998): 235–65, argues that a process of rent substitution for previous beneficiaries of inflation, from monetary to nonmonetary ones, allowed the government to achieve macroeconomic equilibrium. He does not address whether a low rent-seeking equilibrium can be equally set up on the basis of the distribution of state assets, nor whether microeconomic reform can, in fact, accelerate on the basis of the distribution of rents. Hellman, on the other hand, argues in "Winner Takes All," that due to the persistence of rent-seeking behavior, reform remains "partial." While this may be the case for Russia, in Hungary and Poland the persistence of rent-seeking patterns expedited reform instead.

hard property rights" becomes pivotal for the transition from "soft to hard budget constraints," among firms and in the fiscal sector alike. Empowering and expanding winning coalitions, in turn, is conducive to a relatively benign reconcentration at the center, for the government can achieve oversight and control functions, critical in the fluidity of the transformation, at a lower political cost. These "restatizing" tendencies thus create a virtuous circle, a setting in which more market correlates with increasing stateness. State formation takes place along the lines of a capital-intensive path, rather than a coercion-intensive one, making it more compatible with parallel democratization processes. In the specific case of Hungary, these tendencies can be observed in three arenas, as they unfolded after 1995: the design of fiscal policy-making institutions, the privatization of public utilities and banking, and the centralization of authority in the executive.

Reorganizing Macroeconomic Policy Institutions

By 1994, at the time under the leadership of Péter Boross, the conservative government had not been able to accomplish a clean-cut departure from the policy-making practices of the late communist period or reverse the declining trend in the government accounts. As under Németh, the magnitude of the deficit continued to be concealed—for instance, by leaving items out of the balance sheet of the central bank—and the drift toward decentralization persisted. In fact, the Law on Public Finances passed in 1992 ratified the legal status of a number of institutional arrangements left behind by the HSWP government. Accordingly, a large number of extrabudgetary funds, the spending capacity of local governments, and the financial autonomy of a wide variety of spending agencies—known as Central Budgetary Institutions (CBIs)—remained untouched.

Moreover, this drift was reinforced by the failure of the Interest Reconciliation Council (IRC)—a corporatist tripartite forum created in 1988, refurbished and strengthened in 1990—due to the small number of firms represented and the limited capacity of the main labor organization, the National Federation of Hungarian Trade Unions (MSZOSZ), to enforce compliance among the rank and file.[37] Privatization, in turn, for all its effectiveness in coalition-building terms, was not contributing much revenue since most companies had been divested through noncash methods, while welfare expenditures, centerpiece of the political strategy of reform socialism, actually increased during the Antall

---

37. Mária Ladó, "Continuity and Changes in Tripartism in Hungary," in Attila Ágh and Gabriella Ilonszki, eds., *Parliaments and Organized Interests: The Second Steps* (Budapest: Hungarian Centre for Democracy Studies, 1996), 158–72.

government.[38] All this conspired against the conduct of macroeconomic policy. As a result, what at the outset of the transition seemed to be a rather moderate deficit turned out to be the most pressing fiscal situation of all the Visegrád countries. By 1994 Hungary's budget deficit peaked at 8.4 percent of GDP, and the current account deficit reached 9.4 percent of GDP.[39]

The real break with the policy-making legacies and institutions of communism, however, was made by the ex-communists themselves under Gyula Horn's government. The first minister of finance was László Békesi, Horn's main rival within the socialist party who also commanded significant support from the coalition partner AFD. His appointment was the product of compromise politics and was pursued by Horn in response to demands of the Free Democrats.[40] After a nine-month stalemate with the left wing of the socialist party over the nature of the intended stabilization, in February 1995 Horn replaced Békesi with Lajos Bokros (then CEO of Budapest Bank) and appointed Gyorgy Suranyi (a prominent orthodox economist) as governor of the National Bank.

In the meantime, the buildup of the macroeconomic crisis, the effects of the Mexican devaluation of December 1994, and the need to resume servicing the external debt had made the adjustment inevitable. The Bokros-Suranyi team launched a drastic stabilization program in March. It included a temporary tax on imports, a nominal 9 percent devaluation of the forint (which would lead to a real 28 percent devaluation the next year), the introduction of a crawling peg, and a widespread freeze on government spending, which included limits on increases in public sector wages.[41] The package also included interest rate increases and reductions in a number of social welfare entitlements, such as university education, maternity leave, and family allowances. These measures were passed in the midst of protests, internal coalitional conflicts, and the resignation of the minister of welfare.

In addition to measures meant to correct public sector imbalances in the short run, the most significant components of the Bokros agenda consisted of a series of institutional reforms conceived to ensure fiscal stability in the long term. The government saw that it was necessary to dismantle the protracted system of overborrowing and overspending inherited from reform socialism and

---

38. János Kornai, "Paying the Bill for Goulash Communism: Hungarian Development and Macro Stabilization in a Political Economy Perspective," *Social Research* 63, no. 4 (winter 1996): 943–1040.

39. Data from European Bank for Reconstruction and Development, *Transition Report,* 1995.

40. Richard Deming, "Will Békesi (and the Coalition) Survive?" *Budapest Business Journal,* January 27, 1995, 5.

41. Miklos S. Gaspar, "Bokros' 25 Economic Points," *Budapest Business Journal,* February 24, 1995, 17.

replace it with a regime capable of achieving tighter macroeconomic discipline.[42] Early in 1995 Parliament passed the Act on Public Procurement, which created a more transparent purchasing system. The most decisive step in the direction of the centralization of public finances was taken by creating the Treasury in October 1995, the first among the former communist countries. The new agency was given full control of fiscal flows and authority over the transfer of funds to the CBIs, making cash and debt management more efficient. On the basis of this newly centralized decision-making capacity, the government proceeded with the consolidation of extrabudgetary funds, reducing them from thirty to five in one year. Similarly, the Central Bank Act served to consolidate and simplify the central bank's accounting system and to set limits on its ability to finance government deficits.[43]

More agitated, however, was the process surrounding the proposed reform of the health and social security systems, both significant and politically contentious lines in the public sector balance. In the case of health, the initial proposal by Bokros contemplated the total elimination of the fund and its replacement by central budget financing. Strong opposition on the part of affected interest groups emerged during the preparation of the 1996 budget. By March the conflict led to the resignation of Bokros, who refused to compromise his budgetary goals by giving in to the health organizations. His successor, Péter Medgyessy, adopted a more pragmatic and less confrontational approach in order to implement some degree of reform. In social security, in turn, the initial government reform anticipated the creation of private-owned pension funds, estimated to be twice the size of the public, pay-as-you-go system. In overt opposition to the reform plan, the welfare ministry and the pension funds themselves elaborated their own proposals. After a period of vacillation that coincided with Bokros's resignation, here, too, Medgyessy found a middle-of-the-road alternative. The minister accepted the existence of a large public pension system along with the privatized "pillar," in order to gather support from the unions and its Parliamentary wing. The government retracted from the initial

---

42. As Gyorgy Suranyi put it, "the Kádár era in Hungary is over for good." *Budapest Business Journal,* April 7, 1995, 14.

43. For a detailed examination of this period and process, see Stephan Haggard, Robert R. Kaufman, and Matthew S. Shugart, "Politics, Institutions, and Macroeconomic Adjustment: Hungarian Fiscal Policy-Making in Comparative Perspective," in János Kornai, Stephan Haggard, and Robert R. Kaufman, eds., *Reforming the State: Fiscal and Welfare Reform in Post-Socialist Countries* (Cambridge: Cambridge University Press, 2000); and László Csaba, "Twists and Turns: The History of the Hungarian Public Finance Reform," in Lajos Bokros and Jean-Jacques Dethier, eds., *Public Finance Reform During the Transition: The Experience of Hungary* (Washington, D.C.: World Bank, 1998), 127–53.

plan, but this way managed to divide what initially constituted a solid bloc in opposition to any kind of privatization of social security.[44] Consequently, pension reform legislation was passed in 1997. However partial, it made Hungary the first former communist country to include private pension funds in its social security system.

Privatizing Public Utilities and Banking

Whatever fiscal savings were forgone due to the rather limited reorganization of the health and social security systems, they were compensated for by the proceeds of an aggressive privatization effort. Upon coming to office in May 1994, the Horn government merged the State Privatization Agency (SPA) with the State Asset Holding Company (ÁV Rt.) into the new Privatization and State Holding Company (ÁPV Rt.). In February 1995, along with the nomination of Bokros and Suranyi, Horn created the position of "minister in charge of privatization without portfolio" and named Tamás Suchman for the post to "supervise but not to direct" privatization operations.[45] Subsequently, in May of that year Parliament passed Act XXXIX, the new privatization law. The new law stressed revenue maximization and the creation of real owners. In contrast to the spontaneous and self-privatization methods, which had produced fuzzy property rights and cross-ownership ties, this new emphasis sought to set more precise boundaries between the public and private sectors, thus leading to the transformation of a relatively large number of "hybrids"—companies in which private and state owners could exercise mutual blocking power—into fully private-owned firms. Cabinet reshuffle, institutional redesign, and the high priority assigned to macroeconomic stabilization gave momentum to this phase of privatization.

The trend toward stricter specification of property rights was a prerequisite to initiate privatization in two crucial revenue-producing areas: public utilities and banking. At the same time, building on previous familiarity with Western economies and their more recent experience with spontaneous and self-privatization, the new managerial class was now in a position to benefit from

---

44. One of the most effective strategies consisted of allowing unions to appoint fund managers in exchange for their acceptance of the private pillar. Contrast with Menem's approach, who instead granted friendly unions the right to run their own "privatized" pension fund, and with Pinochet's, who virtually eliminated the public social security system altogether. See Joan Nelson, "The Politics of Pension and Health Care Delivery Reforms in Hungary and Poland," Collegium Budapest, *Discussion Papers Series* 52 (October 1998).

45. Susan Skiles, "Privatization Minister Designate Draws Fire," *Budapest Business Journal,* February 24, 1995, 3, quoting minister Bokros.

a more extensive divestiture process.[46] Given their significant parliamentary presence, their role was also fundamental to neutralize dissident voices within the socialist camp, for example the MSZOSZ, and reach out to the pro-reform groups among the Free Democrats. This balance of forces proved effective when the government needed to mobilize political resources and circumvent opposition and low public opinion support for the divestiture of the natural monopolies. All in all, these conditions facilitated a rapid divestiture in the electricity sector, and by 1996 it was for the most part under control of French, German, and Italian consortia.

The case of the oil conglomerate Hungarian Oil and Gas Company (MOL Rt.) was politically more controversial. Given the widespread presence of political appointees in the board and management offices, the proposal for its privatization was met by active resistance by trade unions and the industrial lobby associated with the HSWP. Both groups were opposed to giving up control of energy resources to foreign investors. The government designed a formula to get around the problem: divestiture "by installments," that is, privatization limited to only 25 percent of the stock, with the option of another 25 percent two years later. This way, the government sought and managed to placate opposition, but it also dissuaded investors. Thus, by the time the first 25 percent was offered in November 1995, only 19 percent was sold. In an effort to raise more revenue, the government attempted to go beyond the original targets, and by the summer of 1997, 58 percent of MOL was in private hands with the state retaining 40 percent. Despite majoritarian control by private investors, MOL remained as a hybrid. The government continues to appoint the majority of the board, and widespread limitations on shareholders' rights prevail. Nonetheless, the privatization of MOL has been the most radical of its kind in the former communist world and, unlike other hybrids, thriving profits—twenty times between 1995 and 1996 alone—have allowed the company to continue attracting the interest of private investors.[47]

In banking, the precarious state of the industry in 1994 forced privatization and significantly limited the number of available strategies. The Antall government had refrained from privatizing the banks but had simultaneously eliminated barriers of entry for foreign banks. As under reform socialism, soft budget constraints persisted, generating incentives for state banks to continue giving away loans, most of them among public sector firms. The bankruptcy law of

46. Iván Szelényi, "The Rise of Managerialism: The 'New Class' After the Fall of Communism," *Collegium Budapest, Discussion Paper Series* 16 (November 1996).

47. Vitali Silitski, "Constraints and Coalitions: The Politics of Economic Reform in Central and Eastern Europe after the Return of the Left" (Ph.D. diss., Rutgers University, 1999).

1991 drove a large number of firms into insolvency and default, compounding the bad-loan problem of the banks, which mounted to one-third of the total portfolio by 1993. Given the delay of macroeconomic adjustment, the banks did not face incentives to improve their lending policies and relied, instead, on eventual recapitalization, debt consolidation, and other available bailout mechanisms. As a result, a dual banking system developed, one state-owned, plagued by inefficiencies and liabilities, and the other, well capitalized and administered, controlled by prestigious international banks. The immediate risk was that the Hungarian banks were going to be wiped out by foreign competitors, and any revenue from their privatization would be forgone.[48] A banking sector insider himself, Bokros sought rapid privatization, trying to spend as little as possible in cleaning up the banks' finances and collect as much foreign exchange as possible from their sales, in order to set up an efficient and fully integrated financial sector.

On this account, the program yielded indisputable results. By 1998, 75 percent of the banking sector was privatized, and twenty-seven of the country's forty-two financial institutions were foreign-owned.[49] In addition to the banks, the overall proceeds would suggest that the privatization phase of the Horn government was a resounding success: revenue from privatization in 1995 alone surpassed all the previous years combined, reaching HUF 480 billion—85 percent of it in hard currency. Though a sizable share of that revenue—5 percent in 1995, 35 percent in 1996, and 14 percent in 1997—was used in debt relief and equity capital provided to the banks and other SOEs, the overall privatization effort accomplished a number of crucial goals. By 1997 property rights had been clarified across the board (with three-quarters of the Hungarian economy unmistakably in private hands), the budget deficit had been reduced to less than half of its 1994 level, and the current account deficit had been brought down from 9.4 to 2 percent of GDP in the same period. International integration, in

48. See Kalman Miszei, "Property Rights Reform during Democratization," in Joan Nelson et al., *Intricate Links: Democratization and Market Reforms in Latin America and Eastern Europe* (New Brunswick: Transaction, 1994), 105–45; and I. Ábel and L. Szakadát, "Bank Restructuring in Hungary," *Acta Oeconomica* 49, no. 1–2 (1997–98): 157–90.

49. A positive consequence of this type of privatization was to avoid cross-ownership between banks and public utility firms—as in Chile and Mexico—which in a context of currency appreciation, capital account openness, and financial deregulation typically leads to unhealthy lending practices and to recurrent financial crises. With the banks in foreign hands and the adoption of an exchange rate band that prevented appreciation, Hungary managed to circumvent the types of sequencing problems discussed in previous chapters and deflect the effects of the Mexican devaluation of December 1994 and the Czech speculative attacks of May 1997. See Zs. Árvai and J. Vincze, "Vulnerability of Currencies—Financial Crises in the 1990s," *Acta Oeconomica* 43, no. 3–4 (1997–98): 243–69, for a discussion of the problem applied to the Hungarian case.

turn, proceeded steadily in other areas as well, attracting 34 percent of all foreign investment into the former socialist world, and including a fully open trade regime and rapid growth of the multinational export sector.[50] In sum, if the "Change and Reform" debate of 1987 can be considered the foundational moment of Hungary's capitalist transformation, the economic policies introduced by Gyula Horn and Lajos Bokros have to be seen as the culmination of that process.[51]

Centralizing Executive Authority

The expansion of the coalition of beneficiaries of privatization, the recomposition of public finances and budgetary practices, and the redesign of policy-making institutional domains all contributed to a reconcentration of power at the center. By February 1995 the magnitude of the macroeconomic crisis and the official termination of the negotiations of the Social and Economic Agreement (TGM) taking place within the IRC[52] gave the government a window of opportunity to distance itself from a number of social groups and institutions, and to replace a consultative approach with speed and decisiveness. The failure of earlier attempts at public finance reform through bargaining and coordination, in turn, prompted the new minister of finance, Lajos Bokros, to impose major budgets cuts unilaterally, leading to opposition among public servants and also to partial defeats, as discussed in the cases of health and pension reforms.

Opposition on the part of entrenched sectors of the spending bureaucracy had, to a great degree, been predictable. Austerity deprived those agencies of the fiscal transfers they used to enjoy in the past; thus, to fulfill the stabilization goals, the decision-making process began to circumvent them. Left short of financial and political resources, a good part of the administration displayed open hostility toward the program. Bokros generally responded with resolve and surprise, centralizing policy design and implementation in his office. The very initiation of the adjustment program, conceived in secrecy by no more than six economists, conforms to this pattern.[53] This tendency was further reinforced by

---

50. Data from Állami Privatizációs és Vagyonkezelö Rt. (Hungarian Privatization and State Holding Company, Ápv Rt.), "The Ten Years of Hungarian Privatization (1988–1997)," June 1998.

51. Bokros was one of the authors of "Change and Reform."

52. Lajos Héthy, "Negotiated Social Peace? An Attempt to Reach a Social and Economic Agreement in Hungary," in Ágh and Ilonszki, eds., *Parliaments and Organized Interests*, 147–57.

53. See Béla Greskovits, "Brothers-in-Arms or Rival in Politics? Top Politicians and Top Policy Makers in the Hungarian Transformation," *Collegium Budapest, Discussion Paper Series* 55 (November 1998). One should highlight that, in addition to Bokros, one of the six economists was László Antal, also part of "Change and Reform."

the methodology employed to accelerate privatization. Divestiture operations were centralized in legal, administrative, and political terms. Transactions were carried out in the premises of the ÁPV Rt. and under previously specified guidelines. Suchman, in turn, reported directly to Bokros and Horn. More important, revenues were directly channeled to the Treasury.[54]

Effective macroeconomic coordination with the central bank and the support of the prime minister constituted Bokros's and Suchman's main political basis. Horn complemented the expeditious and technocratic style of the reform team with skillful parliamentary maneuvering. The consolidation of the oversized coalition with the Free Democrats expanded the range of strategies available to the prime minister. The option of resorting to the coalition partner to gather support constituted a deterrent for parliamentary groups linked to the radical side of the HSP and the old communist unions. An effective use of the oversized coalition allowed Horn to neutralize opposition and discipline his own party to get the economic package passed and to play his potential rivals against each other to secure his own authority. Later in 1996–97, when Bokros was replaced by Medgyessy, the government adopted a more conciliatory and moderate approach vis-à-vis dissident parliamentary and bureacratic strongholds, revealed, for example, in the process leading to the health and pension reforms.[55] But this has to be explained by three important factors. First, by that time the most contentious measures of the stabilization package had been passed. Second, with Sandor Nagy relegated from the leadership of the MSZOSZ, the capacity of mobilization of opposition groups significantly decreased. And third, the reorganization of fiscal and budgetary institutions had allowed pro-reform policymakers to cement their power and their primacy over rival spending agencies.

In sum, irrespective of the specifics of the different cases examined in this book, the thrust toward concentration of authority in the executive and centralization of power on financial and fiscal policy-making domains appears to be a common feature during the height of reform experiments. For example, in Chile, the minister of finance became "superminister," subordinating all other ministers to his command. In Britain under Thatcher, informal advisory bodies reporting to the prime minister—for example, the No. 10 Policy Unit—expanded at the expense of institutionalized domains—for example, Cabinet and the Civil Service. In Mexico, once the government succeeded in packaging liberalization as an anti-inflation device, decision-making power was concentrated in public

---

54. Anita Papp et al., "Privatization: Restructuring Property Rights in Hungary," in Bokros and Dethier, eds., *Public Finance Reform During the Transition,* 339–75.

55. According to Greskovits, "Brothers-in-Arms," the appointment of Medgyessy was also part of a strategy to co-opt Sandor Nagy, top labor leader and Horn's main rival inside the socialist party.

financial institutions—the ministry of budget and planning, and the central bank—at the expense of industrial policy and other developmentalist agencies. And in Argentina, the ministry of public works, supervisory body of most SOEs, was subsumed under the economy and finance ministry in order to centralize control of the revenue from privatization. The common feature in all cases appears to be the need to accelerate the reform process, catch rivals by surprise, and, allegedly, avoid bureaucratic (and parliamentary) delays.

In this study, these institutional changes are seen as components of a state formation strategy designed by reform governments. It is an even modest claim compared with how former minister Lajos Bokros conceptualized the process: "public finance reform is a societal transformation of much larger proportion than the political systemic changes of 1989. [It is] a profound social revolution requiring the definition of social values, individual behavior, and internalized motivations of everyday life."[56]

Conclusion

In a number of respects, the Hungarian case conforms to the stylized argument of this book. Rent-seeking behavior on the part of dominant distributional coalitions shifts from controlling fiscal resources to taking over state assets. These changing incentives often account for the initiation and acceleration of privatization and other economic reforms. Once under way, marketization gives impetus to significant changes in pivotal institutional configurations. Not only are property rights redefined, but revenue-collecting mechanisms reorganized, and policy-making procedures and routines redesigned. Here the process of economic reform brings about state formation activities, and state formation generally entails a significant centralization of administrative and political resources.

On this basis, three theoretical points should be reemphasized in this conclusion. First, as the main impetus for reform comes from the beneficiaries of state and reform socialism, the fundamental assumptions of a collective action theory inspired by neoclassical economics should be reconsidered. Liberalization appears to be a necessary condition for dissipating rents and dismantling distributional coalitions, but it is by no means a sufficient one. Collusion between economic and political elites can, in fact, easily be reproduced during reform experiments on the basis of expected distributional outcomes, including the reproduction of market reserves. This suggests, in contrast to an Olsonian approach,

---

56. Lajos Bokros, "The Unfinished Agenda," in Bokros and Dethier, eds., *Public Finance Reform During the Transition,* 539.

that with this type of liberalization benefits are concentrated and costs dispersed. *Winners* thus have incentives to organize and mobilize political resources *in support* of marketization. Nomenklatura privatization in this sense exhibits very similar characteristics to the Chilean privatization, where the top policymakers of the Pinochet government ended up themselves on the boards of the firms divested along with domestic and foreign investors. A paradoxically similar pattern of elite fusion under state socialism in the east and market authoritarianism in the south can be seen through their respective reform experiments. If this is so, arguments that view autonomous, insulated, and heroic policymakers as the main explanatory variable of successful reform are exaggerated at best.

Second, seen under East European light, where the nature of the transformation suggests nothing less than state formation, other comprehensive marketization experiments can be more clearly seen as such as well. The comprehensive penetration of market forces has not exactly shrunk or weakened the state, as a good part of the literature on globalization and on privatization has suggested. On the contrary, a stricter specification and enforcement of property rights, the recomposition of fiscal and budgetary institutions, and the centralization of administration have translated into a more assertive state. The state may have withdrawn from certain markets and allocative functions by leaving them to the private sector, but this was all done to increase stateness by concentrating on the specifics: property rights, extraction, and centralization. One of the puzzling discoveries of the East European transformation is precisely that the socialist state was a very weak one. Marketization has strengthened it, largely by triggering state formation processes.

Third, the simultaneous processes of capitalism, democracy, and state building have not produced major mutually obstructive effects, at least not in and of themselves. Even simultaneous nation-building processes have not triggered across-the-board destabilizing conflicts. The traditional approach to state formation stylized after West European experience—which identifies a path where state building is later followed by capitalist development, and capitalism by democracy centuries later—should be reconsidered on the basis of the postsocialist transformation. Not only have all these processes taken place at once, but even democratic development has not necessarily conflicted with state formation. Once again, in light of the Hungarian and other East European experiences, we can reinterpret the character of market reform and privatization in the South and the West, but we can also speculate about the conditions under which state formation—naturally exhibiting tendencies toward centralization and extensive deployment of coercion—can nevertheless go together with democratization. I address these issues in the next, and concluding, chapter.

PART 4

———

Conclusions

Chapter 8

Economic Reform, State Formation, and Democracy

Inconvenient Facts and Avenues for Future Research

The task of this concluding chapter is threefold. First, it summarizes the argument. With reference to the main theoretical foils of the study and on the basis of the findings presented in previous chapters, it highlights the main deficiencies of those competing theories. Second, it goes back to the political economy approach used, which supports the main theoretical propositions advanced, and to the logic of comparison employed, which explains the criterion for case selection. And third, this chapter speculates on some related arguments, issues not fully developed or not examined in the book but that are relevant to ongoing controversies in comparative politics: debates on state formation in general, and on the relationship between economic reform and democratization in particular. Building on the argument and findings of the book, this last set of issues brings to the discussion possible avenues for future research.

The Argument

This book has pursued two broad lines of inquiry. The first one has examined the collective action patterns and the coalition-building processes leading to comprehensive marketization. In so doing, this study has engaged prominent contributions, in economics and in political science, to the study of economic policy-making in general and market reform in particular. The second line of investigation has examined the institutional effects of privatization and has challenged the idea that the state retreats and shrinks in the face of openness and large-scale marketization. On the contrary, the state is re-formed. This section recapitulates these two arguments.

Distributional Coalitions

Dominant reasoning in economics treats a liberal economic order as a public good. It is therefore subject to typical collective action problems: the gains of liberalization benefit all groups in society, but vested interests who enjoy specific protections will favor a closed economy. Thus, the former are prone to free riding, while the latter have incentives to organize against an open economy. On this basis, the neoclassical political economy field—an approach that brings together the insights of public choice theory, Olson's collective action, and the literature on the rent-seeking society—has explained state intervention as the result of continuous attempts to secure market reserves on the part of rent seekers and distributional coalitions who capture policy-making arenas and collude with the policymakers.

Consequently, and in contrast to this pattern, since liberalization will disperse gains and concentrate costs, those approaches expect marketization efforts to dissipate rents and to dissolve distributional coalitions. A broad research program in political economy, which I have examined under the heading "the politics of economic adjustment," picked up on this insight and used it to explain comprehensive reform experiments in the developing world. Since the losers of liberalization are prone to engage in collective action, whereas prospective winners, facing uncertainty about the payoffs, remain disorganized, gathering political support for market reform is considered a difficult and improbable task, at least in the early stages of the program. The pro-reform coalition is seen as fragile vis-à-vis forces seeking tariffs, subsidies, and regulations. Only cohesive and insulated reform elites, thus, can deliver reform packages successfully. In a nutshell, while the neoclassical political economy approach has furnished only a theory of the "interventionist" state, the literature on the politics of economic adjustment has mainly advanced a theory of the "autonomous" state.

Both approaches overlook a most crucial aspect of the reform processes, one I have highlighted throughout this book: how coalitions organize in support of marketization on the basis of rents they expect to appropriate. Oftentimes, the privatization and reform experiments examined in previous chapters have preserved market reserves for actors that provided crucial political support to policy-making elites. Reform scenarios have thus reproduced incentives for rent-seeking behavior and the organization of distributional coalitions, even in the presence of comprehensive liberalization. In these settings benefits appear to have been concentrated and costs dispersed, suggesting that the influence of winners and their capacity for collective action has offset that of the losers. On the basis of this modified payoff matrix, I have advanced two interrelated theoretical claims. First, that distributional coalitions may also proliferate when the state withdraws from the economy, not only when it intervenes. And second, that interest-based variables retain key explanatory power in political economy—which state autonomy arguments generally reject—irrespective of whether the economy is closed or open—which neoclassical perspectives overlook.

The evidence presented in the previous chapters shows that in the most ambitious market reform experiments in Latin America, collusion between political and economic power and the rent-seeking behavior of industrial-financial conglomerates shaped the pace and content of these programs, especially in the area of privatization. In Chile, for example, such collusion was made explicit by revolving-door relationships between corporate and executive posts. This translated, in the 1970s, into a divestiture method that distributed the majority of the stock of manufacturing firms, banks, and private pension funds among no more than four economic consortia—the so-called *grupos*—while, in the 1980s, the privatization of traditional SOEs and public utilities brought cabinet and central bank officials to the boards of the very companies they divested.

In Mexico, the pressure of a small group of business elites organized under the CCE allowed them to enjoy frequent and transparent access to top executive offices since the mid-1980s. In the 1990s, favoritism in the conduct of bank divestiture operations turned those firms into the beneficiaries of the process, achieving significant levels of sectoral diversification and leading to integration of financial and industrial firms into private economic conglomerates. In Argentina, in turn, the most successful contractors and purveyors of the state during the 1970s became the beneficiaries of industrial and financial subsidies in the 1980s, one of the most significant items in the public sector deficit. This group, so-called captains of industry, also took over the assets divested in the 1990s, when the Menem government used privatization as the crucial revenue collection mechanism. In most sectors in all three nations, privatization translated into the preservation of market reserves through which private economic groups consolidated monopoly positions.

Similar patterns of collective action were seen in the postcommunist transformation. Most notably in Hungary and Poland, though not only, the dissolution of state socialism triggered peculiar forms of marketization. The divestiture schemes implemented were instrumental for company directors to take over ownership of the companies they used to administer, for party apparatchiks to collude in order to control the distribution of the shares, and for state managers to obstruct forms of privatization meant to increase competitive biddings. Terms like political capitalism, spontaneous privatization, and nomenklatura privatization, among many others, capture the process by which well-positioned communist party officials transformed their vanishing political power into economic power, becoming the main beneficiaries of the sweeping changes in the property structures of these nations. Throughout much of the postcommunist transformation, rents extracted from privatization have turned a decomposing political party into little more than a distributional coalition.

The British case is in some ways a different one, useful to introduce nuances to the argument. No comparable capture of policy-making arenas, like the ones seen in Latin America and in Eastern Europe, took place during the implementation of Margaret Thatcher's privatization program. No equivalent collusion, followed by the preservation of market reserves and the appropriation of rents, characterized the U.K. divestiture process. In contrast to the other cases examined, the Thatcher government took the initiative and launched these policies in a rather independent fashion, largely to alter electoral competition in the short term and change the makeup of long-standing political coalitions. The idea that social groups would alter their material incentives by becoming homeowners and shareholders, and therefore also shift their electoral preferences, marked the implementation of crucial components of the program, such as the privatization of council housing and the sale of shares to wage earners. Nevertheless, to the extent that these coalitions were built on the basis of the redistribution of existing wealth, rather than being concerned with expanding output, the Olsonian definition of distributional coalition still holds for the beneficiaries of the government-sponsored "nation of shareholders" and "nation of homeowners." Theoretically, moreover, even when privatization was initiated by the government, later convergence in the behavior of political elites and the goals of interest groups point, once again, to the limitations of state autonomy arguments.

In sum, neither the proposition that only state intervention creates opportunities for the organization of distributional coalitions (and, thus, that rent seekers necessarily prefer a closed economy and dirigisme) nor the claim that liberalization flows from insulated policymakers because losers are better organized than winners conforms to the empirical materials discussed in this book. As discussed in the chapter on Hungary, the litmus test for these propositions has, to a great degree, come from the very fact that the rent seekers of state socialism—enterprise directors, state managers, and party officialdom—reinvented themselves as the new private sector elite, accelerated the marketization process (in the last days of communist rule and when elected in the mid-1990s), and secured important market reserves on the basis of the privatization methods employed. If, despite the dramatic collapse of the system that had created them, those distributional coalitions were able to survive and readapt to the new context with such ease, one can expect these actors to have even better prospects in cases where the rules of economic interaction are not as radically altered.

State Building

The second line of investigation of this book has examined the institutional effects of privatization and has challenged the conventional wisdom on the impact of market opening upon state structures. The literature on globalization has viewed the increasing penetration of market forces into the national space as the source of the erosion and weakening of state power. In the face of global production, fully mobile financial capital, and extensive technological change, states are supposed to lose their autonomy and their capacity to choose domestic policy that does not conform to the international norm. As a result, the state is in retreat, as the traditional conceptions of sovereignty and, ultimately, the very idea of the nation-state, are considered to be under assault by openness and large-scale marketization.

Substantial research on privatization in the advanced, developing, and post-communist worlds has viewed "state shrinking" as the domestic counterpart of "state retreat." According to this argument, withdrawing from the market, massively transferring assets and allocation processes to the market, and downsizing programs and agencies have made the state recede in the face of comprehensive divestiture programs. Starting in the 1980s and well into the 1990s privatization was commonly characterized as a state-shrinking phenomenon. I have suggested, however, that these claims (and the language used) miss a most critical political aspect involved in marketization efforts: the reassertion of state power. To assume that, just by withdrawing from a number of markets and leaving allocative functions to the private sector, the state shrinks, erodes, or otherwise retreats provides a superficial reading of the state, one that, limited to the size of the "apparatus," would be more characteristic of the public administration field than of the political economy one.[1] In contrast, the evidence presented in this book has indicated that, to the extent that market reform experiments involve, among others, a stricter definition and enforcement of property rights (a "hardening" of property rights), seek to revamp revenue collection procedures (a "hard-

---

1. As in John Shields and B. Mitchell Evans, *Shrinking the State: Globalization and Public Administration "Reform"* (Halifax: Fernwood Publishing, 1998).

ening" of budget constraints), and lead to the centralization of economic policy-making processes, they can hardly be associated with "less" state but, rather, with "more."

In a nutshell, this study has treated marketization as institution building. Since governments' credibility is a function of the belief in the inalterability of the resulting normative framework, those that embark on reform experiments explicitly aim at changing basic economic rules. This is one of the reasons behind attempts to privatize public enterprise, balance the budget, make the central bank independent, and marketize social provisions, among other institutional redesigns. In so doing, however, governments "re-form" the state, as they specify new property rights, overhaul extractive methods, and centralize administrative and political resources. The evidence presented has suggested that privatization, the emergence of a new edifice of property relations (generally accompanied by a concentration of benefits on small distributional coalitions), appears as the key component of this state-building effort.

This would be of no surprise for the literature on property rights, for it expects stricter specifications of private property rights to increase efficiency, reduce transaction costs, maximize gains from trade, and increase revenues accruing to the government.[2] Similar reasoning comes from a vast scholarship on state formation. For North, for example, the state's ultimate capacity to tax depends on its power to enforce property rights.[3] This suggests that rulers count on a constituency of beneficiaries of property rights in order to collect revenue and ensure stable rule. For Levi, Lane, and others, revenue is the core of state domination because it allows the ruler to monopolize the means of force and achieve economies of scale in the provision of protection.[4] This view is con-

---

2. See, for example, Harold Demsetz, "Toward a Theory of Property Rights," *American Economic Review* 57 (1967): 347–59; Eirik Furobotn and Svetozar Pejovich, "Property Rights and Economic Theory: A Survey of Recent Literature," *Journal of Economic Literature* 10, no. 4 (1972): 1137–62; and Gary Libecap, "Property Rights in Economic History: Implications for Research," *Explorations in Economic History* 23, no. 3 (1986): 227–52; and *Contracting for Property Rights* (Cambridge: Cambridge University Press, 1989).

3. Douglass C. North, *Structure and Change in Economic History,* chap. 3. Necessary complements within this approach are Douglass C. North and Robert Paul Thomas, *The Rise of the Western World: A New Economic History* (Cambridge: Cambridge University Press, 1973); and Douglass C. North, *Institutions, Institutional Change and Economic Performance* (Cambridge: Cambridge University Press, 1990).

4. Margaret Levi, *Of Rule and Revenue* (Berkeley: University of California Press, 1988); Frederic Lane, *Profits from Power: Readings in Protection Rent and Violence-Controlling Enterprises* (Albany: SUNY Press, 1979). For an argument on how changes in property rights produce changes in the organization of coercion, see also Allan Silver, "The Demands for Order in Civil Society: A Review of Some Themes in the History of Urban Crime, Police, and Riot," in David Bordua, ed., *The Police: Six Sociological Essays* (New York: John Wiley & Sons, 1967), 1–24.

sistent with Tilly's historical analysis, in which extraction, needed to fund protection from internal rivals and external enemies, is the catalyst by which the wielders of coercion combined with the owners of capital to accomplish the centralization process that gave rise to the state.[5]

I have borrowed these insights from the literatures on property rights and on state formation to highlight the state forms emerging from contemporary experiments of economic reform and privatization. Take the case of Chile, where the acceleration and broadening of the economic reform process was followed by unprecedented alterations in the country's institutional configuration. As shown, piece by piece, the market reforms were locked into new norms, rules, and organizational blueprints. These range from a new labor code—useful in dissolving rigidities of the labor market but also in demobilizing unions—to a private social security system—effective in creating competitive capital markets but also in introducing new patterns of socialization among wage earners—and to a new constitution—which sanctioned the autonomy of the central bank (with a balanced budget amendment) but also established the new political order, the so-called protected democracy. Along the way, these economic and institutional reforms converged in reinforcing the centralization of coercive, symbolic, and administrative resources in the executive.

It was often considered that those reforms—forcefully imposed from above—and the frequently accompanying pattern of concentration of authority, were the by-product of military authoritarianism and unthinkable in a democratic polity. I have argued, in contrast, that the explanation for this process has less to do with regime type and more with the form and content of the economic reform program itself; that is, with the extent to which changes in policy and in one type of institution (the redrawing of property rights) spill over the organizational configuration of the state, irrespective of the nature of the political regime. Unlike Pinochet's, in fact, not only did other market-oriented, authoritarian governments in Latin America fail to leave any significant institutional legacy behind,[6] but some governments in established democratic polities, like Margaret Thatcher's, have redrawn historical institutional blueprints.

---

5. Charles Tilly, *Coercion, Capital, and European States* (Cambridge and Oxford: Blackwell, 1992); and also "War Making and State Making as Organized Crime," in Peter Evans, Dietrich Rueschemeyer, and Theda Skocpol, eds., *Bringing the State Back In* (Cambridge: Cambridge University Press, 1985), 169–91; and his edited volume *The Formation of National States in Western Europe* (Princeton: Princeton University Press, 1975); and also see Gianfranco Poggi, *The Development of the Modern State* (Stanford: Stanford University Press, 1978).

6. For example, the military, and often more repressive, governments in Argentina (1976–83) and Uruguay (1973–85).

In Britain in the 1980s, once the initially modest divestiture process gained momentum, it brought about unprecedented changes in the structure of the state. The institutional consequences of Thatcherism included, among others, the marketization of administrative functions (which privatized or subcontracted a range of services, from garbage collection to the NHS's catering and laundry), the reorganization of the civil service (which created a two-tier officialdom that insulated political appointees from career public servants), and legislation that increased the prerogatives of the central government over the control of revenue and spending policies of councils (which dramatically reduced the financial autonomy of local governments). In Britain, one can conclude, the resolute quest for a private, decentralized, market-based allocation pursued by the Conservative governments in the 1980s and 1990s was paralleled by an unabashed centralization of political authority. One of the main arguments of this book has been that, if the former constitutes a state formation process, the latter could hardly be surprising.

In Mexico, in turn, the privatization program ran in parallel with a constitutional reform process aimed at strengthening private property rights. Departing from the "Economic Chapter" of the 1917 constitution, the De la Madrid and Salinas administrations passed unprecedented amendments between 1985 and 1993. These reforms increased the overall status of private initiative and modified the legal specificity of banking, allowing private firms into the sector while eliminating the possibility of nationalization, as in 1982. Reinforcing this trend, reforms to the *Ejido,* the communal land system introduced in the 1930s, authorized local authorities to grant property rights to occupants of parcels. By 1993 another amendment sanctioned the autonomy of the central bank. As shown, this process of constitutional reform, coupled with increasingly close and transparent relations established between the government and the largest private firms, prompted the Salinas administration to undo the main institution of governance in postrevolutionary Mexico—corporatism—and supersede it with an organization more suitable for the economic reform goals and directly overseen by the president and his close advisers—the Solidarity program. Seen in retrospect, this centralization of political authority was effective for the presidency to recover the political initiative it had lost in the aftermath of the 1982 debt crisis, and for the dominant party to continue to be a viable political option throughout the 1990s, even when its "natural life span" had, in the wake of the collapse of hegemonic party regimes across the world, seemed to have come to an end.

The Argentine reform experience displays fewer long-term institutional consequences than the other cases, yet similar patterns of centralization. Unlike in Chile and Mexico, none of the economic reforms adopted constitutional status and, unlike in Britain, no comparable reorganization of the main civil service agencies took place. Instead, the new constitution, passed in 1994, appears as little more than a vehicle for reelecting the incumbent president and an instrument for "legalizing" de facto increases in executive discretionary authority. The implementation of economic reform by presidential decree, the expansion of formal powers of the ministry of the economy, and the overuse of executive vetoes was the birthmark of the Menem program. A veritable fence-in of the state followed, as the executive used these prerogatives, initially, to pass legislation that suspended the right to litigate against the state and, later, to pack the Supreme Court.

Unlike Latin America and Western Europe, the postcommunist transformations were faced with multiple and more fundamental challenges: nothing less than building capitalism and democracy, if not the nation-state, "from scratch and in a hurry." In some cases, however, clearly that of Hungary, the simultaneous creation of market and democratic institutions reinforced one another, rapidly overcoming the destructuration effects associated with the collapse of the ruling party. In fact, if nomenklatura privatization was instrumental in giving the ex-communist elite a stake in widespread marketization, empowering these winning coalitions was conducive to a relatively benign reconcentration at the center—so critical in the extremely fluid and uncertain transitional context—at a lower political cost. Paraphrasing Charles Tilly, state formation has taken place along a "capital intensive" path, leading, in the second half of the 1990s, to the reorganization of macroeconomic policy institutions, the divestiture of public utilities and banking, and the concentration of policy-making authority in the hands of Prime Minister Gyula Horn and his finance minister, Lajos Bokros.

In sum, neither "state retreat" nor "state shrinking" capture the deeper institutional effects of marketization, much less that, instead, current privatization and economic reform experiments constitute state-building efforts. Accordingly, this study has stressed not only the flaws of much of the literature on globalization and privatization but also the limitations of historical-institutionalism and other state-centered approaches in political economy. Based on the assumption that organizational configurations and agencies are resilient structures outliving the interests and ideas that create them, most state-centered perspectives commonly posit state institutions as autonomous domains with explanatory power over a variety of political outcomes, government economic policy among them. Because of this, little light can be shed, within this approach, on the conditions and processes that shape, instead, institutional domains. This book has attempted to do so by placing institutions as the dependent variable; that is, by examining the impact of distributive considerations on economic reforms and emphasizing the centrality of privatization for the emerging institutional designs. More generally, this argument has spoken to one of the building blocks of the political economy field: the relationship between economic policy and state structures. This, in turn, highlights the main attributes of the political economy approach adopted and the logic of comparison applied in this study.

The Approach

This book has examined the relevance of interest-group behavior for marketization programs and the institutional effects of those programs through a cross-regional framework of analysis. This section summarizes the political economy approach adopted in this study as well as the method of case selection and the logic of comparison employed.

Political Economy

This book has advanced a political economy approach that gives primacy to distributional considerations—a phenomenon typical of interventionist policy settings—but has extended this emphasis to current economic reform experiments. To the extent that asymmetries among social groups are based on differences in market power, it is plausible to assume that groups will seek market reserves, and the concomitant rents, to increase their market power. I have thus applied the conceptual apparatus of the neoclassical political economy to the study of economic reform and privatization, to point to ex-ante links between interest groups and policymakers, as well as to the manner in which societal support for these reforms mobilizes on the basis of expected distributional consequences. This approach has sought to bring interests to the forefront of our theorization in political economy—which state autonomy arguments omit—irrespective of whether the economy is closed or open—which neoclassical perspectives overlook.

I thus argue that Olsonian reasoning about the behavior of groups applies to privatization contexts as well. To the extent that distributional coalitions are defined as groups whose preferences are oriented toward the redistribution of wealth and income among themselves, rather than toward the maximization of additional output, they will prefer to privatize assets. I have thus shown that the supporters of reform experiments organized around short-term distributional considerations, and I have highlighted that their behavior, instrumental in getting their preferences translated into policy, did not really differ from the behavior necessary to obtain tariffs, subsidies, or any other form of protection. Moreover, I have shown that, by deviating from aggregate efficiency, the methods used in divestiture programs have often produced suboptimal outcomes, further magnifying the pivotal character of distributional considerations. This is the result of the fact that these programs represent an important source of revenue, affect competition and the price structure of the economy, and bring about the alteration of institutional domains. As such, I have examined privatization programs in the context of broader reform efforts, for privatization is used as an instrument for macroeconomic stabilization, microeconomic restructuring, and the design of institutions.

I have also argued, however, that the pursuit of these simultaneous goals is likely to translate into a mix and sequence of policies that neutralize each other or, worse, work across purposes. On this basis, the conclusion is that while privatization is the key component of the overall market reform, it also exacerbates distributional conflicts and becomes the locus of interest-group politics. For example, under far-reaching privatization, private sector demand for credit in domestic and international capital markets increases. Privatization thus contributes to open the capital account, which puts downward pressure on the exchange rate. Currency appreciation will lead to the accumulation of current account deficits, generally financed by the inflow of short-term capital, and will increase pressure on the real sector of the economy, greatly accelerating industrial restructuring. This setting can be worsened by across-the-board deregulation of the domestic financial sector, for increasing incentives for arbitrage will produce a massive reallocation of resources from the real to the financial sector, generating efficiency losses that partially offset the welfare effects of liberalization. These inconsistencies between the real exchange rate and the microeconomic regime, greatly magnified by (widely adopted) fixed exchange rate regimes, have been at the roots of several crises in emerging markets in the 1990s. Typically, these crises have ensued when difficulties financing the current account deficit led to more expansive fiscal and monetary policies, followed by attacks on the currency, loss of reserves and, inevitably, a large devaluation.

If privatization is initiated in the midst of high inflation, as in most Latin American and East European nations in the 1990s, this context interferes with the microeconomic objectives. Price distortions and macroeconomic instability make it difficult to value assets. Because of this, the price of the firms on the block tend to be determined more by projected earnings and future market share than by their book value and present proceeds. The more severe the budget deficit, the more incentives governments have to tender the companies undivided and with monopoly rights, as in most divestiture programs in the developing world. In this context, revenue maximization offsets the expected increases in allocative efficiency associated with decentralized private ownership.

These considerations are also relevant for the analysis of the process in Britain. Since the Thatcher government gave private ownership a higher priority than increasing efficiency and competition, the program resulted in the transfer of several monopolies largely intact and the preservation of market privileges. This decision was meant to maximize revenue as well, but most especially to boost the flotation of the shares, and with it the support of the managers, the employees of the firms, and the popular capitalists. Decreases in costs and increases in shares, rates, and profits of the utilities raised their productive efficiency at the expense of consumers—a trade-off that was made evident in 1997, when payments of large dividends and substantial increases in the salaries of the directors of the electricity, gas, and water companies were disclosed to the British press.

Governments with budget constraints also prioritize the speed of privatization, avoiding the breakup of the firms and impairing the design of a regulatory framework prior to the divestiture process, one of the main flaws of the Argentine privatization program of the 1990s. This creates additional incentives for the transfer of public utilities as vertically integrated monopolies. If, simultaneously, privatization takes place in the banking sector, it will lead to concentration of assets and interlocking ownership, often resulting in unhealthy lending practices with significant moral hazard consequences, as exemplified by the Chilean and Mexican bank privatizations and their widespread bank defaults in 1982–83 and 1995–96, respectively. This context is propitious for collusion between policymakers and business groups involved in divestiture operations. It also allows newly private firms to enjoy skyrocketing rates and windfall profits, without any tangible benefits for consumers. The presence of insiders in the process, in turn, may make things even worse for, as in Hungary and Poland, they can take over the assets through noncash methods, reproducing monopoly tendencies while forgoing much needed fiscal proceeds.

These attributes of the political economy of reform and privatization are central to the theory of institutional change advanced, for they highlight the connection between policy and institutions. If actors are informed of the distributional effects of economic policy, they can also anticipate that, once policy becomes embedded in a set of norms, rules, and organizations, future conflicts over these policies can be avoided, or at least mitigated. Actors' policy preferences thus have institutional implications. It is plausible to argue that interest groups will seek to invest resources in institutional configurations that are overly redistributive, rather than efficient, on the basis of the same Olsonian logic that expects them to aim their strategies at redirecting wealth toward themselves rather than at maximizing output. Neoclassical and state-centered perspectives generally stress the role of institutions in securing greater prosperity and in constraining behavior and shaping outcomes, respectively. In contrast, the political economy approach adopted in this study has highlighted that institutions affect the distribution of wealth; that is, they provide the framework for the distribution of the gains. As such, institutions often become the battlegrounds for interest-group politics. In sum, the cases examined in this book support the claim that institutions are neither autonomous nor created by actors pursuing optimal choices; rather, they are the product of the strategies of actors whose main goal is to secure their preferred distributional outcome.

Logic of Comparison

The theoretical argument and the political economy approach were evaluated in a series of cross-regional cases. I have inductively stylized the argument on the basis of the Chilean reform and privatization experiment for a number of reasons. First, Chile constituted the first nation to embark on comprehensive marketization and to turn it into state strategy and purpose. Second, the alleged success of the Chilean reform experiment turned it into a showcase, particularly for policymakers in the developing and postcommunist worlds. And third, but most important, the causal relationship among rent-seeking opportunities, distributional coalition building, and market reform policies appears consistently throughout the country's extended policy reform program.

I have subsequently introduced more cases in my narrative and assessed whether the argument retains more or less power in explaining later reform experiments. Thus I have examined the reform processes in Britain, Mexico, Argentina, and Hungary. In so doing, I reproduced the most different systems design, a strategy based on expected similar outcomes across a range of dissimilar contexts. However, I have also examined variations in the type of interaction between interest groups and policymakers, differences in the mix and sequence of policies pursued, and contrasts in the ensuing state formation strategies and processes, both across and within cases over time. Increasing the number of observations, while keeping the number of explanatory variables to a minimum, has allowed me to introduce nuances to the argument through a detailed analysis of the causal flow of events and a systematic look at similarities and differences.

Acknowledging renewed methodological debates in comparative politics, I have admitted that, to the extent that the observations were chosen on the basis of the prominence of their economic reform and privatization experiments, the logic of case selection can be criticized by sampling on the same value of the dependent variable; namely, the selection bias problem. However, I have also advanced a series of arguments in support of the choice of cases. First, selecting on the dependent variable has been useful in eliminating a range of plausible causes, an important first step in any process of scientific inquiry. To prove wrong the propositions that rent-seeking behavior necessarily leads to state intervention, and that reform programs lack organized political support, I selected cases where market reform was present and verified the extent to which the organization of distributional coalitions has persisted. The higher the frequency of this type of scenario, the weaker the propositions advanced by the main rival approaches of this study become.

Second, the impact of rent-seeking behavior has mainly been analyzed during marketization experiments but, to the extent that the analysis has pursued a historical narrative, its role was also examined during previous strategies of development in all three regions: ISI in Latin America, Keynesian demand-management in Western Europe, and state and reform socialism in East-Central Europe. This way, I have compared each case with itself, increasing the number of empirical observations drawn from each case. Even if it is not strictly necessary for this study, given the fact that the causal force of rent-seeking behavior and distributional coalitions on different forms of state interventionism has been amply documented in the political economy field, this procedure nonetheless introduced variation in the dependent variable.

Third, while the main comparison has been a cross-regional one, another subset of more or less explicit comparisons addressed variance among roughly analogous cases. Thus, I have treated Chile, Mexico, and Argentina in the context of the terminal crisis of ISI in Latin America, I have examined the British case as a manifestation of the general problem of Keynesian decline in Western Europe, and I have investigated the Hungarian case as a significant example within the broader postcommunist transition in East-Central Europe. This way I have also selected observations on the basis of the independent variable, adding a most similar systems perspective.

Finally, as I proceeded from the examination of the factors that explain market reform to the analysis of the institutional consequences of privatization, I introduced a diachronic dimension to the argument. Thus, by developing a more complete picture of the politics of economic reform over time, its causes and effects across different cases, but also across similar ones, I have attenuated the problem of selection bias. With this procedure, I have held economic reform constant across the cases, in order to address variance in the mode and timing of institution-building strategies and state formation processes emerging from similar marketization programs in different countries. In the next section I come back to this issue and its relationship with democracy.

In Conclusion: Unexamined Issues, Unanswered Questions

In the process of explaining the institutional consequences of marketization, I have highlighted how, by restructuring property regimes, altering extractive mechanisms, and centralizing political and administrative resources, these economic reform efforts become state-building projects. The concentration of authority in the executive examined across a variety of contexts, however, leaves open fundamental questions: why has this tendency, unsurprising in authoritarian regimes, also been noticeable in polyarchical settings, and how has it affected the very process of democratic governance? These issues exceed the goals of this book. Nevertheless, in the remainder of this chapter I advance some speculations and suggest some avenues for future research on the implications of these state formation tendencies for simultaneous democratization processes.

Economic Reform, State Formation, and Democracy:
Some Inconvenient Facts

This study has treated marketization as a state formation process. The cases examined previously exhibit variation in the extent to which their respective economic reform experiments were consolidated in new institutional designs. Specifically, while some cases locked in stricter private property rights in new constitutions and in comprehensive reorganizations of the main policy-making domains, others achieved more superficial, and perhaps ephemeral, institutional changes. As has also been discussed, however, there has been more of a convergence among the cases in the centralization of political authority concomitant to the economic reforms. Many of the institutional reforms associated with marketization have, in fact, gone in the direction of a relentless concentration of power in the executive. Prioritizing speed and decisiveness, reform governments have generally sought firm control over policy-making routines, and repudiated "unnecessary delays in the bureaucratic arena."[7]

---

7. A typical example of this view can be seen in Carlos Menem, *Discursos del Presidente* Secretaria de Prensa y Difusión, Presidencia de la Nación, República Argentina, 1989.

While centralization in the executive was predictable in the context of reforms implemented under authoritarian rule, civil in Mexico and military in Chile, this tendency was reproduced across regime types. In transitional contexts in Latin America, for example, reform policies were generally implemented by circumventing regular legislative procedures with practices of dubious legitimacy: bypassing congressional legislative prerogatives, packing supreme courts, and drafting constitutions "tailor-made" for the incumbent, to name a few.[8] On this basis, several scholars have highlighted that reform experiments have adopted an autocratic quality. Some have even engaged in a reconceptualization of this peculiar type of polity, one characterized by a relatively effective enforcement of political rights coexisting with systematic and blatant violations of the rule of law on the part of office holders; a combination that has led, in Guillermo O'Donnell's terms, to a "delegative" democracy.[9]

Similar attributes were present in the postcommunist transformation. As discussed above, the resiliency of economic practices inherited from state socialism gave former party officials a stake in the new market economy, but it also provided the bulk of the population—in the form of informal activities and nonmonetary market outlets—with escape valves from the transformational recession. Concurrently, the persistence of institutional legacies meant to inhibit collective action—for example, the tradition of collusion between unions and management—has shielded the new systems from the politically destabilizing mobilization of affected groups but has also contributed to insulate political elites and create a context conducive for behind-the-doors pacts and negotiations. Because of this, the path to a liberal economic order after the collapse of the party state has been faster, and the recomposition of the political center smoother, than early predictions had anticipated. This stability, however, seems

---

8. Theoretical formulations on this issue by Matthew Soberg Shugart and John M. Carey, *Presidents and Assemblies* (New York: Cambridge University Press, 1992), were applied in broad comparative analyses in John M. Carey and Matthew Soberg Shugart, eds., *Executive Decree Authority* (Cambridge: Cambridge University Press, 1998).

9. Among his several contributions on this issue, see "Delegative Democracy," *Journal of Democracy* 5, no. 1 (1994): 55–69; "Polyarchies and the (Un)Rule of Law in Latin America," in Juan Méndez, Guillermo O'Donnell, and Paulo Sergio Pinheiro, eds., *The Rule of Law and the Unprivileged in Latin America* (Notre Dame: University of Notre Dame Press, 1999), 303–37; and "Democratic Theory and Comparative Politics" (paper presented at the Mellon-Sawyer Seminar on Democratization, Cornell University, April 1999). See also Stephan Haggard and Robert Kaufman, *The Political Economy of Democratic Transitions,* chap. 10; and Luiz Carlos Bresser Pereira, José María Maravall, and Adam Przeworski, *Economic Reforms in New Democracies* (New York: Cambridge University Press, 1993), 199–220 for similar concerns. In contrast, however, Ben Ross Schneider argues that a reliance on centralized organizational patterns of business elites in Latin America may nevertheless be conducive to democratization. See his "The State and Collective Action: Business Politics in Latin America," unpublished ms, January 1999.

to be stranded at a "low-level equilibrium," one characterized by the presence of significant institutional configurations and collective action patterns of the past. As a result, a hybrid system has emerged, a poorly functioning, imperfect market economy in combination with an exclusionary, semidemocratic regime.[10]

It appears, then, that in the transitional polities of Latin America and Eastern Europe the simultaneous implementation of comprehensive economic reforms has, by deviating from a typical Western model, affected the quality of democracy. A prevalent explanation offered by the literature on democratization highlights the very newness of democratic institutions in these two regions and points out that accountability, rule of law, inclusiveness, and checks and balances, among other attributes that define fully democratic orders and are absent in these nations, are characteristic of *consolidated* democracies. Accordingly, the literature on consolidation has underlined the sequential nature of the process; namely, that it takes time for democracy to become "the only game in town," as Adam Przeworski put it.[11]

The problem with this line of argument, however, is highlighted by looking at Thatcher's policy reform experiment, one that certainly took place in a consolidated democratic system. Her economic program, too, led to unprecedented levels of concentration of executive authority, particularly in the office of the prime minister. The outcome of a reform zeal that restructured major institutional arenas and decision-making routines by stripping power away from the civil service, local government, and cabinet, a wealth of literature has rendered this cen-

10. The term "low-level equilibrium" is from Béla Greskovits, *The Political Economy of Protest and Patience,* chap. 10. Similar discussions are in Joan Nelson, "Overview: How Market Reforms and Democratization Affect Each Other," in Nelson, ed., *Intricate Links: Democratization and Market Reforms in Latin America and Eastern Europe* (New Brunswick, N.J.: Transaction, 1994), 1–36; David Ost, "Labor, Class, and Democracy: Shaping Political Antagonisms in Post-Communist Society," in Beverly Crawford, ed., *The Political Economy of Post-Communist Transformation* (Boulder: Westview Press, 1995), 177–203; and Valerie Bunce, "Comparative Democratization: Big and Bounded Generalizations," *Comparative Political Studies* 33, no. 6–7 (August-September 2000): 703–34. For the term "hybrid" in the Latin American context, see Terry Lynn Karl, "The Hybrid Regimes of Central America," *Journal of Democracy* 6 (1995): 72–86.

11. *Democracy and the Market: Political and Economic Reforms in Eastern Europe and Latin America* (Cambridge: Cambridge University Press, 1991). For the concepts of democratic transition and consolidation, see Guillermo O'Donnell and Philippe Schmitter, *Tentative Conclusions About Uncertain Democracies* (Baltimore: Johns Hopkins University Press, 1986); Giuseppe Di Palma, *To Craft Democracies: An Essay on Democratic Transitions* (Berkeley: University of California Press, 1990); John Higley and Richard Gunther, eds., *Elites and Democratic Consolidation in Latin America and Southern Europe* (New York: Cambridge University Press, 1992); Guillermo O'Donnell, "Illusions about Consolidation," *Journal of Democracy* 7 (1996): 34–51; and Andreas Schedler, "What Is Consolidation?" *Journal of Democracy* 9 (1998): 91–107.

tralization as plain authoritarianism. Some saw in it a distinctive characteristic of Thatcherism,[12] while others viewed in this trend the accentuation of attributes of the polity more deeply rooted in Britain's constitutional design.[13]

In sum, these considerations suggest that by altering property relations, overhauling extractive mechanisms, and reorganizing allocative processes, reform governments in radically different systems and with diametrically contrasting economic and political trajectories share, nonetheless, one important commonality. They have all concentrated extraordinary levels of power in the executive, certainly in autocratic regimes but also in a variety of more or less polyarchical systems: consolidated and unconsolidated, parliamentary and presidential, federal and unitary. Perhaps it is because of this that democracy has become in some way compromised; "half-baked democracy," as the qualifications previously mentioned suggest. Across the board, therefore, economic decentralization has gone hand in hand with centralized executive power. Far from suggesting incompatibilities between an open market economy and a democratic system, these considerations are meant to highlight the presence of "inconvenient facts" between comprehensive marketization programs and the "democraticness" of the polity. I elaborate on this in the next section and, as a conclusion, I suggest some avenues for future research.

Avenues for Future Research: Disaggregating "Stateness"

There has never been a fully democratic political order in a command economy. However, implementing market reforms while simultaneously maintaining or expanding democratic mechanisms may have conflicting logics. To the extent that the creation of market institutions entails state-building activities, becoming in the long run a state formation process, it is reasonable to expect a significant centralization of administrative and political resources. Thus, while marketization has generally implied a concentration of authority, the critical

---

12. For a lively discussion on this characterization among British intellectuals, see Bob Jessop et al., "Authoritarian Populism, Two Nations, and Thatcherism," *New Left Review* 147 (September/October 1984): 10–60; Stuart Hall, "Authoritarian Populism: A Reply to Jessop et al.," *New Left Review* 151 (March/April 1985): 115–24; Alan Norrie and Sammy Adelman, " 'Consensual Authoritarianism' and Criminal Justice in Thatcher's Britain," *Journal of Law and Society* 16, no. 1 (spring 1989): 112–28; Andrew Gamble, *The Free Economy and the Strong State: The Politics of Thatcherism* (London: Macmillan, 1988); and articles in Andrew Gamble and Celia Wells, eds., *Thatcher's Law* (Cardiff: GPC Books, 1989).

13. For this emphasis, see *Political Quarterly* 60, no. 1 (January 1989), entitled "Is Britain Becoming Authoritarian?" especially Shirley Williams, "The New Authoritarianism," 4–9; see also Paddy Hillyard and Janie Percy-Smith, *The Coercive State* (London: Pinter, 1988).

tasks of a democratization process and the building blocks of democratic governance run in the opposite direction, as they seek to establish devices that promote the dispersion of power across the polity and to fix in place decision-making procedures that hold leaders accountable to the citizenry.

In other words, state formation and democratization exhibit contradictory logics. It is not an accident that, stylized on the basis of European history, much of the literature on state formation has identified a well-defined sequential path, one in which state and nation building are eventually followed by capitalist development, and capitalism by democracy centuries later. State building, that is, the creation of political order, is often a violent venture, one that moves forward through war, conquest, expropriation, and the deployment of coercive resources.[14] Bearing these considerations in mind, it is difficult to even imagine democracy in a context of state formation, and this is why, in fact, the path to state building and the path to democratization rarely cross each other in this literature.

However, while this research has provided invaluable insight on the conditions under which epochal political change occurs, and this book has borrowed from it, the widespread and simultaneous processes of marketization and democratization currently taking place in East-Central Europe and in Latin America suggest the need to rethink some of its key postulates. The specific theoretical challenge is how to make sense of the fact that state formation— exhibiting intrinsic tendencies toward the centralization of administrative, symbolic, and coercive resources—has nonetheless been taking place concurrently with democratization—which is supposed to promote the diffusion of those resources. In other words, can state formation take place within the boundaries of a democratic political regime and, if so, how can the scholarship on state formation be reconciled with the literature on democratic transition and consolidation?[15]

In response to these theoretical quandaries one should highlight that the current economic and political transformations in East-Central Europe and Latin America offer a rather unusual empirical opportunity to see the path of democracy and the path of state formation intersecting. In terms of a research agenda, then, the key question is not whether economic reform and democratization are

---

14. Borrowing from Tilly, Poggi, and others, an explicit emphasis on this is in Youssef Cohen, Brian Brown, and A. F. K. Organski, "The Paradoxical Nature of State Making: The Violent Creation of Order," *American Political Science Review* 75, no. 4 (December 1981): 901–10.

15. A recent book by Doug McAdam, Sidney Tarrow, and Charles Tilly, *Dynamics of Contention* (New York: Cambridge University Press, 2001) integrates processes of state formation and patterns of contention into an analytical framework that explains long-term democratization across a variety of contexts.

per se mutually reinforcing or mutually destabilizing, as most of the literature on the "dual transitions" in the East and the South has debated for a decade.[16] Rather, it seems more promising to explore nuanced scenarios across both regions, from those where simultaneous political and economic reforms have created the conditions for robust democracy and robust capitalism to emerge, to those where the opening of the polity and the deregulation of the economy have, instead, led to patterns of fragmentation and political destructuration under which democracy became unsustainable and capitalism substandard. In short, the key question is why, while some reform strategies have been conducive to contexts of high stateness, other trajectories of change have, in contrast, produced scenarios of virtual statelessness.

This is important, for stateness is a function of state formation strategy and a prerequisite for the stability of democracy and the market economy. As Linz and Stepan have pointed out, stateness problems are the result of differences regarding the territorial boundaries of the political community's state and differences as to who has the right of citizenship in that state.[17] In other words, where there is more than one political community within a state, that is, when the demarcation lines of the nation and the state do not overlap and are contested, the ensuing conflicts pose serious challenges to the prospects of democracy. Yet this understanding of stateness, which I call the "horizontal" dimension, should be complemented with what I label "vertical stateness." Treated in a vertical sense, stateness refers less to the national and territorial question and addresses, instead, variation in the capacity of the state to specify the terms of economic interaction, to extract resources, and to centralize administrative procedures and coercive means. Accordingly, stateness problems also arise in a polity where property rights are loosely defined and poorly enforced, revenue collection is insufficient, policy-making routines are ineffective, and the government does not monopolize the legitimate use of force. In such contexts as well, the chances of democracy, but also of capitalism, are at risk.

---

16. For example, Adam Przeworski, *Democracy and the Market;* Claus Offe, "Capitalism by Democratic Design? Democratic Theory Facing the Triple Transition in East Central Europe"; Luiz Carlos Bresser Pereira, José María Maravall, and Adam Przeworski, *Economic Reforms in New Democracies;* Jon Elster, "The Necessity and Impossibility of Simultaneous Economic and Political Reform"; Joan Nelson, ed., *Intricate Links;* Stephan Haggard and Robert R. Kaufman, *The Political Economy of Democratic Transitions;* Valerie Bunce, "Regional Differences in Democratization," *Post-Soviet Affairs* 14 (1998): 187–211; Steven Fish, "The Determinants of Economic Reform in the Post-communist World," *East European Politics and Societies* 12 (1998): 31–78, among others.

17. Juan Linz and Alfred Stepan, *Problems of Democratic Transition and Consolidation* (Baltimore: Johns Hopkins University Press, 1996), chap. 2.

With the hindsight of this definition, which covers a wider range of situations as it addresses stateness problems in countries with contested state and/or territory but also in those without such conflicts, we can illustrate the point. Take the examples of countries that, in their transformation trajectory, have pursued a fast and radical break with the previous order. In some of them the introduction of democratic and market mechanisms contributed to enforcing civil rights, protecting property rights, and improving public finances. In this group of countries—among others, the Czech Republic and Slovakia in the East and Bolivia in the South—the reforms translated into increases in revenue collection, sharp decreases of inflation, and a relative improvement of public administration. Contrast this scenario with other reform experiments based on similar ruptures with the previous order, for example, in Russia and Romania in the East and in Nicaragua and Paraguay in the South. In these countries, however, the introduction of sweeping political and economic reforms did not succeed in reversing a poor enforcement of civil and property rights, plummeting tax revenues, a pervasive informalization of economic activities (which in some countries equates to a demonetized economy), and a widely corrupt public administration. The first group thus exhibits higher stateness levels; it is no accident that both democracy and capitalism perform better than in the second group.

These variations in stateness can also be seen in reform countries that exhibit a slower path to reform. In some of them—for example, Hungary, Poland, Slovenia, Argentina, Chile, and Costa Rica—and perhaps because they had relatively higher levels of political freedom and economic openness prior to the full-fledged transformation, their gradual and sequential reform trajectory translated into increases in stateness in most key areas: stricter property rights, small informal economies, low inflation rates, and an effective centralization. In other countries, however, and to the extent that the process has been permeated by the persistence of inherited liabilities (in the form of Leninism, authoritarianism, the resiliency of fully isolated state socialist economies, or widespread backwardness), gradualism has translated into scenarios that fall short of being capitalist, or democratic, or both.

Take the examples of Ukraine and Belarus, where their productive profile under state socialism, largely specialized in heavy industry until the very end, left them ill-prepared to jump onto the bandwagon of marketization, producing a rapid deterioration of the living standard of the population and stalling their political transition. Consider the cases of the war-torn economies of Croatia, Georgia, and Serbia, among others, where whatever state capacity was left in a context marked by the primacy of ethnic and regional conflict was used by rulers for state making through war making, in a dynamic reminiscent of the coercion-intensive path of early European state formation. And note the "functional equivalent" in Colombia, Peru, Ecuador, Venezuela, and much of Central America, where fragmentation, destructuration of the center, and the pervasiveness of patrimonial forms of political domination have allowed drug lords, local bosses, and revolutionary groups to act as competing sovereigns; that is, private entities that perform statelike functions such as enforcing property rights, collecting revenue, and providing order. In this last group of countries, whatever reconcentration at the center was attempted it was done at the price of a severe erosion of their democratic institutions. All of these examples, East and South, point to the existence of quasi-stateless political economies, ones where democracy and capitalism are definitely in danger.[18]

In sum, and on the basis of these examples, three concluding comments are in order. First, stateness makes all the difference between success and failure. Stateness problems in "horizontal" terms refer to situations in which contestation over the nation and over the borders of the state jeopardize the course of democratization. Variations in what I have called "vertical" stateness apply to all countries in transition, with or without contested nation and/or territory. It is likely that deficits of horizontal stateness will be conducive to stateness problems in a vertical sense; namely, it is unrealistic to expect an effective enforcement of rights, collection of revenue, and accountable administration in contexts where the state itself is challenged. However, to the extent that the reverse is not true—that is, that countries without horizontal stateness problems are nevertheless susceptible of vertical stateness deficits (in fact, a frequent scenario in Latin America)—the analytical distinction remains a necessary one.

Second, vertical stateness captures a number of political economy issues. Because of this, it complements, though not necessarily replaces, the horizontal notion. A clear definition and enforcement of property rights, an efficient collection of revenue, and the centralization of administrative and coercive resources all translate into a robust economic performance. But they all provide political order as well. Stateness is thus necessary for dynamic capitalism, but it is imperative for stable democratic institutions. Democracy is, before it is anything else, a form of political order. In the absence of order, that is, in the absence of stateness, democracy collapses, and collapses faster than nondemocratic regimes, at the very least because nondemocratic governments have a much larger discretion and autonomy to resort to the use of force in order to remain in office.

---

18. The preceding discussion is borrowed from Béla Greskovits and Hector E. Schamis, "Democratic Capitalism and the State in Eastern Europe and Latin America" (paper presented at the Annual Meeting of the American Political Science Association, Atlanta, Ga., September 2–5, 1999).

Finally, if stateness is so central to the prospects of marketization and de-mocratization, then state building and democratization may go together, and the literature on state formation and the one on transition and consolidation may be reconciled. In other words, the market and democracy are, in fact, mutually re-inforcing, but not so much because economic freedom and political freedom go together, or because there are no democratic command economies (though there have been countless authoritarian capitalist experiments). Marketization con-tributes to democracy because, by strengthening property rights, reorganizing revenue collection systems, and centralizing administrative and coercive re-sources, market reform experiments are potentially conducive to significant in-creases in stateness. Even if the concentration of power in the executive may make democracy suboptimal in the short run, in the long run, however, it gen-erates the conditions under which a democratic political order can thrive. As I said at the beginning of this book, the state is "re-formed" through marketiza-tion, and this is a sine qua non condition for robust capitalism and healthy de-mocracy.

Index